IN THE
WORLD

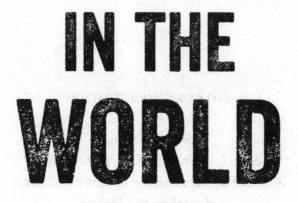

IN THE WORLD

FROM THE BIG HOUSE
TO HOLLYWOOD

RICHARD STRATTON

Arcade Publishing • New York

First Edition

Arcade Publishing books may be purchased in bulk at special discounts for sales promotion, corporate gifts, fund-raising, or educational purposes. Special editions can also be created to specifications. For details, contact the Special Sales Department, Arcade Publishing, 307 West 36th Street, 11th Floor, New York, NY 10018 or arcade@skyhorsepublishing.com.

Arcade Publishing® is a registered trademark of Skyhorse Publishing, Inc.®, a Delaware corporation.

Visit our website at www.arcadepub.com.

10 9 8 7 6 5 4 3 2 1

Library of Congress Cataloging-in-Publication Data

Names: Stratton, Richard (Richard H.), author.
Title: In the world: from the big house to Hollywood / Richard Stratton.
Description: First edition. | New York: Arcade Publishing, [2020]
Identifiers: LCCN 2019035674 (print) | LCCN 2019035675 (ebook) | ISBN 9781628727272 (hardcover) | ISBN 9781628727296 (ebook)
Subjects: LCSH: Stratton, Richard (Richard H.) | Ex-convicts—United States—Biography. | Screenwriters—United States—Biography.
Classification: LCC HV9468.S77 A3 2020 (print) | LCC HV9468.S77 (ebook) | DDC 812/.54 [B—dc23
LC record available at https://lccn.loc.gov/2019035674
LC ebook record available at https://lccn.loc.gov/2019035675

Cover design by Erin Seaward-Hiatt
Cover photograph courtesy of Ray Vanacore

Printed in the United States of America

I returned, and saw under the sun
that the race is not to the swift,
nor the battle to the strong,
neither yet bread to the wise,
nor riches to men of understanding,
nor yet favor to men of skill,
but time and chance happens
to them all.

Ecclesiastes 9:11

Ain't life grand . . . ?

Bank robber Clyde Barrow,
from the movie *Bonnie and Clyde*

CONTENTS

PART TWO

PART THREE

Author's Note

DÉTENTE IN THE WAR ON PLANTS

FOR THIS, VOLUME three of my *Cannabis Americana: Remembrance of the War on Plants* trilogy, I pick up the story on that unforgettable day, Monday, June 25, 1990, when they opened the front gate at the Federal Correctional Institution (FCI) in Ashland, Kentucky, and I was allowed to walk out. After eight straight years in custody of the US Bureau of Prisons, I was suddenly free.

The outside world felt like a different reality—a heightened new dimension of existence where anything is possible. The simple act of walking without high stone walls and chain-link fences strung with coils of gleaming razor wire penning me in; the horizon no longer assaulted with manned gun towers; no shackles and chains around my ankles to restrict my stride; no handcuffs linked to a belly chain around my waist to hinder my reach; no sullen, beefy guards loitering, watching, poised to order me to drop my drawers, bend over, and spread 'em so they could peer up my asshole—yes, I was a man again, a human being, no longer an inmate identification number, no longer a prisoner. After a struggle worthy of Kafka with faceless authorities in an unfathomable criminal justice system, I was free at last.

MY FIFTEEN-YEAR CAREER as an international marijuana and hash-ish smuggler prior to my arrest in 1982 is recounted in volume one,

Smuggler's Blues: A True Story of the Hippie Mafia. That book ends with my capture by DEA agents, deputy US marshals with the Fugitive Task Force, and LAPD cops in the lobby of the Sheraton Senator Hotel at the airport in Los Angeles. I went to trial twice—once in the District of Maine and a second time in the Southern District of New York. In the Maine case I was convicted of conspiracy to possess with intent to distribute marijuana and sentenced to the maximum: fifteen years. On my way to the penitentiary to serve that sentence, I was waylaid in New York and told that unless I was ready to cooperate with the government and become a rat, I would be charged again, this time under the so-called kingpin statute, Title 21, United States Code, Section 848, with being the manager and organizer of a continuing criminal enterprise. I faced anywhere from a minimum of ten years up to life in prison with no possibility of parole. I chose not to cooperate and went to trial again. After a second conviction, I was sentenced to a total of twenty-five years and six months in prison.

While in prison, I became a jailhouse lawyer. I studied the law and discovered an illegality in my sentence. I appealed the sentence and won in the Second Circuit Court of Appeals. The appellate court vacated my twenty-five-year sentence and remanded me for resentencing before a different judge. After more legal wrangling, I was resentenced to ten years. I maxed out that sentence, but I then had to litigate with the Federal Bureau of Prisons (BOP) and ultimately have the judge order the bureau to release me. Both federal cases and the years of legal warfare, my eight-year sojourn in the vast, brutal American penal system in custody of the BOP, and my eventual courtroom victory that resulted in my being released are detailed in volume two: *Kingpin: Prisoner of the War on Drugs.*

RELEASE WAS A heady time. My novel, *Smack Goddess*, about a lady kingpin drug dealer, written while in prison, was about to be published. I had an advance from my publisher of $20,000 waiting for me— the most legal money I had ever earned. Anything seemed possible.

Freedom beckoned, and challenged: *Get your life back*. Or, better still: *Make a new life for yourself.* And a reminder: *Obey the law, asshole. Stay the fuck out of prison.*

Several of the friends I made while in prison who had been released were unable to make it out here in the world. They were busted for violating conditions of their parole, or they picked up a new case and were soon back behind bars. Doing serious time—anything over five, ten, or more years in a maximum-security penitentiary—will change you no matter how strong you are—it's inevitable. I had a lot going for me, far more than most ex-cons coming out of prison. But I was still wrestling with internal demons, doppelgangers, and the self-sabotaging tricksters of my character that had not been fully exorcised even after eight years of punishment, and were just lying in wait to resurface and play havoc with my peace of mind. As I was about to learn, getting out of prison, and staying out, and really getting free from the prison in one's head is in many ways more of a challenge than surviving long-term imprisonment.

SOME NAMES HAVE been changed to protect the privacy of dear friends and lovers, as well as those who have never been captured, and who may still be active in the marijuana underground and cannabis black market even as the mysterious outlaw spiky green-leafed plant becomes semi-legal. The status of cannabis has changed dramatically since my arrest and imprisonment. It has gone from the "weed with roots in hell" to legal medicine and recreational refreshment available over the counter in some thirty American states, and in foreign countries, including our enlightened neighbor to the north, Canada.

One could argue that we were right, that we were ahead of our time, those of us in the so-called hippie mafia, the outlaws and freak entrepreneurs who risked their freedom and their lives and continued to defy laws that were not only wrong but ridiculous, unenforceable, and downright un-American. Over a tumultuous three decades we were able to change the culture in the United States by continuing to smuggle, cultivate, and distribute this remarkable, and yet still controversial, plant. We questioned and resisted the so-called authorities, the federal government; we fought them not only in the war on pot, but in the ongoing civil rights struggle, the anti–Vietnam War movement, and in opposition to the police state and ever-expanding prison-industrial complex that still represses us today.

As far back as the Nixon presidency in the 1970s, the war on drugs has been used by the government as a means of social control over blacks and the counterculture through arresting the leaders and disrupting their communities. Yet all these years later America's longest and costliest war—the war on plants—rages on. Thousands of men and women are locked up, serving long sentences, even life sentences, with no possibility of parole for trafficking in an herb that has proven to be a remarkable medicine and a disobedient friend of mankind. As I write, the old-guard reactionary right has once more assumed power in America. Already the forces of repression have begun to mount a new propaganda campaign against cannabis. It is long past time for our politicians to wake up and understand that this plant and the people who use it will not be controlled. It is too late to try to put the genie back in the bottle. It is time to get smart and to end this destructive government fiasco.

Free the prisoners of the war on plants.

IN THE
WORLD

Prologue

TIME AND CHANCE

June 25, 1990

FREE AT LAST! Although . . . not so fast.

Monday morning at 9:00 a.m., as I am ready to leave the prison through the front gate at the FCI in Ashland, Kentucky, my case manager—a guy I call Axelrod, not a bad guy as far as these Bureau of Prisons types go—pulls me into his office and hands me some papers. He informs that I have forty-eight hours to report to my parole officer in the Eastern District of New York, Brooklyn office. If I fail to show up, if I do not report on time, Axelrod says, I will be deemed an escaped prisoner and pursued as a fugitive.

"What did you say? Parole? No. Wait a minute. That's wrong. My sentence is *nonparoleable*. Remember? Look."

I show him my commitment papers and sentence computation sheet where it specifies that I am serving a nonparoleable sentence and therefore not subject to parole.

"Yes, that's true," Axelrod tells me. "You won't be on parole. You'll be on *supervised release*."

"Supervised release? What the fuck is that?"

"Well," he says, "the good-time you earned while you were locked up—a little over two years—that good-time is forfeited as you walk out the door."

He smiles a smug captor's smirk.

"You still owe the government that time on the street."

Oh, okay. I get it now. Supervised release is simply another term—government doublespeak—for parole. It's another way of saying that I am still under the scrutiny and ostensible control of federal authorities. This is fucked up—typical Uncle Sam double-dealing. You can't trust these federal fuckers. They dole it out with one hand, snatch it away with the other.

"You can refuse to sign the release papers if you choose," Axelrod says, still with a knowing smile. "You could go back to your cell . . . and do the remaining two-plus years here with us."

No. I'm tempted out of sheer defiance, but no, never mind that. I have had more than enough of the prison existence, this half-life of the convict—of the world but not in it. I want out now, today, not after two-plus-more years, not after two more days. Anything could happen in that time. I could pick up a new case by strangling some motherfucker who disrespects me. I could get caught smoking or dealing pot. I'm ready to leave now, today, with or without supervised release. Fuck that noise. I am ready to live again in the free world. And to hell with these lying *federales* and their supervised release. I never gave credence to these people or obeyed their rules in the first place. I never kissed ass and adhered to their ridiculous regulations. Why start now? Any bureaucracy that is run by supposedly intelligent human beings who outlaw and wage war on a plant cannot be trusted. Aren't these the same so-called authorities that told us we could free the people of Vietnam by bombing the shit out of them, murdering hundreds of thousands of women and children? I didn't believe them then, and I don't believe them now.

I live by the maxim "Question authority." I don't trust anything these government stiffs tell me. After eight years of being subjected to total Bureau of Prisons control down to regular asshole inspections, I will leave prison, yes, I will walk out of here today with new respect for the frightening power of my government and its minions, but also with new disdain for their legitimacy, their veracity. They lie, they cheat—they don't even abide by their own rules. They fuck us over all in the name of justice. They have usurped the American dream of personal liberty. But they do it with such authority, with such willful power, and such guile, such arrogance and zeal that you must pay attention and remain mindful of what it means to be an American in the first place, or you will find yourself cowering in the face of fierce governmental repression.

To Axelrod I say, "No way. Gimme the fucking papers and show me where to sign."

In my own personal war with the government over time, I got lucky—twice. First, I was sentenced in October 1984, nota bene. Had I been sentenced fourteen months later, in 1986, when the feds enacted new mandatory sentences under the kingpin statute, my judge would have been required by law to impose a *mandatory life sentence with no possibility of parole*. I would have been sentenced to life in prison for smuggling cannabis. Instead of walking out the gate, my release plan would have called for a wooden box and a grave in the pauper's cemetery outside the prison.

I would still be locked up serving a life sentence instead of out here in the world writing this book and bringing attention to the government's criminal war on drugs. Under mandatory federal sentencing guidelines judges have no discretion; they must impose the sentence called for by the guidelines—unless one "cooperates" and becomes a rat for the government. This federal law is still on the books.

I got lucky a second time in the New York prosecution when my sentencing judge, United States District Court Judge Constance Baker Motley, made it clear that she was enhancing my sentence, giving me more time, because I "refused to cooperate with the government," that is, I refused to rat on my friends and enemies. Her language on the record tended to make my sentence *coercive* rather than *punitive*. And for a judge to do that, to try to force a defendant to cooperate and become a rat by giving them more time rather than simply punishing them for their illegal behavior, higher courts have ruled to be illegal. You can give a defendant less time for snitching, but you cannot give them more time for refusing to become a snitch. Judges do that all the time, of course, but they don't usually make the mistake of stating on the record in plain unequivocal English that that is what they are doing. Judge Motley, however, made it clear she had determined to give me a total of twenty-five years and six months "for the reason," as she put it, "that it might convince you that cooperation with the government is in your best interest."

Well, dear Judge Motley—may you rest in peace, gone off to that great courthouse in the sky where we will all be judged one day— perhaps not. You see, things are not always as they seem. Sometimes it is better to keep your mouth shut—hold your mud, as they say. Admit nothing. Deny everything. Make them prove it. Rat on no one. Go to trial. Tell them they are wrong. Tell them to go fuck themselves. Their laws are asinine. Take a stand—but not the witness stand. Insist this war on drugs is bullshit—it's a lie; it's a war on the American people.

As Americans we have a constitutional right to keep our mouths shut, to not incriminate others or ourselves even after we have been arrested and convicted. When I was locked up in the early eighties, the feds were hot on a drug-fueled celebrity witch hunt not unlike the McCarthy-era pursuit of presumed communists. They were determined to indict my close friend and mentor, the world-renowned novelist, frequent TV talk show guest, author of Pulitzer Prize–winning books, husband of several wives, and perennial government critic and alleged enemy, Norman Mailer. They hoped to disgrace Mailer by branding him a drug dealer, convicting him as a co-conspirator in my far-flung pot-smuggling enterprise, and locking him up in prison. Mailer had held a position on the government's enemies list since the Nixon regime primarily due to his opposition to the war in Vietnam. Government prosecutors in New York figured that if they put enough pressure on me, I would flip, roll over, and implicate

Mailer and testify against him as well as my friend the writer Hunter Thompson, my attorney and friend Richard N. Goodwin, and his wife, Doris Kearns Goodwin, and anyone else I knew whom they hoped to indict, convict, and imprison, destroying lives in order to enhance their careers.

Mailer and I had known each other and been friends for more than a decade by the time I was arrested. We owned a horse farm together in Maine that was ultimately seized by the government. Certainly, we were close; we remained in regular contact during the time I was a fugitive and after I was arrested. Next to my mother, Mailer was my most loyal prison visitor all the years I was locked up. And he welcomed me into his home when I was released. It was my choice based on personal convictions not to serve the government by creating false evidence and giving testimony against Mailer or anyone else.

At my first trial in federal court in the District of Maine I presented a somewhat fallacious defense—not entirely bogus but a bit farfetched. I claimed that I was not a dope smuggler at all, not a criminal, but rather a writer, a journalist who was engaged in research on the illegal dope trade. This was half true. I was a writer before I was arrested. I had published short stories and some journalism. And, when I was twenty-one, I had been granted a writing fellowship at the Fine Arts Work Center in Provincetown, Massachusetts, where I first met and became friends with Mailer. At the time I was busted, I was writing magazine articles and doing research for a book on the worldwide cultivation and illegal traffic in cannabis.

It was while on assignment for *Rolling Stone* to write an article on infamous Rochdale College in Toronto, a center for soft-drug distribution throughout North America, that I met and befriended iconic hippie godfather Robert "Rosie" Rowbotham. Rosie is a legendary character in the marijuana underground. The Bachman-Turner Overdrive song "Takin' Care of Business" was inspired by Rosie. While at work on the *Rolling Stone* piece, I partnered with Rosie to import and distribute multiton loads of marijuana and hashish in the US and

Canada. The market was there; it was booming, and the pot business paid better than journalism. I used to tell people that I supported my writing habit by smuggling pot.

Ultimately, the sheer intensity of the outlaw marijuana business, and the intoxicating insanity of the outlaw lifestyle, came to dominate my days. I became a junkie, addicted not to dope but to the adrenaline rush I got from getting over on the Man. I wrote less and smuggled more and bigger loads of cannabis. As North America's appetite for the illegal herb grew exponentially, and the business of importing marijuana and hashish continued to ramp up during the 1970s and into the 1980s, I became a full-time, 24–7 dedicated dope-smuggling outlaw.

Yet always in the back of my mind there was the dormant commitment that once the craziness ended—however it ended, whether in a prison cell or as a fugitive in exile, as long as I was alive and still in possession of my faculties—I would use the experience to write about the global war on drugs, and, specifically, about our government's ill-advised criminalization of cannabis. I became obsessed with the metaphoric implications of what I came to think of as a war on plants: a specific plant, *Cannabis sativa, Cannabis indica,* and eventually the American-grown *Cannabis Americana* that has come to dominate the domestic market. There were stunning images on the nightly news: black helicopters descending into the lush green mountains of Northern California's Emerald Triangle; paramilitary drug warriors dressed in black flak jackets, bulletproof vests, and dark-visored helmets to hide their faces and wielding assault weapons as they charged out of police choppers—to do what? Raid an encampment of enemy forces? Attack a heavily fortified criminal redoubt? No, these grown men, armed agents of the law, were there to uproot lovely, peaceful, verdant plants as they luxuriated in the sunshine. They were there to rip these plants from the bosom of Mother Earth.

The story took me all over the world. I began by smuggling a few kilos of commercial weed across the Mexican border while still in college at Arizona State University. Later, I felt I needed to embed myself in the international illegal cannabis trade to fully understand it, to get to know the players, to visit the countries of origin and meet the growers in order to write about it knowingly. I came to appreciate that the government's anticannabis effort is not about the dangers to one's mental or physical health posed by consuming cannabis; rather it is about perpetuating the crime-control establishment. It is about law enforcement dominance encroaching upon the realm of private behavior and government control over how we alter our consciousness—indeed, how we think. And so resistance is tantamount to expressing personal freedom: the freedom that we as Americans are guaranteed by the Constitution to life, liberty, and the pursuit of happiness. Surely that must also include the right to alter our consciousness as we see fit so long as we are not harming anyone else.

The pot smuggler's life is about defiance. We defied specific laws we knew were wrong. The outlaw life for me was also about high adventure in foreign lands, and risk, serious risk with real consequences—all contributing to the intense adrenaline rush of being a renegade and a free spirit, of waking up every day and wondering if this will be the day cops and federal dope agents finally catch you. Soon I came to realize that the outlaw lifestyle is itself a drug. It becomes an addiction that can only lead to death or imprisonment. That day of reckoning came when a small army of LAPD cops, DEA agents, and deputy US marshals with the Fugitive Task Force finally brought me to ground. They surrounded me with guns drawn, slapped handcuffs on my wrists, and hustled me off to jail. After years on the run, my first thought was, "Okay, now it's over. At last I can stop running and write about it."

And write I did, all during the time I was locked up. In addition to the legal writing I did as a jailhouse lawyer—which resulted in my getting myself as well as a few others released from prison—whenever I had an opportunity I wrote short stories, one of which, "A Skyline Turkey," won the 1989 PEN Prison Writing Award for short fiction. And I wrote a novel, *Smack Goddess*, loosely based on a lady kingpin dope dealer I met when we were both locked up in the Metropolitan Correctional Center (MCC) in New York City. The novel was accepted for publication just weeks before I was due to be released.

TODAY, AS I walk out through the prison gate with my reputation, my dignity, and my asshole intact, the possibility of a new, legitimate career as a working professional writer is every bit as real in my mind as the prison cell I leave behind. If I fail to make it out here in the world, if I let the twin demons of hubris and megalomania regain control, I will have no one to blame but myself.

PART ONE

PAROLE:

DOING TIME ON THE STREET

Chapter One

LAWLESS

Outside the prison gate in Ashland, Kentucky, a taxi waits to take me to the Tri-State Airport in Credo, West Virginia. The Bureau of Prisons has provided me with a one-way ticket to New York City, where I am to be paroled. I was also given $100 in cash and a government check for whatever was left in my commissary account, $27.33 of the eleven cents per hour I earned working as a clerk in the prison law library.

When I change planes at the airport in Charlotte, North Carolina, suddenly it hits me: I'm free. I'm out of prison. I'm going home. It all feels so new: a virtual midlife transformation. Rebirth at age forty-five. Prisoner one moment—in custody, confined behind bars and walls and fences, watched over by grim keepers, in constant peril—free man the next, walking around surrounded by male and female civilians. It's disorienting, it's surreal, it's amazing to be able to move around and mingle with normal people, no longer in the company of brooding convicts dressed in khakis or blaze-orange jumpsuits, but in close proximity with free American citizens wearing civilian clothes—and, yes, no doubt, there are women out here, actual living humans of the opposite sex, those endlessly fascinating and alluring creatures without whom I have existed for so many solitary years. Now to be in their company once again, to be assured that women still move freely among the population, strikes me with an almost dizzying rush of liberation and optimism—a zest for life.

Can this really be happening? Is it real, or am I imagining it? Dreaming it, as I dreamed of freedom so many times while locked up, only to wake and realize I was still in prison.

This is good, Stratton, I assure myself, very good indeed for a man who loves women, to find that they exist out here in the world—and lots of them, all sizes and shapes, and dressed not in the garb of a prison guard but in skirts, dresses and blouses, shorts and tank tops; smelling deliciously of female; infusing the atmosphere with their intoxicating pheromones—it gives me new hope for the future, new joy to think that I might yet live again in close proximity with a woman, oh, God, yes, and to love her and cherish her, perhaps even have a wife and a family, children—something I had all but given up, something I wanted with all my mind and soul.

It is all so fantastic and bewildering even to entertain these thoughts when not so long ago it appeared hopeless. There were times during my years as a prisoner when it did not seem likely or possible that I would ever get out and be in a position to contemplate having a family, a wife and children of my own. The prospect of fatherhood seemed doubtful if not impossible. Locked up at thirty-seven with a twenty-five-year, nonparoleable sentence, had I not won my appeal and been resentenced, I would have had to do somewhere around seventeen or eighteen years at the very least. That would have meant I'd be in my midfifties when I was released—if I made it out at all. And by then, there is no telling what shape I would have been in mentally and emotionally. As it is, after eight years in maximum- and high-medium-security joints, it remains to be seen how sane I am, how well I will be able to adjust to living in the free world. The longer you do, the harder it is to get out, and the harder it is to assimilate back into society, to free yourself of the mindset and distorted code of ethics of the convict.

Doing time in prison becomes a way of life; like anything else, you get used to it. You lose touch with the outside world. You adapt to a whole new culture and morality. You shut down and deny tender feelings, feelings of love and compassion. You forget the skills and manners it takes to live in society. You learn to live by the convict code: lying and deceiving the authorities simply to get by without becoming that most despised creature of the prisoner population—the jailhouse snitch. And it's easy to fuck up and lose acquired good-time, even to pick up a new case, especially if you are inured to rehabilitation, still and always an outlaw in the eyes of the authorities.

I nearly blew my release date by getting into a fight in the prison TV room and getting locked up in the Hole when I was just weeks from release. And all the time I was in prison I continued to use and deal pot—of course I did; I wasn't about to admit I was wrong. I daily violated any number of rules and regulations imposed by my Bureau of Prisons keepers that could have resulted in a new prosecution had I been caught. There is also the psychological effect of imprisonment to contend with. The long-term prisoner begins to fear freedom, if not consciously, then at some deeper level. One questions one's ability to make it out there in the world. Ex-con. No job. No place to live. Fucked-up value system. Will I find someone to love me? And, if I do, will I know how to love and respect another person after so many years of living in close custody with nothing but brutal keepers and damaged men? There was no prerelease counseling to prepare me, only all these bad habits, these unsavory relationships, these inner demons and self-destructive impulses to contend with. The convict may even self-sabotage and fuck up on purpose as his release date draws near, what's known as short-timer syndrome. Or get out, find he can't make it on the street, and hasten his return to the cloistered life he has come to know so well.

But I am in no frame of mind to contemplate failure. No, I will not succumb to fear of what I have longed for and dreamed of, worked so hard to achieve, and prepared myself for. I am in a far better situation than most ex-cons hitting the street. I have a novel about to be published. I have a job in a law firm waiting for me. I have a place to go to live until I can find a place of my own. And, above all, I have friends and family who love me, believe in me, and support me. I have nothing to complain about. I have no excuse if I fail out here. I should fall to my knees right here in the airport terminal and praise God that I lived through the last eight years in prison to experience the incredible high of resurrection in midlife.

Enjoy it, Stratton. And whatever you do, don't blow it.

WHEN I ARRIVE at La Guardia Airport in New York it's just 2:00 p.m. and I am at a loss where to go, what to do next. I call my parole officer, Joe Veltri, in Manhattan. I know Veltri; he's a decent guy. He was assigned to prepare my presentence report, and he came to interview me at the MCC before my sentencing. Veltri tells me that my case has been transferred to Brooklyn, where I will be residing temporarily at Norman Mailer's home in Brooklyn Heights. Veltri gives me the number and address for the Brooklyn, Eastern District Parole Office. He also informs me that once I report, I will not be allowed to leave the district. I will have to wait for some time to get myself established, and then apply for written permission to go beyond the five boroughs of New York.

With still nearly two days before I'm required to report, I decide to continue on to Massachusetts to see my long-suffering parents, who have been waiting for this day with almost as much anticipation as I. When I call my friend and attorney, Ivan Fisher—who is to be my employer—Ivan whoops for joy. He cries, "Mazel tov!" and declares for the whole office to hear: "Stratton is out of jail!"

I walk to the Trump Shuttle, no longer the Eastern Airlines Shuttle, where I learn that the airfare to Boston is $119. I have only $77 left from the hundred the Bureau of Prisons gave me upon my release. After a few more calls, I take a cab to Brooklyn Heights where I meet with Judith McNally, Norman Mailer's secretary, who gives me $100 and the keys to the Mailer home at 142 Columbia Heights.

Norman calls while I'm with Judith. He and the family are at his home in Provincetown, Massachusetts, for the summer. He tells me he's hard at work on a new book, his long-anticipated novel of the CIA, *Harlot's Ghost*, which now stands at over two thousand pages and is, he believes, no more than half done. Norman faxes his daily output of handwritten pages to Judith, who transcribes them on a computer, prints out the pages, and faxes them back to Norman. Ah, the wonders of all this new technology.

"This is great news, Rick," Norman tells me. "Get yourself settled, and then come see us here in P-town. . . . Stay as long as you like."

I catch a six o'clock shuttle to Logan Airport in Boston. My mother, Mary, my father, Emery, my sister Judith, who we call GiGi, and her oldest son, my nephew Robert, meet me at the arrivals gate for a full-on, joyous reunion—the prodigal son back in the bosom of his family. On the way to my parents' home, we stop for a celebratory dinner at Legal Seafood, a restaurant in Brookline. I order lobster and a bottle of champagne. Yes, this must be freedom, and it's a far cry from the mess hall at the FCI at Ashland, Kentucky. Two sips of the wine and I'm already feeling light-headed.

EARLY THE NEXT morning, unable to sleep past dawn, I finally realize my one abiding prison fantasy of life in the free world. I get up, get dressed, and walk out the front door of my parents' home unobstructed. I continue to walk for several blocks with nothing or no one to impede me until I reach the town square in Wellesley, Massachusetts. There I use actual US currency to buy today's edition of the *New York Times*. I find a coffee shop and order a cup of real, brewed coffee. Then I sit down and read the paper and drink my coffee with no one watching over me, no one to question me, no one to demand that I recite my name and federal prisoner number, no one to tell me to drop my drawers, bend over, and spread my cheeks so they can peer up my asshole, no one to tell what I can or cannot do, where I must report, whom I must report to and when. No more controlled movements— that's all over; the control, the constant supervision has ended. Walking down the street, buying a newspaper and a cup of coffee, sitting down and being left alone to read my paper and drink my coffee—this, more than anything else, this simple act has come to define what it means to me finally to be a free man living in the free world.

A few days before I was released from prison, while I was still in the Hole after the fight, I got a visit from my unit manager, Axelrod. He cut me a break. He released me from the Hole and went to bat for me before the disciplinary committee so there were no new charges and no loss of good-time. Axelrod advised me that I should seek help when I got out. He warned that the psychological defenses and character traits, the physical and mental demands of getting and giving respect that one develops and builds upon to survive in prison do not easily translate to the free world. That was the extent of the prerelease counseling I would receive. I knew what he said is true. I'd seen it in how I reacted to even the most insignificant perceived threat to my character while locked up. You could not cut in line in front of me in the mess hall and not expect to be challenged. To let something like that go in prison is the beginning of the end of your dignity and the integrity of your personal space. Once the other convicts suspect that you will break weak, the next thing you know they will be demanding you go to commissary and buy things for them—or worse. I believed that I didn't need any help. I imagined that I would adapt to freedom as well as I had conformed to life inside.

And so it seemed, sitting with my parents, my sister, and my nephew in the restaurant the night before. I probably appeared normal then, and I felt one with my family like someone who has returned from a long journey. But now, alone, as I look around and try to appreciate what I've achieved, the euphoria, the sense of wonder, and the optimism slip away. As a new reality sets in, I perceive a distance, a sense of alienation, of not belonging, of not being one of these people in this world, out here, these civilians with their humdrum workaday lives. And yet I must try to fit in, to be one of them. I can't go on defining myself as a convict, an outlaw living by a different moral code, a different set of laws and values, or I will surely end up back in prison. I imagine this is how veterans must feel upon returning from war, and why some choose to reenlist while others sink into despair, drugs, or alcohol, or succumb to mental illness. Post-traumatic stress disorder: that's what I am feeling. There is a whole depth of experience one cannot hope to share with normal people. And why share it? Why not just forget it?

Because you can't. Because it's who you have become.

I CALL MY friend Shane, another ex-con who lives nearby in Brookline, and who was released a year before I got out. This is a violation of the terms of my release; I know even without having heard it from my soon-to-be parole officer that I am not allowed to communicate with, associate with, or have anything to do with anyone I met and became friends with while I was in prison—just another of their ridiculous and virtually unenforceable rules. Forget that. Who else am I going to hang out with? Who else can I talk to who might understand what I'm going through, might even be going through it himself?

I met Shane and we became close friends while we were both locked up on the ninth floor at the Metropolitan Correctional Center, the infamous federal jail in downtown Manhattan, known among convicts as the Criminal Hilton. Shane is a former hashish smuggler, so we also have that in common, as well as our home state of Massachusetts. His family is originally from Iran. They fled after the revolution and settled in Boston. I met Shane's sister, Diana, in the visiting room at the MCC. Diana and my mother began coming to New York together to visit us. After Shane shipped out, back to FCI Otisville in Upstate New York, where he completed his sentence, Diana and I stayed in touch. We spoke on the telephone several times a week. I wrote to her, and she came to visit. She is gorgeous, a Persian beauty, tall, with long, thick black hair and a proud bearing; smart, sophisticated; divorced, with a teenage son. I thought we were falling in love. I know I was.

But then, just as suddenly as it began, it was over. No more letters or phone calls, no more visits. It's not easy to sustain these love affairs when one-half of the relationship is in prison. Shane had warned me that his sister was emotionally traumatized after having discovered her father, who committed suicide by hanging himself in the basement of their home. There was certainly a deep, profound sadness I hoped to be able to dispel.

Shane picks me up at my parents' home and we go for a two-hour workout at his gym in Alston, just outside Boston. It's a whole new experience working out with all these state-of-the-art exercise machines after the crude equipment one finds on a typical prison weight pile. Coming off eight years of near daily regimented exercise—even while I was in the Hole and restricted to push-ups and sit-ups—working out has become so much of who I am, a part of my daily routine, a psychological as well as physical means of keeping my shit together, that I intend to remain that creature of habit, the person of self-discipline and mental focus that sustained me in prison.

After the workout, we take a drive into Boston's Back Bay to stop by and check the progress on a townhouse on Beacon Street Shane bought and is in the process of renovating. He tells me Diana is in Europe and advises me to forget about her. "She's not a happy person, and probably never will be. You don't need that in your life right now, Richard—or even any time in the future."

Shane takes us out to dinner—my mother, my nephew, and me. After the meal, outside the restaurant, I meet up with another jailhouse friend, Dr. David Buckley. The Doc, as I call him, is a defrocked psychiatrist who was implicated in his younger brother's marijuana importing business. A sailboat full of Colombian pot was offloaded and landed successfully on the coast of Maine. The pot was distributed, everybody got paid, and they all went away happy. One of the partners got busted on another trip some years later, but not long enough to have exceeded the five-year statute of limitations. He made a deal and ratted out the Doc, his brother, and anyone else connected to the original smuggle.

Doctor Buckley was running a successful if unorthodox business as a shrink in Fort Lauderdale, liberally prescribing quaaludes and other mood-altering drugs, when he was arrested and charged in the marijuana conspiracy. He went to trial in Portland, Maine, maintaining a not-guilty-by-reason-of-insanity defense. During his sentencing, he gave an impassioned allocution, ending with the classic line, "Give me liberty, or give me death!" and then he jumped out the window of the courtroom, landing, as he knew he would, on the roof of a lower wing of the building and sustaining no physical harm. He was quickly recaptured and sentenced to the maximum at that time, five years, and designated to a minimum-security prison camp.

By the time I met Doctor Buckley in holdover at MCC in New York, he had so pissed off Bureau of Prisons staff at every institution to which he was designated that he was being shipped from a minimum-security camp to one of the higher-level prisons, possibly even the infamous gothic penitentiary at Lewisburg, Pennsylvania—one of the oldest and toughest federal joints in the country and a major transit hub in the Bureau of Prisons system, a kind of intelligence communications center for all things happening at certain levels in international criminal circles. Doctor Buckley didn't seem to mind; he'd heard that the guards and staff in the higher-level facilities were less apt to harass prisoners for infractions of minor rules and regulations since the convicts in those joints were doing serious time for serious crimes. My advice to him was that, true as it might be with regard to the level of one's custody, he did not want to pick up a new case and end up spending much more than the five years he'd been sentenced to in the custody of the US attorney's designated authority, the Bureau of Prisons.

"This is no joke, Doc," I told him during one of our talks at MCC. "You can't fuck with these people. They are in total control. Just do the time. Keep your head down, keep your mouth shut, and get the fuck out, or you will end up being even crazier than you already are."

The Doc took my advice, sort of. We were to meet again a few years later when we were both doing time at a high-medium-security FCI in

Petersburg, Virginia. We used to gather out on the exercise yard in the evening for what we called a meeting of the Riviera Club. We'd smoke pot and fantasize that we were not in prison at all but rather ensconced at some exclusive resort on the French Mediterranean coast, Cannes or Saint-Tropez, surrounded by bare-breasted, beautiful women. The idea was to tell each other stories, no matter how fantastic, weave tales of life in the world that would have nothing to do with the facts of our separate cases or the conditions of our incarceration. No bitching allowed. The hope was to escape the prison at least in our minds; and it worked . . . as long as the reefer was good.

All of the members of the Riviera Club were doing time for drugs except one other guy from the Boston vicinity, who was a bank and armored car robber from Charleston, Massachusetts, the US capital of bank robbers. Stevie Burke is his name. A tough kid, and a sweet guy, but steeped in the harsh mentality of the convict. He'd been in and out of prison most of his adult life. Stevie and I became close, along with another Boston guy, Lance McMahon. In time, further violating the terms of my release, I will reconnect with all these guys and bear witness to how they readjust to the world, or reoffend and go back to prison.

LATER, BACK AT my parents, I unpack, sort through, and then repack all the cartons—eleven total—filled with my prison writings—short stories, poems, the manuscript of my novel, hundreds of letters, a dozen journals, legal briefs and memoranda I wrote on my own case and for several other cases I worked on for prisoners who, if they could afford it, paid me in commissary—cartons of cigarettes (though I didn't smoke tobacco, cigarettes are a negotiable currency in prison), ice cream, morsels of weed. I'm a packrat when it comes to paperwork, a hoarder of written records, any documents that might provide written evidence of having lived this life and help locate meaning in the experience through the words committed there. I shipped home reams of papers amounting to a trove of manuscripts over the years of my captivity in the Federal Bureau of Prisons. While still a prisoner, I would be charged twice with running a business from prison, though never convicted. This was yet another violation of the rules and regulations of the institution that I chose to ignore. They charged me with providing services as a jailhouse lawyer, which was true, though they could never prove that I accepted payment. And they tried to punish me for operating a business as a writer. I was ordered to pack up all my manuscripts and send them home. But they were never able to show that I had been paid for my work.

I will leave the cartons stored at my parents' home until I can get a place of my own. *Ah!* Just the sound of those few words, "a place of my own," fills me with anticipation. Some long-term prisoners come to call their cell their "house"; I never did. I never thought of the many cells I occupied as anything more than stops along the way to where I was going—to a place of my own.

My mother and my sister drive me from Massachusetts back to Brooklyn Heights. We walk along the promenade overlooking the East River and downtown Manhattan, to arrive on Montague Street where we dine at a Japanese restaurant. To say that I am enjoying the variety of restaurant food after so many years of bland and sometimes barely edible institutional fare is to touch on a subject that often comes up when people learn that you spent a number of years in prison: food. "How was the food?" they might ask. In general, it was pretty bad, some things worse than others. I've always been a good eater. At twenty-one, I quit eating beef, pork, lamb—except during those times when I was in Lebanon and felt it would have offended my hosts. In prison, it's not just that the food is bad or at best mediocre; it's that the whole ritual of eating goes from the communal enjoyment of breaking bread with family, loved ones, and friends to rushing to line up in a crowded mess hall with a bunch of hungry, angry, tough convicts who brook no delays in getting their fare and wolfing it down in the allotted few minutes. Most of the violence that takes place in prison happens in the mess hall: stabbings, riots, beatdowns. At the penitentiary in Lewisburg, Pennsylvania, I once witnessed a prisoner get shanked, near gutted, and left to bleed out on the red top, the area of red brick tiles just outside the mess hall doors. It was the favored spot for eviscerations, right in front of the guards. All this by way of saying that, immediately following my release from prison, to enjoy good food with family and friends is a blessed experience, one that will never pale, and a pleasure that can only be compared to that other basic, cherished human inter-course—sexual intercourse. I'll get to that. I've only been out . . . what, two full days?

BACK IN MAILER'S apartment, his top floor aerie and multitiered loft complete with rope ladders, parapets, narrow ledges that must be scaled to reach a crow's nest writing perch high above the rest of the dwelling, we find Judith McNally and are soon joined by Maggie Mailer, Norman's youngest daughter, and one of his sons, Steven, whom I've known since he was a boy when we lived in Provincetown, at the tip of Cape Cod in Massachusetts. It was during a winter sea-son on a writing fellowship at the Fine Arts Work Center in Province-town that I first met and became friends with Norman. The Mailers (Norman was then with his wife Carol, Maggie's mother) lived in a big brick house on the bay side of the cape. My wife and I became friendly with Norman's cook, a young woman named Bobbi, who lived in the apartment below ours across the street from the Mailers. One evening the phone rang; my wife answered and handed me the receiver. "It's Norman Mailer," she said. Norman told me that he'd heard a lot about me from Bobbi, and he wondered if I'd care to come over and watch *Monday Night Football* with him. We ended up drinking a fifth of brandy and half a bottle of scotch (my wife helped somewhat) and staggered home at dawn. Mailer and I became close friends, sharing our interests in writing, boxing, women, music, and marijuana. When Mailer and his friend, the former whiz kid and

Kennedy speechwriter Richard N. Goodwin, bought a farm in rural Western Maine, my wife and I lived there for a time and eventually bought Mailer and Goodwin out. That transaction and my long close friendship with Mailer would lead the government agents and prosecutors who arrested and prosecuted me to believe that Mailer was an investor, money launderer, and knowing co-conspirator in my cannabis smuggling and distribution enterprise.

My mother, GiGi, and I all spend the night at the Mailers. GiGi and my mother sleep in Norman and Norris's room with the air conditioner. The past couple of days have been sweltering. I sleep in their youngest son's, John Buffalo's, room and am not troubled by the heat. That's another of the few advantages to having spent time in prison; not only does it increase one's enjoyment of good food, but after living through harsh conditions you might be subjected to in any number of jails and prisons in the vast American prison system, you can handle just about any discomfort you might encounter out here in the civilized world. As a wrestler in high school and college I used to say, "After wrestling, everything else is easy." I can now say that about prison. Very little in the way of lack of creature comforts fazes me.

Mother Mary—can a man, a loving son, say enough good things about his mother when she is so selflessly devoted to the welfare of her child? I used to say about my mother that you could go to her and complain, "Mrs. Stratton, your son just murdered a whole family down the block and chopped them to pieces," and she would reply, "Well, they must have been very bad people." I am her only son; there is just me along with my older sister. When I wrestled in high school, my mother was my most loyal fan. She very rarely missed a match or, when I played fullback on the Wellesley High School Red Raiders team, a football game. All during the years I was locked up, she and Mailer were regular visitors and correspondents. My mother came to adore Norman, and he her. This trip from Massachusetts was rough on her—she's not in the greatest physical shape—but I know that to see her wayward son finally released from prison, and to be here to help him as he embarks on a whole new phase of his checkered life, has been nearly as uplifting and gratifying for her as it has been for me.

First thing the next morning I walk several blocks from Mailer's apartment to the United States Parole and Probation Office for the Eastern District of New York. I am there when the doors open at 8:00 a.m. My parole officer is a young African American woman with the unlikely name of Gloria Lawless. I begin by asking her how it is that I am on parole in the first place when my sentence under the continuing criminal enterprise statute is nonparoleable. Lawless gives me much the same explanation as my case manager back at the prison: good-time earned in prison is not actually deducted from one's sentence. It is credited toward one's release date but then must be accounted for under supervision after release. It still doesn't make sense, but I am not here to argue. I'm here—as I was in prison—to do the time and get it over with. Ms. Lawless assures me that, if I abide by the rules and regulations of supervised release—which are exactly the same rules and regulations that apply to being on parole—there should be no problem. Then she hands me a bottle and tells me to pee.

"Here?" I ask and reach for my fly.

She's not amused. "No. Take it to the men's room. And it better be warm."

I piss in the bottle, return to her office, and hand it to her. "Steaming," I say.

"Am I going to have a problem with you, Mr. Stratton?" she asks.

"No," I tell her.

"I hope not. But I can already see we have an issue that needs attention—this job of yours. You say you are employed in the law offices of Ivan S. Fisher. Is that correct?"

"Yes."

"Are you a lawyer?"

"No."

"What will you be doing for Mr. Fisher?" she asks.

"Writing, mostly. Doing legal research, then writing briefs, letters, whatever Mr. Fisher needs drafted—"

She cuts me off. "Do you know that Mr. Fisher is on probation in this office?"

This comes as a surprise. I am aware that Ivan has had some tax issues, to which he pled guilty, but I had no idea he was on probation in the Eastern District.

"No, I didn't know that."

"Well, he is," she says and gives me a stern look. "I don't believe I will be able to approve your employment."

I'm stymied. Once again, I'm reminded how dealing with these people—the government functionaries in the Bureau of Prisons, and now their counterparts in the Probation and Parole Department—calls to mind when I was a kid in grade school and was sent to the principal's office after getting in trouble with the teacher. Naughty boy, in trouble again. I feel like telling her: "Dear Ms. Lawless, at forty-five, as a career criminal from my late teens and having just served eight years in some of your most secure institutions, all the while never adhering to the rules and regulations, I hate to tell you this, but I am the one who is really lawless here, and there is no way I am going to look for another job."

Instead, I say, "Well, then we will have a problem. Because that's the job I have. So, please, take it up with your supervisor. I'll wait to hear from you."

Jesus, Lord, does it ever end? Pee in a bottle. We may not approve your employment. These people are out of their federal fucking minds. I'm not supposed to be on parole in the first place! But, predictably, when I call Lawless later from Mailer's apartment, she tells me that she spoke to her supervisor—who is actually the probation officer assigned to supervise Ivan—and, no, my employment will not be approved. "You will have to find other employment," Lawless says.

I hang up. We'll see about that. I didn't do my time in prison obeying the petty rules and regulations of the various institutions, and I'm not about to give in. No, if need be I will take the Parole Commission to court. I doubt there is a judge in either the Eastern or the Southern Districts of New York who does not know Ivan S. Fisher and who, knowing Mr. Fisher, does not regard him as a good, law-abiding professional who may have had some financial issues in the past but who nevertheless is not going to lead me further astray. Still, it's upsetting. Here I thought I was through having to deal with this intrusive government supervision, and now it's taken on a whole new dimension. At least in prison I knew where I stood.

No, no, please, Stratton, don't say that. Don't even think such thoughts: that is a sure bet you are headed back to prison. This is just another test, another trial, and a mere hiccup in the great feast of life out here in the world. You've been through much worse. Stay strong. Just—as you have advised so many—put your head down, pull up your pants, tighten your belt, and figure this shit out. Come up with a game plan, a strategy, and resist, resist, always resist, even while appearing to go along to get along.

I remind myself that I once stood trial in the Southern District of New York facing a possible life sentence without possibility of parole. That is serious: fighting for my life against the awesome power of the United States Department of Justice. This is a minor skirmish compared to that. Look on the bright side. They're not going to lock me back up—or are they? Is that their objective, to see me fail at my reintegration into law-abiding society? What can they do if I refuse to get another job?

Just to prove to myself if to no one else that I am in fact employed in the law offices of Ivan S. Fisher and intend to remain so employed, I take the train to Manhattan and check in at Ivan's offices on the seventeenth floor at 425 Park Avenue. Charlie Kelly, Ivan's investigator, is there. Charlie's another ex-con, a former NYPD narcotics detective who got caught up in a big cop drug scandal and went to prison in the state system. Good guy, Charlie. Kept his mouth shut. Did his time. And now he works for Fisher. We hit it off immediately. Ivan's secretary,

Karen, tells me Fisher is in Florida on a case. When he calls in, she puts me on with him, and I tell him of my meeting with Lawless. Fisher agrees; if need be we will take it to court and let a judge decide. But in the meantime, he says he will call his probation officer, with whom he claims to have a good relationship, and see what he has to say.

From Ivan's office, I walk the few blocks to the Birch Lane Publishing Company on Madison Avenue. There I pick up ten copies of the bound galleys of my novel, *Smack Goddess*. My editor, Hillel Black, a veteran New York editor, isn't in, but the rest of the staff could not have been more welcoming. I meet Hillel's secretary, who gives me the galleys. She introduces me to Fern Edison, who is in charge of the publicity department. Fern wants to see if she can generate magazine articles to promote the book. She asks if I can send her copies of whatever news clippings I have on my criminal cases in Maine and New York. Another young editor congratulates me on my release and tells me, "You paid for the alleged sins of a generation of Americans."

From Birch Lane I continue on to Scott Meredith's office, where I meet with my literary agent, Jack Scovil, and pick up a check for $9,000. The remaining $9,000 will be paid upon publication for a total of $20,000, minus the agent's 10 percent. Scovil tells me he has agents working on selling foreign rights to the novel, as well as film rights. We discuss the collection of short stories I have in manuscript. Scovil wants to wait until the novel is published before taking the collection out to publishers. The day is definitely improving after my early morning meeting with my parole officer.

My next stop is the Thurgood Marshall Federal Courthouse in Foley Square. It is here, in this majestic edifice named for one of the true heroes in the world of American jurisprudence—the first black man to be named a justice of the Supreme Court—that I stood trial before the Honorable Constance Baker Motley, who was the first African American woman appointed to the federal judiciary. I encounter a bevy of news reporters and cameramen jockeying for position behind police barricades as I mount the wide granite steps into the courthouse.

I find the courtroom where John Mulheren, another friend I made while housed at the Metropolitan Correctional Center, is on trial. I arrive just in time to hear Mulheren's lawyer, Thomas Puccio, a former federal prosecutor who supervised the Abscam investigation, deliver his closing argument.

When Puccio finishes his summation and court is adjourned, John gives me an enthusiastic welcome. He introduces me to his wife, Nancy, and his sister and father as well as Puccio, who is a close friend of Ivan Fisher. John is a legendary Wall Street bond trader whom I met the day he was locked up, charged with various white-collar crimes, something known as "stock parking," and, more seriously, with allegedly plotting and actually being on his way to murder the infamous Wall Street trader Ivan Boesky.

I was in the bullpen at MCC having just returned from court when John was brought in. John is a big man, over six feet, with a full head of thick iron-gray hair and a prominent brow that gives him an intense, brooding presence. When I first saw him on the day of his arrest, I made him for a prizefighter and never would have guessed he was a white-collar defendant until I spoke with him. Even then he put on no pretenses. The guards at the MCC claimed the elevators were out of order, and we were made to walk up the nine flights of stairs with guards in front of us and guards in back. In fact, I knew, there was a major rat move going on. The elevators were being used to take newly designated organized crime snitches from Nine South down to the third floor, where the Witness Protection Program houses cooperators whose lives may be in danger if they are kept in general population, or even in segregation.

Mulheren and I began a conversation during the long trudge up the stairs. I had spent so much time on the ninth floor at MCC—more than two years while the courts decided an interlocutory appeal to determine if I could be tried a second time after already having been tried and convicted and sentenced on various marijuana-related charges—I had acquired a fair amount of influence on the unit. I was in a position to have minor housekeeping details as well as some other conveniences arranged. At that time, I was back in MCC on a subpoena ad testificandum while the government tried to force me to testify against Mailer before the grand jury. For John Mulheren's brief stay with us on Nine North, I was able to get him assigned to a cell with another amenable white-collar crook. I got him some time on the phone, as well as a few basics from the commissary.

John wasn't with us for long, a couple of days. He made bail and was released to a private psychiatric facility, where he was to be examined and treated for a long-standing manic-depressive condition while awaiting trial. During the brief time we spent together at MCC we became friends. John told me that while succumbing to a manic episode, after having foregone his usual regimen of lithium, he loaded a high-powered rifle into his car and set out to kill Boesky. He claimed Boesky had falsely implicated him in an allegedly illegal stock transaction in order to make a deal with the prosecution to lessen his own exposure. I know all about that drill. I counseled John on the inner workings of the federal criminal justice system based on my by then quite extensive experience. Criminal lawyers may know a lot about how the law works, but someone who has been through multiple arrests, prosecutions, federal criminal trials, and years of imprisonment and had a mind to study the process and the law from the inside can gain and impart invaluable understanding of how the system really works: the day-to-day machinations, the intimidations, frustrations, calculations, falsifications, and the petty and not-so-petty bullshit one has to put up with in order to survive and stay sane during the process.

We stayed in touch after John was released on bail and I shipped back out to Ashland, Kentucky, for the remainder of my bid. When I tell John of the difficulty I was having with the parole office, he immediately offers me a job. "Why not come work on the exchange?" he asks. "What do you want to do? Just let me know, whatever you want, we'll find you something."

John says he is offering me the job for selfish reasons. "It's hard to find people who will stick by you."

I'm not sure how that would go over with Ms. Lawless, and anyway, I have no inclination to work in the financial world. John invites me to join him and his family, catch the helicopter back to his home on the Jersey Shore for dinner. But I tell him I need written permission from my parole officer to leave the five boroughs, and I doubt they would give me permission to visit with another former resident of Nine North at the MCC.

Once the Mulheren party departs for the heliport, I can't resist the urge to take a walk around the neighborhood. This is the bastion of federal law enforcement power in New York City. The FBI's monolithic New York headquarters faces the courthouse from the west side of Foley Square. I pass by and gaze up at the federal lockup, MCC, also known as the rock 'n' roll jail. MCC is attached to the courthouse by an elevated walkway that serves to deliver a fresh supply of prisoners into the courthouse building without their ever having to step outside. The jail is a grim, brooding, concrete, fortress-like structure with barred windows and a rooftop recreation area covered with steel netting strung with fat round obstructions to keep prisoners from escaping by helicopter. I remember the many days and months and years that I lived in that building—more uninterrupted time than I spent in any other structure in my entire life. I recall the hours spent gazing out the windows at the streets of New York City, so near and yet a world away, and where I now stand as a free man—well, almost free, still partially under the auspices of my keepers. And to be here on the outside alone, with no guards or deputy US marshals escorting me, no chains on my ankles or handcuffs on my wrists, standing in these longed-for city streets and looking back at that building—I am overwhelmed with a whole new sense of relief.

Yes, damn it, I did it! I made it out. I got my skinny white ass out of prison. This is nothing less than a waking dream come true, an imagined future that has now become reality.

Chapter Two

GET MY MONKEY LAID

COME ON, STRATTON—LET'S get to the sex. A horny motherfucker like you, man, when are you gonna get your dick wet?

Not so fast.

You have got to think these things through. You can't be impetuous when it comes to something as important as making love to a woman, not after eight years of enforced celibacy, not ever. I consult my mental checklist of things to do upon release from prison. First on the list: visit my parents. Okay, I did that. It was a deeply moving reunion with family. It was a nostalgic trip back to my childhood environs that I am still internalizing and will continue to reflect upon as I seek to understand who I am now in relation to who I was before my arrest and imprisonment, and in relation to who my family and loved ones still are.

Next: check in with my parole officer. Also done. This was and still is a frustrating and upsetting encounter with the agents of authority that I am still entangled with, still seeking a workable resolution to an essentially antagonistic relationship. Then: visit my employer. Okay, did that as well. I haven't actually seen Ivan yet, but I did speak with him on the phone. It's touch and go whether I'll be allowed to continue working for Ivan given the situation with the parole commission. We will see how that plays out. There is no way I'm going to knuckle under and give up without a fight. I may be forced to take the issue before a judge. And there are other alternatives to consider if that doesn't work.

Next: stop by my publishers to pick up copies of the bound galleys of my novel. That was unequivocally a hugely gratifying experience, without doubt the best possible result of having spent all those years in prison next to actually getting myself out. I wrote the book while I was locked up—not an easy thing to do. Yes, you have plenty of time as a prisoner, but almost no privacy, no opportunity to do something that requires as much concentration as writing. Now the book is on schedule to be published—that in itself is amazing. And as part of that good fortune, I picked up a check for nine grand from my agent. Fucking wonderful! To get paid for doing something I love doing, what could be better? Next on the list: gather together all my prison writings. Also done. And, finally: find and secure somewhere to live—a place of my own. I'm working on it.

Nowhere on my list do I see: get laid.

Good to know I am keeping my priorities straight. Still, eight years without the love of a woman, it was rough, it was lonely as hell; it hurt, it was physically and emotionally painful. Enforced celibacy, reluctant onanism is no fun. Being denied the company of women is psychological torture. The loneliness is soul killing. It does bad things to one's character. Much as I may love my male friends, including and even especially some of the men I met in prison, it's not the same as the deep, intimate love I feel for the women in my life. I am not sexually attracted to other men. What happens in prison—I am talking about men's prisons here; from all I'm told it's different in women's prisons—sexuality becomes perverted. It's not about love and tenderness; it's about dominance and power. Judging by what I saw during my time in prison, I would have to say that there is a lot less sex in men's prisons than one might imagine having watched prison life depicted in the movies and on TV. I was in federal prison; people tell me buggery is more prevalent in state joints. Maybe so. The point is, I think most men doing a long bid just shut down emotionally and close off the whole side of their nature that thrives on interaction with women as most intimately experienced in making love. Sex becomes relegated to the imagination. Sure, you may jerk off from time to time, but even that is awkward, given that one is almost never alone. Prison is aptly described as the loneliest place in the world, where you are never alone but always surrounded by other men. Even in the Hole, in solitary confinement, the guards are watching.

For an ex-con, everything about being free is measured against what it was like to be in custody, how it feels to be deprived of fundamental liberties we take for granted. It's the shock of release after imprisonment that is at the center of my life right now, and how to deal with this radical change. Basic freedoms such as the ability to move in space as one chooses as opposed to being locked behind bars, confined to an eight-by-ten-foot cell; having your dignity and self-respect constantly demeaned; forfeiting all privacy, even the privacy of your asshole; and to be lonely, deeply lonely, lonely in your bones: that is the prison experience. You are forced to shut down and cauterize a whole range of human experience and emotion; you are forced to embrace a code of conduct where to show weakness or vulnerability is to start down a path that leads to total subjugation and humiliation. You live under a regime that seeks to diminish your humanity, thwart your individuality. And so you are forced to live by a set of values that rewards dishonesty and subterfuge to survive in a perverse world.

As I taste life anew, I'm not going to dine at the nearest greasy spoon or pig out on junk food. No way, Jose. I'm going to eat well. I'm going to dine in as many good restaurants as I possibly can. And I'm not going to take up residence in the men's room at Pennsylvania Station, which is, out here in the world, the closest example I can give of what it's like to live in jail. You are confined to one giant fucking men's toilet with some weird dudes hanging around and measuring you. I'm going to seek a clean, well-lighted place to live and work in solitude—not loneliness but solitude—and to do my work in privacy. So it makes sense that while imagining and dreaming of the long-anticipated return to the land of men and women, the last thing I desire, and the last thing I longed for while dreaming of love while in prison is a quickie wham-bam-thank-you-ma'am with a virtual stranger. I never was good at one-night stands. I'm into intimacy. Sex without love, without real physical attraction and more—the desire to know someone deeply—does not excite me. So I know that coming out of prison my first intimate connection with a woman is not going to be with a pro, not going to be a rushed chance random encounter, not even a mercy fuck. I'm in no hurry. I just want to take my time, enjoy the realm of possibilities, see how things play out, give it to God, and experience what life in the world of men and women has in store for me. This, however, does not preclude me from making some phone calls.

THE FIRST WOMAN I call I met while in prison. Her name is Naomi Klein. She's a civilian who worked as director of the college education program at the FCI in Otisville, New York.

Just eighty miles north of the city, FCI Otisville was for much of the time I was locked up considered to be one of the better stops on the Bureau of Prisons national tour—a preferred place to do time for anyone from New York or New England. My friend Shane did most of his bid at Otisville. I tried a few times to get transferred to Otisville, but my security level was too high. Once the federal prison system became enormously overcrowded during the crack epidemic at the height of the war on drugs in the mid- and late 1980s, when the MCC in Manhattan could no longer house all the prisoners awaiting trial in New York, and before they opened the huge new federal jail in Brooklyn, the Metropolitan Detention Center, known as MDC, they turned Otisville into half a transit stop where prisoners were housed while awaiting transfer to a permanent institution or while awaiting a trial date in one of New York City's federal district courts. There were still a couple of units for prisoners designated to Otisville as a work cadre when I arrived, and there was also one whole separate unit specifically for Witness Security (WITSEC) prisoners: high-level government snitches either doing time or awaiting their day to testify in court.

Because of the WITSEC unit, security at Otisville was high: controlled movement, meaning prisoners could go only from the housing units to the yard or mess hall or education department on the hour during the ten minutes allotted for prisoner moves; regular cell shakedowns; impromptu asshole inspections; and uptight guards and Bureau of Prisons staff with an attitude. But still it was a lot better than doing time at MCC, where one rarely, if ever, got to see the light of day other than through a barred window. Otisville had a big, open recreation yard and fully equipped weight pile. The housing units had large, two-man cells. The food was decent and the commissary exceptional. All of this one might attribute to the number of New York City heavyweight mafiosi doing time at Otisville.

In New York, while housed at MCC to be called to testify before the grand jury investigating Mailer and while researching the issue in the law library, I found case law that held a US judge could not immunize a potential witness and force them to testify if they were also facing charges in a foreign jurisdiction. Wonderful. Sometimes having several cases can work to one's advantage. I was charged with over sixty defendants in a huge hash and marijuana smuggling prosecution in Canada. When I brought this to the attention of the judge overseeing the New York grand jury, much to the government's chagrin, the *writ ad testificandum* was dismissed, and I was due to be shipped out of MCC. While the Bureau of Prisons puppet masters were still trying to figure out what to do with me, I was sent to Otisville in holdover status.

In fact, I was shipped out of MCC precipitously when I got caught allegedly having sex with a civilian female sociology professor in the education department. The supervisor of the education department claimed he walked in to one of the classrooms on the third floor and found me sitting on the teacher's desk, with the teacher poised to give me head. What can I say? These things happen. You put men in prison and give them an opportunity to have sex with female staff members or contract civilian employees, and it's bound to happen. Horniness prevails. Once at Otisville, I again gravitated to the education department.

Not looking to get laid necessarily, but rather seeking to continue my education. In time, I would complete a bachelor's degree program while in Bureau of Prisons custody.

This was before they shut down most higher education programs in federal prisons—another politically driven, counterproductive move on the part of our ill-advised government representatives. The major cause of crime in America is illiteracy, lack of a decent education, and lack of access to decent jobs that comes with some degree of secondary education. People who don't know what they're talking about believe it is wrong to give prisoners access to education programs. But you have to ask yourself: Whom do you want coming out of prison to be released back into the community? Most of these men and women are going to get out one day. Do you want someone who has been further brutalized, dehumanized, and educated only in how to continue their criminal careers to be let loose and move in down the block? Or do you want someone who has had their mind and character given a whole new positive dimension and new hope for integration back into society by exposure to an education program? It's a no-brainer. And in the end, it saves taxpayers money. The rate of recidivism drops significantly for ex-cons who have participated in some educational programming while in custody.

As a sentenced federal prisoner one is required to work in order to earn what is known as meritorious good-time. It's a joke, really; most of these prison jobs are just a way to keep convicts busy while they do their time. There is what is known as UNICOR, comprising real jobs in federal prison industries, a kind of modified version of slave labor. But I never signed up for that. I nearly always looked for some easy job in the education department where I might have access to a typewriter and be able to get some of my own work done. Or I looked to get a job in the recreation department so I could spend most of my day working out, playing tennis, or just hanging out in the yard picking up a few cigarette butts and pretending to be busy. And, whenever possible, I looked to get assigned to the prison law library to continue working on my own case as well as to help other prisoners with their various legal issues.

At Otisville, it wasn't so much a job that brought me into contact with Naomi Klein in the education department. Because I wasn't designated to that prison, I wasn't required to work. But I wanted to stay busy, so I signed up each day to go to the education department. I got a pass from the guard assigned to my unit, and I went there to help out in any way I could—but primarily I went there to work on my novel and short stories, to use the typewriters whenever available, and to read or write in a relatively quiet environment.

And it was there while working on my novel that I met Naomi Klein. She's an attractive, upbeat, intelligent, and compassionate woman—a ray of light in what can be a dark place. Naomi brought a lot of positive energy into the prison with her each day. She would smile when she said hello to us convicts, and she has a great smile. Her whole face lights up. That's not something you see very often in prison, people smiling. Grimaces, yes, and leers, sneers, looks of disgust. Pained expressions. Hateful, angry looks. The bland, bored bureaucratic demeanor that says, "You are nothing to me." The faces of men who seem void of emotion. But a real smile from a good-looking woman—that's a good thing, a rare and good thing indeed in prison.

There was a song popular at the time, "Sweet Child of Mine," sung by Axl Rose of Guns N' Roses. Naomi loved that song. Whenever it came on the radio in the education department, she turned up the volume and sang along. We became friends. She was interested in my literary efforts and helped me further them by giving me access to a typewriter, paper, carbon paper, and envelopes. Naomi read some of my work. By then, it looked like I might actually have a life as a professional witer after prison, and with my various appeals working their way through the courts, I had hope that I could actually be released before too much longer. Naomi gave me her home address and asked me to stay in touch.

I did, when I arrived at FCI Ashland and settled back in to a routine to complete my sentence. I wrote to Naomi and she wrote back. We began writing to each other regularly, several times a week, and as sometimes happens in jailhouse correspondences, the letters soon turned torrid with pent up lust. She was separated, not actually divorced because she had never been legally married, a mother of two young boys living in the country in a home on several acres of land with a large vegetable garden in Upstate New York. Naomi is a progressive intellectual, an activist, college educated and a college educator. She dresses in long, colorful skirts. She has a beautiful body and open, attractive face with that bright, engaging smile. She sent me her home phone number and I began to call her once or twice a week during those final months in prison.

But it was the letters that got to me—got to both of us. I wrote to her about the many and varied ways that I would fuck her. Yes, we would make love, I said, but we were also going to fuck, fuck seriously, fuck passionately, fuck long and hard, fuck gently and slowly—fuck all these years of not fucking out of me. She wrote back of the many ways she was going to receive me, take me into her soft places, her special places, and let me feel everything good and wonderful to be felt inside a woman. Those letters—love letters, sex letters, long letters about life and prison and literature, and a hoped-for time of freedom regained—I still have them in my voluminous hoard of prison correspondence.

Now it has happened, the longed-for release. Here I am *at large*. I am back in the world, a newly minted free man about to meet a woman with whom I carried on a provocative, X-rated correspondence. It seems only right and fitting that I—that we—should realize the full extent, the full dimension and sensational spectrum of the male-female relationship we envisioned, imagined, and described in such felt detail in those letters.

It is Monday, the second of July. I have been out of prison exactly one week. After over two years of writing to each other, talking on the phone, at last Naomi and I are to meet again face to face.

NAOMI DRIVES HER car into Brooklyn from Upstate. I meet her in the street outside the Mailers' home in Brooklyn Heights. There she is, in the flesh, and looking every bit as lovely as I imagined her. I take her in my arms and we kiss. My cock immediately jumps to attention. But there are things to do, places to go, people to see before we spend time alone together. We leave her car parked in a garage and take the train into Manhattan, to Foley Square, to the federal courthouse where I am eager to follow results in the federal trial of my friend John Mulheren.

We sit through the government's summation. Stock parking, which is what John is charged with, is a measure by which a broker arranges to sell shares to another party (supposedly Ivan Boesky, in John's case) to reduce their position for disclosure deadlines, with the understanding that the original broker will purchase the shares back later at a profit to their receiving broker. The more serious charges of threatening to kill Boesky were dismissed prior to trial. Given the complexity of the alleged security violations, in an effort to try to explain to a lay jury what exactly John is accused of having done, the assistant United States attorney chooses to use a heroin conspiracy as an analogy. This, he posits, is how the stock transaction would have taken place if it were a heroin deal: Dealer Number One buys kilos of heroin for a set wholesale price. He then sells the kilos to Dealer Number Two at the same price he bought them for to appease the wholesaler by moving the product quickly. Both dealers then wait until the price of heroin goes up as supply becomes scarce. Dealer Number Two then sells the kilos of junk that Dealer Number One "parked" with him at the increased price, and in turn he shares the profits with Dealer Number One.

"Very subtle," I say to John. "I've heard of junk bonds, but . . . how long have you been in the heroin business?" which provokes laughter from Mulheren's team.

Again, John and his wife Nancy invite me, and now Naomi, to their home in New Jersey. Again, I must decline the invitation. One can only violate so many different conditions of one's parole on any given day. As I know it is a violation for me to have prolonged social contact with someone I met while in prison, that is, Naomi, I can only imagine how dear Ms. Lawless and her supervisor would react to my having a romantic relationship with a former Bureau of Prisons contract employee, cohabiting with her however briefly in the home of another alleged criminal I met while at the MCC, and at the same time leaving the borough of Manhattan without written permission. This would undoubtedly constitute a parole violation overload that would necessarily call for an immediate return to custody.

We choose instead to dine at a Vietnamese restaurant in Chinatown near the courthouse. This time is all about prolonging the anticipation of how the day will end, filling the hours with errands—I buy an address book; we take a copy of the *Smack Goddess* galleys uptown to deliver to Ivan—before we return to Brooklyn Heights for the long-anticipated, years-in-the-making hours of intimacy.

Back at Mailer's we get no further than Norman's writing studio on the floor below his loft apartment before we stop to undress each other. It's not the frenzied ripping off of clothes one sees in movies. Rather each slowly disrobes the other, taking time to delight in the gradual revelation of the other's longed-for naked body. I'm awkward at first but Naomi is the ideal lover companion for a man not sure of himself. It's not a question of performance; my long-neglected dick is as stiff as a cue stick. It's more a matter of remembering one's way around something as mysterious and delightful as a female's body. One must not rush these things. It's akin to a pilgrimage, like entering a new land, a holy place, and a whole new continent with unfamiliar yet sensational topography. I'm ready to move into this land and take up residence. But when you've been so long in the wasteland, so long in the cold, empty places, you must first familiarize yourself with all the hot nooks and crannies, the hidden erogenous zones, the veiled moist valleys, and the engorged promontories: the ridges, lips, vulva; the secret spots. Good to be here with someone who knows the way and is in no hurry to show me where to discover and how to cherish each new territory of sensation, to communicate feelings without speaking but rather with subtle moves, gestures, utterances of delight: grunts, moans, whimpers. These are my lips. Kiss them. These are my breasts. Suck them. This is my pussy. Eat it.

Hours go by, and we climb back up out of slumber to look around and visit this new land of love all over again.

"You good?" I ask her.

"I'm fine," she says.

"Yes. Yes, Naomi Klein, you are fine. . . . Thank you."

"Believe me when I tell you it was—*it is* my pleasure," Naomi tells me. "I am honored to be your first in so long. It's like . . . like being virgins and yet knowing all there is to know."

"I feel like I learned some things I never knew."

We have a late dinner at an Italian restaurant, and then return to the studio to make love all over again. Saturday morning before breakfast, more fucking, harder this time, with gusto, and each time it keeps getting better.

My FIRST CALL Saturday is from my encumbered employer, Ivan Fisher. I am to start work for him Monday morning despite the ultimatum from my parole officer that I seek and secure new employment. Ivan says he has two jobs he wants me to begin working on immediately. I am to research Eleventh Circuit Appellate Court cases on exigent circumstances. Then I am to draft a motion to suppress to be submitted in district court in Tampa, Florida, in hopes of getting the judge to grant an evidentiary hearing. Ivan is at home in Manhattan; he's due to go back to Tampa on Monday and says he needs the suppression motion no later than Wednesday. He is of the opinion that I have a month in which I am obliged to find a new job before my parole officer will have cause to reprimand me and possibly charge me with a violation of the terms of my parole—the parole I was never supposed to be on. So for now I continue to work for Ivan even as I plot my counterattack and appear to go through the moves of adhering to Ms. Lawless's demand that I seek alternative employment.

During the day Naomi and I go over to SoHo to meet my friend Shane and another ex-con, Robert Sterling, for a three-way parole violation luncheon and the makings of what might be perceived as a new conspiracy, given that all three of us were convicted of the rarefied crime of "operating a continuing criminal enterprise" under United States Code Title 21, Section 848, whereas we thought we were smuggling cannabis, pot, weed, herb, reefer, dope, merely trying to meet a demand and to supply millions of Americans with a substance meant only to provide enjoyment and relaxation. Sterling says he's hoping to get back into the movie business, and not the marijuana business; he was a producer on the film *Winter Kills*. Shane hands me three thick files given him by my mother; they are filled with newspaper clippings on my arrest and two federal trials and are to be provided to my publisher's publicity department.

After lunch Naomi and I return to the apartment for some afternoon delight. More sexual healing for the libido. Fortunately, Naomi is as horny and energetic in her performance as I am. We spend a quiet evening in Brooklyn Heights, have dinner and margaritas at a Mexican restaurant, then back to bed for more lovemaking. It just keeps getting better. By that evening, it's nothing short of wonderful, as though we have been lovers for years and yet we still can't get enough of each other.

SUNDAY MORNING I get a phone call from Richard Goodwin. When I met Goodwin, he had left politics and withdrawn to his farm in Kingfield, Maine, to write a play and practice shooting his collection of handguns in a homemade pistol range. Goodwin is also a lawyer. He graduated summa cum laude from Harvard Law School. For a time, he acted as my attorney. The film *Quiz Show* with Robert Redford is based on Goodwin's book *Remembering America*. Now he has a project he says might interest me. He wants to introduce me to a producer who is putting together a film project based on the career of singer/songwriter and philanthropist Harry Chapin, who died in an automobile accident on the Brooklyn-Queens Expressway. The producer is looking for someone to do research, interview Chapin's widow and family, and write a treatment for the film on the singer's life and career. Dick says it pays a grand a week. Sure, I say, have the guy call me.

After Naomi leaves to go back to her home and job upstate, I immediately call Nora, another woman contract employee, a professor of sociology I met while taking courses at the MCC. It was the fellatio interuptus with Nora that brought about my abrupt transfer to Otisville. We make plans to get together tomorrow night. I'm like an addict after a long withdrawal. I got that first taste, and now I just want more.

LIFE IS GOOD, more or less, though not without challenges, obviously the first being my questionable employment status in the view of the US Parole and Probation Department. I am gainfully employed as a "forensic specialist" in the offices of criminal defense attorney Ivan S. Fisher located on Park Avenue in midtown Manhattan. What I do is study the facts of various criminal cases, research the relevant law, and then draft pleadings, briefs, motions, letters, and memoranda as a self-educated jailhouse lawyer.

This is real work, not some bogus no-show job simply to bamboozle the parole people. Ivan represented one of my co-defendants in the New York prosecution, and he helped me in my self-representation at trial. Years later he argued the appeal I wrote before the Second Circuit Court of Appeals that resulted in my ultimately being released from prison after eight years rather than having to serve close to twenty. The appellate court's decision and my eventual release were based on legal work I did in the prison law library researching and writing my own brief and then litigating with the Bureau of Prisons to force them to give me a new release date. That work convinced Ivan to hire me.

Lawless denies my appeal for reconsideration of her decision not to approve my employment. She refuses to approve my working for

Ivan on the grounds that he is on probation. So what? How is that supposed to affect me? She says she does not object to me working for a lawyer, just not a lawyer who is also under supervision. Then she out-and-out lies. She tells me that her supervisor, Ivan's probation officer, some guy named Dorbacher, reached the decision with her. That's not true; I know for a fact that Dorbacher had no part in her decision. Dorbacher told Ivan he is not against my working for him. Ivan went to see Dorbacher, who told him that, to make it look good and give Lawless a way out, Ivan should refer me to another lawyer, one of his associates who will become my official employer while I in fact continue to work for Ivan. In other words, he advised that I lie and cheat the system. Which reminds me of nothing so much as the way we convicts were able to get around the rules and regulations while in prison: just tell them what they want to hear, and then go about your business. Never mind the rules and regulations; that's all nonsense.

But Lawless won't budge. It's become personal for her. She does not want me to prevail and make her look bad, so she is determined to force me to give up my job and find new employment. Now she has come up with a different rationale to deny my appeal. She claims that while working in Ivan's offices, in addition to coming in contact with others engaged in or charged with engaging in criminal activity, I will also have access to confidential client files and information about ongoing criminal cases that I might be inclined to share with others.

Fuck her, this is bullshit. Let her try to lock me back up. I'm not going to give up this job. I'll take it to court. We'll let a judge decide what to do with me. I'll go back to prison before I cave in and look for other employment. Lawless wants to make it difficult for me, okay, I'll fight her every step of the way. I like my job. It pays well. And I'm not about to give it up and look for another shitty job I will end up hating and soon find myself in even more trouble with the government. Lawless and I are clearly on a collision course regarding my future.

Why should I give up this job? I have a nice office overlooking Park Avenue with a view of Central Park through the Manhattan cityscape. I am fond of Ivan, and I am sufficiently intrigued by the law to keep me engaged in my work while I continue to pursue a career as a writer. It's all about words: the language of the law or of writing fiction. So much of the work I do depends on composing a compelling statement of facts, being able to tell an engaging story and capture the judges' interest. I have been considering going to law school and taking the bar exam. New York is one of a few states where convicted felons can go through a process known as "relief from civil disabilities," meaning being allowed to regain some of the privileges of citizenship that are revoked upon a felony conviction. After a thorough vetting, it may be possible for an ex-con to become accepted as a member of the bar. The lawyer licensing process goes beyond competence to evaluate character and fitness. I note that "revelation or discovery of unlawful conduct should be treated as cause for further inquiry before the bar decides whether the applicant possesses the character and fitness to practice law." My charges and convictions are all related to the importation and distribution of vegetable matter, that is, cannabis.

But of course, I know all this might well be just a distraction to keep me from concentrating on what I really want to do, which is to support myself as a professional writer. The conditions of my parole require that I have steady employment with a verifiable and approved employer; being a freelance writer is not acceptable. The job with Ivan is meant to satisfy the parole employment requirement while allowing me the time and opportunity to pursue my true calling. Now that I am embroiled in this dispute with Lawless over my job with Ivan, I must not let that distract me from pursuing a career as a writer. Meanwhile there have been some positive developments in my nascent writing career.

Ivan shares office space with another famous criminal defense attorney, Michael Kennedy, perhaps the nation's foremost attorney advocate for marijuana decriminalization and legalization. Michael represented my former sometimes partner, the founder of *High Times* magazine, Tom Forcade. Tom was a dope smuggler turned publisher, a brilliant manic-depressive who killed himself, blew his brains out not long after he launched the magazine. Michael is the trustee of the family trust Tom set up to retain ownership of Trans High Corporation, publisher of *High Times*. Michael is aware of my relationship with Tom and the magazine prior to my arrest. He read *Smack Goddess* and loved it. Michael offers me a position writing a monthly column and occasional feature for *High Times*.

And then there is the novel, *Smack Goddess*, with an imminent publication date. I am at work proofing the edited galleys. My career as a professional writer may actually offer real possibilities as a remunerative occupation. So what am I to do? I admit to experiencing critical internal conflict over this question of what career to pursue—how to spend my days for the rest of this brief stay on planet earth.

Do I go to law school, take the bar exam, endeavor to become a licensed attorney, and write briefs and argue cases in court? Could be interesting, especially given my background and contacts in the prison system and criminal underground. Ultimately, however, knowing me, I would use the very real demands of the legal profession as an excuse for not embracing the more risky alternative of working to support myself as a writer. Are the two occupations mutually exclusive? No, not necessarily. John Grisham and Scott Turow, to name a couple of the better-known lawyer novelists, do or did both. But understanding how I am, if I were to choose to study and then to practice law, I would devote myself to the profession with the same monomaniacal zeal that characterized my career as a dope smuggler. I would take on more and more challenging cases. I would revel in legal combat with the government, and inevitably my creative writing would suffer, atrophy, and ultimately cease altogether. I'd end up drinking heavily, sitting in bars half shitfaced talking about the books I was going to write, and deeply frustrated that I did not pursue my true passion. I am reminded of what Sigmund Freud said to his student, Theodor Reik. "You want to be a big man, piss in one spot."

"A Skyline Turkey," the story that won the PEN Prison Writing Award for fiction, is to be published in *Fortune News*, the publication of the Fortune Society, an organization devoted to helping people released from prison to find their way in the free world. I have been invited to attend a meeting of the writers asked to read at the PEN Prison Writing Awards Ceremony. "A Skyline Turkey" is also to be anthologized in a collection of prison writings called *Doing Time*.

It is not unrealistic to think that this writing gig could actually turn into a real paying vocation. Isn't this what I always wanted? Going back to a postgraduate year I spent at Wilbraham Academy after a near fatal motorcycle accident my senior year in high school, it was my English teacher at Wilbraham, a man named Dudley Cloud, a former editor of the esteemed *Atlantic Monthly* magazine, who encouraged me to write. He complimented me on an essay I had written, and he urged me to continue to pursue the craft. During my freshman year at Arizona State University, when I told my faculty advisor what I wanted to do with my life, he advised me to quit college, read everything I could get my hands on, and go live in Europe for a while like Hemingway and Fitzgerald. "Just write," he told me. "And live a life worth writing about." He confessed to being a frustrated novelist himself, and he warned me to avoid the trap of academia.

Like most monomaniacs, however, I have a deeply divided nature and am always seeking unity, trying to find compromise between the man of action and the contemplative artist. I immerse myself in whatever I am doing with single-mindedness in an effort to quell the other rebellious half of my nature yammering for attention. Write— or live the outlaw life. Write—or become a trial lawyer and take on the government. I heeded my college faculty advisor's advice and spent two years writing short stories while living in England and later in Spain on the Mediterranean Island of Mallorca, where I met my first wife. When I returned to the US, I enrolled in a summer creative writing program at Harvard. Again, the professor, a lovely Lithuanian named Vida Chesnulis, encouraged me to pursue creative writing. By then I had published a short story, "The Artists of Déya," in a respected literary magazine. I applied for and was granted a writing fellowship at the Fine Arts Work Center in Provincetown, Massachusetts.

In Provincetown, while a Fellow at the Fine Arts Work Center, I was again confronted with this internal conflict. I had vowed to quit smuggling pot and focus on writing after a failed off-load from a sailboat of three thousand pounds of Jamaican ganja resulted in several arrests. I tried and was unable to give up the outlaw life. I needed the money, and I was addicted to the adrenaline rush of smuggling marijuana and hashish. Even in prison I couldn't control the evil twin in my head, the doppelganger who demands a divided attention, and who always seems to want me to risk it all and possibly fall short and fail at whatever I am attempting to accomplish just as the effort seems on the verge of success. Call it self-sabotage. Call it a need to continually test myself. Call it disdain for convention. Fear and loathing of mediocrity. Call it lack of confidence or too much confidence—hubris. A sense of unworthiness, a feeling somewhere deep inside that I was a bad kid who became an adult criminal, an ingrate who had no excuse for seeking a life of crime and so deserve to fuck up everything I attempt to do, get arrested, get sentenced to a shitload of time, and molder in a prison cell.

Ah, yes, that's the problem, Dickhead Stratton. The problem is that I refuse to abide by the rules. Always been that way. A juvenile delinquent kicked out of junior high school for getting into a fistfight with the student gym teacher. A rebel without a cause. From a good home, with a good education, but way too much TV, watching episodes of *The Untouchables* and *Dragnet* and relating to the criminals instead of the supposed good guys. Sent off to do a year on Thompson's Island in Boston Harbor, a kind of junior Alcatraz for wayward boys where there was no television. And that rock 'n' roll music I listen to, that's the devil's music. That shit I smoke, that wacky weed . . . no wonder I became a career outlaw thumbing my nose at any number of criminal statutes. I even smuggled pot and burned herb on a fairly regular basis all the while I was locked up. Good Jesus, will I never learn to obey the law? What the fuck is wrong with me? And now that I'm finally out of prison, free after all those years of longing for freedom, I seem hell-bent to defy the rules and regulations of the terms of my parole or supervised release or whatever it is and say, "Fuck you. Send me back to jail."

Yep, that's right. Figure it out. This supervised release shit is worse than being in the joint. At least there I knew where I stood—firmly on the side of the convict. Give and get respect from staff and prisoner alike or there will be serious consequences. Out here, anything goes. People have no respect. They act like there are no consequences for rude behavior. Better be careful whom you disrespect.

Just the other day I took the Mailers' dog for his morning walk. He's an ugly little brute, a pug named Hubert for his resemblance to Hubert Humphrey. Leave it to Norman to name his dog after a politician. Hubert and I were in front of Mailer's brownstone on Columbia Heights when the dog decided to lift his leg and pee on the lower section of the balustrade. An irate neighbor verbally attacked me. Who did I think I was to allow my dog to pee on his steps? Apparently, this guy didn't recognize Hubert as the Mailers' dog. He assumed I was some interloper from another building allowing my dog to piss where we don't belong. Instantly, without a moment's hesitation I went into hardcore convict mode, zero to sixty not in a fight-or-flight response but in the fight-or-die response of a convict. I got right up in his face. I shoved him against the stoop, grabbed him by his lapels and told him to back off before I broke his neck. The guy was stunned. He looked like he was ready to shit his pants. I was appalled by my sudden lack of self-control and reversion to the hardcore convict mindset.

What am I going to do? Beat the shit out of some hapless citizen? Kill some poor fool who doesn't realize he's confronting a man who has just survived years in the penitentiary? I recalled my case manager at FCI Ashland had advised me to seek counseling. I thought I could handle the transition. Now I have to wonder.

How am I ever gonna make it out here?

IT'S TIME FOR a visit with my friend and mentor, Norman Mailer. In fact, I'm long overdue. If anyone can understand my malaise, it is Mailer, author of the classic essay "The White Negro," which might as well be about me. I first became interested in Mailer's work not as a writer but as a filmmaker. I was living in Wellesley, Massachusetts, when I read in the Boston underground press that Mailer's film *Beyond the Law*, about a long night in a New York City police precinct, was to be screened at Brandeis University in nearby Waltham. I went to see the film, and it inspired me to read *The Naked and the Dead* and then everything Mailer had written up until then, most notably *The Armies of the Night*, his nonfiction novel about the the October 1967 march on the Pentagon and anti–Vietnam War rally in Washington, DC. I wrote Mailer a letter after reading another of his essays about the death of Benny "Kid" Paret at the hands of Emile Griffith in a fight Mailer attended at Madison Square Garden. Mailer wrote back and invited me to visit him if I were ever in Provincetown. It was some years later, in 1970, while I was a fellow at the Fine Arts Work Center, that Mailer called me, and I took him up on his invitation to watch *Monday Night Football* at his home.

We became close friends practically overnight. Mailer had written "General Marijuana," perhaps the first confessional essay about smoking pot by a reputable writer. Mailer believed that we all have two complete personalities in our psyches that manifest in our contrary impulses and aspirations. Clearly, this is what I was experiencing. I wonder then if, after having struggled with his own divided psyche, thought about it deeply, written about it extensively, Norman might have some advice for me. But first I had to get permission from my parole officer to leave the district.

To APPEASE Ms. Lawless's demand that I seek employment in another lawyer's offices, I contact two other lawyers I know and ask them to write letters to the parole commission to the effect that although they find me qualified to do the work I'm doing for Mr. Fisher, they are not in a position to hire me at this time. This is designed to document another step that I have taken to at least attempt to find comparable employment. Next, I compose my own letter describing my duties for Mr. Fisher, explaining that my role as a forensic specialist does not require me to come into contact with Ivan's clients. (This is not true; I often meet with clients to discuss their cases.) Further, I write that I occupy an office at the rear of the suite and away from where I might chance to meet clients who are or have been involved in criminal activity. (This is also a lie; yes, my office is well away from Ivan's office, but I am frequently in his office with him during client meetings.) I ignore the claim that my job will give me access to confidential attorney-client correspondence. (Of course it will; that's the nature of the work.) Finally, I maintain that Fisher himself has read and approved of my letter to Lawless and her supervisor, United States Parole Officer Dorbacher. (This is a boldfaced lie. Ivan is out of the country. He has not seen the letter, he does not even know that I have written it, and he won't be back for at least a week.)

The letter is delivered to Lawless without Ivan having reviewed it. I receive permission to leave the district and travel to Massachusetts. I take a bus upstate to New Paltz where Naomi meets me. We spend the night at her home, set out early the next day, first for Wellesley to see my parents and then on to Provincetown to visit Mailer.

By the time we arrive in Wellesley, calls from Ivan looking for me have already begun. I've been found out. I know I am in trouble. How could I have done this? Why tell a lie in a letter to the parole commission, the authorities charged with supervising not only my release but also Ivan's probation? What the fuck was I thinking? Part of me, that defiant outlaw personality I have come to recognize as my evil twin, clearly doesn't give a shit. Yet, the part of my character that wants to belong, that wants to be accepted and respected and even loved, is appalled. You did it again, asshole! You are in deep shit not only with the parole people but also with your friend and employer who has gone out of his way to be good to you. I am beset by guilt and self-loathing throughout the trip.

Things begin to look up when we arrive at Norman's. The Mailers' big brick mansion on the Cape Cod Bay is filled with family and friends. At dinner that evening in a Provincetown restaurant, before a large gathering, Norman tells a ribald story, as is his wont. He says that on Marlon Brando's first visit to Hollywood after his spectacular success on Broadway, Brando was surrounded by publicists, studio flacks, assistants, and gofers anxious to service his every desire. The actor had brought his pet chimpanzee along to Hollywood with him. The ape was agitated by all the attention, he kept leaping about, screeching, tugging at Brando's arms and legs trying to lead him away from the crowd of admirers. Asked over and over again what they could do for him, how to please him during his visit to Hollywood, Brando thought about it for a bit, and then he said, "Get my monkey laid."

Norman and I have a heart-to-heart over a nightcap in the bar in his home just off the deck as the waves at high tide sluice in and wash against the pilings. I don't even need to ask him. I know what he will say: "Obey the risk." He has lived his whole life that way. Norman Mailer is the bravest man I've ever known. He is intellectually brave, not afraid to embrace and expound on—often brilliantly, always eloquently—controversial, even unpopular ideas. He is physically brave to the point of never backing down from a potentially dangerous or even violent confrontation with authority; witness *The Armies of the Night*. And he is artistically brave in that he is never satisfied with convention, never content to rest on his successes, always eager to try new approaches to his art. He's had his own experience with convicts who find it difficult to adjust to the free world. He tells me details of the harrowing weeks with ex-con Jack Henry Abbott, how unprepared Abbott was for the world, and the world for Abbott.

"Stay focused on the work, Rick," Mailer tells me. "The work is its own reward. You don't want to be a lawyer. That's not who you are. You've got a novel coming out. You're a professional writer. Embrace it."

WHEN I MEET with Ivan in his office after the weekend, he is sympathetic. He tells me that Linda Sheffield, a lawyer he works with who specializes in postconviction remedies and in dealing with the parole commission, advised him to fire me for composing and submitting the letter without his prior approval. But Ivan says he understands how one could easily form a habit of giving the authorities false information in order to get by in prison. He then emphasizes how dangerous it is to continue these jailhouse practices and habits and to revert to the convict mindset once one is released, and especially while working in a law office where every communication is subject to legal restrictions and review. He tells me he is capable of getting himself in enough trouble and so he doesn't need any help from me.

Ivan also brings up Jack Henry Abbott. It seems that I am forever destined to be compared to Abbott despite all apparent dissimilarities. Ivan represented Abbott after he was captured and stood trial for manslaughter in the death of Richard Adan, a twenty-two-year-old actor and playwright, who worked as a waiter in a restaurant called the Binibon on Second Avenue. Abbott, who had been out of prison for six weeks at the time, had a dispute with Adan over use of the toilet. They took the beef outside, where Abbott stabbed Adan to death. The next day, the *New York Times* ran a glowing review of Abbott's prison memoir, *In the Belly of the Beast*.

"Prove yourself to be the better man," Ivan tells me.

"Oh, by the way," he says as I am about to leave his office. "We won the suppression motion in Tampa. The judge agreed there were no exigent circumstances to justify a warrantless search. Two million in cash and postarrest statements made by the defendant are not admissible.

The government is appealing, of course. But for now, at least, we are winning."

"That's great, Ivan," I say, and we shake hands. "Congratulations."

"And to you, your first win—no, not your first; your first win for me. . . . Oh, and one other thing. . . ." Now he can't resist a big smile. "I heard back from your parole officer and her supervisor. I'm sure you'll be hearing from them as well. Congratulations, boobie. They approved your working here."

Hah! My criminal monkey perched on my shoulders chortles: No dishonest deed shall go unrewarded.

Chapter Three

A VIOLATION FOR REAL

I'M ON THE subway on my way from Brooklyn to the office in Manhattan, now officially approved to work for Ivan, when I look across the aisle and see this old guy sitting between two burly characters who look like bodyguards.

The old man gazes back at me. "Richie," he rasps and gets to his feet.

No, could it be? Yes, *it is.*

There is no mistaking the man. It is Joe Stassi, the octogenarian original gangster, cohort of such criminal luminaries as Charlie "Lucky" Luciano, Al Capone, Meyer Lansky, and Abner "Longy" Zwillman, to name a few. Joe occupied the cell next to mine for over two years at the FCI in Petersburg, Virginia. He had been locked up for more than twenty years on multiple narcotics violations when, having learned of my reputation as a jailhouse lawyer, he asked me to look into his case.

As I read through the documents in Joe's central file (known as his "jacket" in prison parlance), I discovered an irregularity in his sentence computation. He'd been locked up so long his internment predated the computer-based sentence monitoring system known as SENTRY. Joe had been denied parole for a third time after having served almost twenty years. He was told by the parole board to "bring it all," in other words, max out the thirty-eight-year term he was serving.

By statute at the time, prisoners in federal custody could earn two types of good-time: statutory good-time at a rate of ten days per month just for being there and not violating the rules and regulations of the institution; and meritorious good-time, an added five days per month for working at some bullshit job if the convict's work supervisor saw fit to authorize the request. Joe had been locked up in the Hole at the maximum-security penitentiary at Marion, Illinois. He was under investigation following a failed escape attempt from the MCC in Manhattan. Once it was determined that Joe had no part in the escape planning or attempt, he was released from the Hole at Marion back into population, and he went to work in the prison bakery. At that time, he was entitled to have resumed receiving both statutory and meritorious good-time. As well, he should have been credited for the statutory good-time he would have earned during the ninety days he spent in the Hole. But Joe would have been required to bring this failure to receive his good-time to the attention of his case manager, as Federal Bureau of Prisons functionaries will do nothing to aid a convict unless they are forced to abide by their own rules and regulations. When I told Joe this and asked him if he had requested his good-time, he told me, "I don't ask these people for nothing."

So I did. With Joe's permission, I wrote up and filed what is known as a BP-9, requesting that the old man be credited with what amounted to nearly two years of good-time. I also requested that he receive a new sentence computation to reflect the credited good-time, and to determine a new release date based on the added good-time credit. With the number of years Joe had already served, we figured that if he were to prevail and get credit for all the good-time he deserved, he would have been very close to his mandatory release date. Ordinarily, BP-9s are rejected outright no matter the merits. In order to get any relief, if the convict has a valid issue, it takes a judge in federal court under a writ of habeas corpus or writ of mandamus to compel the Bureau of Prisons to grant the prisoner relief. But one is required to exhaust all administrative remedies before a judge will consider issues brought in a habeas writ.

Joe got lucky. As it happened, the warden at Petersburg when we filed the BP-9 had been Joe's case manager at Marion, and he was familiar with Joe's case. Around this time, I was transferred from Petersburg to the federal prison in Ray Brook, New York, near the Canadian border. Some months later, when another busload of prisoners came to Ray Brook from Petersburg, I learned that the old man—this infamous mobster Joe Stassi, a.k.a. Hoboken Joe, a revered and feared mob hitman—had received credit for all his good-time, and he had been released straight to the street.

Wow! Nice, I thought, I got this aging mafioso out of prison so he could return to his wife of over sixty years—a former Miss America, no less. True, Joe was a serious gangster in his day, a major Mafia figure, and a highly skilled professional assassin who murdered, in his own words, more men than he could remember—including his best friend under orders from his bosses in what was the Genovese Crime Family. But the law is the law. Joe had served his time, he had fulfilled his obligations to the government, and I figured that, going on ninety years of age, perhaps he would mend his ways and live out his days as a law-abiding citizen—or at least without committing any more mob assassinations. Even hitmen retire.

And now here is Joe riding on the Number Four train from Brooklyn into Manhattan. We stand up and embrace. Joe is practically in tears. He can't believe it; I can't believe it. We are in a city of ten million inhabitants, riding on a mass transit system with hundreds of thousands of passengers, and we end up on the same subway car sitting across from each other. Surely this is no coincidence. There is a God, and He has a fine sense of timing, and an even better knack for how to craft a good story.

I ask Joe what he's doing riding on the subway. "It's these fuckin' FBI," he sneers. "They follow me everywhere I go. So I jump on a bus. Then I get off the bus and run down to the subway to try to lose them."

He says he heard I had some success as a writer. "Well, you sure know how to write a brief, that much I know."

I tell him I work for a criminal defense attorney, and I hand him one of my business cards. He pockets the card and says, "I'm gonna look you up, Richie. I got a story I want you to tell."

A week or so passes, and I get a call at the office. Joe invites me to join him for lunch at Docks on Third Avenue. As we enter, Joe tips the hostess with a crisp C-note. He peals off more hundreds to pay the check, and he leaves a big tip. Either he had a healthy stash of cash put aside when he went away, or the old mobster is back in action.

"I got a story to tell, Richie," he says. "I'm not gonna say nothing, you understand? But it's all there—it's in the papers, the documents. I got boxes and boxes full 'a papers and letters and pictures, everything from my life. And I'm gonna turn it all over to you so you can write the story—*my story*. What I seen with my own eyes and what I know to be true. What I personally done! Not some made-up nonsense. *The real story*. How it all began . . . and what it really was, this thing of ours."

I already knew a good deal about Joe's history as a central figure during the origins of organized crime in New York, North America, and eventually Cuba. I'd read the government's version of his long criminal career in his Bureau of Prisons central file. I'd also read about Hoboken Joe in a book on Abner "Longy" Zwillman, a Newark, New Jersey, bootlegger who was an important figure in the national crime syndicate. And I knew details Joe confided about his case. Stassi grew up on the Lower East Side of Manhattan at the turn of the century. His father was an immigrant from Sicily who went to work as a street cleaner. Joe was one of nine kids and out in the streets stealing and running errands for neighborhood gangsters at an early age. He was there from the very beginning, when the Mafia was known as the Black Hand. Joe was a childhood friend of Charlie Luciano and Meyer Lansky, the men who formed Cosa Nostra in America and who established the ruling body of the national criminal organization of Italian and Jewish gangsters known as the Syndicate. Joe was there, in the room, when Luciano unveiled the plan for the Five Families and ruling Mafia Commission to oversee organized crime on the national level. Joe was especially close to Longy Zwillman, whom the government called the Al Capone of New Jersey. Though nominally grandfathered in as a member of the Genovese Crime Family, Joe served as a kind of ambassador-at-large to all the different groups. Due to his Sicilian heritage and close ties to Meyer Lansky, Benjamin "Bugsy" Siegel, and Longy Zwillman, Joe acted as the liaison between the Italians and the Jews. His specialty was setting up, planning, and overseeing high-profile mob hits. He hired the shooters, he chose the location, he was often instrumental in luring the target to the spot, and he stuck around in the vicinity to make sure everyone did what they were supposed to do until the target was dead. He was like the producer and director of the killings of, among others, the infamous public enemy number one, Dutch Schultz, murdered by gunmen in a chophouse in Newark. And, though many so-called mob experts dispute it, Joe confirmed that he also planned and oversaw the hit on Albert Anastasia in the barbershop at the Park Sheraton Hotel in Manhattan in October 1957. He was a partner with Tampa, Florida, mob boss Santo Trafficante in the Sans Souci Hotel and Casino in Havana when Fidel Castro and his men came down from the mountains and drove the mob from Cuba. Joe was close to New Orleans mob boss Carlos Marcello, and he came under intense suspicion after the Kennedy assassination. Joe claimed his arrest and subsequent lack of relief from the Parole Commission had been orchestrated by Bobby Kennedy to try to force him into revealing what he knew about the murder of JFK. Joe and Jack Kennedy's father, Joseph Kennedy, once shared the same girlfriend. Joe claimed he and Kennedy Senior hated each other.

For a writer with an interest in the history of organized crime and the government, to have someone with Joe's firsthand, encyclopedic knowledge and his high-level participation in major historical events in the formation of the American criminal syndicate from the earliest days up through the Kennedy killing was a rare opportunity indeed.

Access to his boxes full of mob memorabilia, that was a rich bonus. We make our deal on the spot. Joe wants nothing but to tell his story. "My story, the way it happened *to me*. You understand me, Richie? I'm not gonna talk about nobody else. I'm just gonna tell you *what I know, what I did, what I saw with my own eyes*, and what really happened. Not all this crap you read in books by people who know nothing about what they're writing. People who were never there. People who only heard stories from other people who were never there. This book will be the truth."

We part outside the restaurant. Joe says he will be in touch, and that I should be prepared to come to his home in Brooklyn and sort through his archives, go through his collection of letters and legal papers, transcripts, memos, and reports, photographs and mob mementos, and then choose what I will need to document his story.

"It's all right there," he assures me. "It's in the papers. You understand? You got everything you need to tell the real story right there in them papers."

I'm excited as I leave Joe and walk back to my office. Still, I can't help but wonder what my parole officer, young Ms. Lawless, will have to say if I tell her about my lunch meeting and planned collaboration with a major organized crime figure.

"Ah, well, Mr. Stratton. I don't think so. . . . I'm not sure we can approve that."

DAYS, WEEKS, MONTHS, and eventually years go by, and I hear nothing from Joe Stassi. The old mobster just seems to disappear. It isn't until the fall of 2000 when I am directing a short film about parolees and parole officers that we are shooting in the parole offices in Brooklyn that I learn from one of the parole officers what happened to Joe. Not long after our lunch date, Joe violated his parole. He was caught consorting with other known organized crime figures, and he was sent back to prison at the age of eighty-nine.

"We knew he was back in the narcotics business," the parole officer tells me. "But we couldn't catch him dirty. The old guy was too sharp. So we violated him for association with other known LCN members. We had photographs of him meeting with half a dozen made wiseguys, and we locked him back up."

This, however, was not to be the last I would see of Joe Stassi. The man and I had some obscure karmic connection. We were destined to meet again through an even more remarkable and seemingly coincidental sequence of events.

Chapter Four

A MAN HAS GOT TO GET HIS TEETH FIXED

(With respect, Edward Bunker,
December 31, 1933–July 19, 2005)

As I RECLINE in the dentist's chair in the offices of Dr. Noah Eisenberg, DDM, on Fifty-Eighth Street, just down the block from my old stomping grounds at the Plaza Hotel, something else is happening. I'm getting more than my teeth fixed.

I met Doc Eisenberg a few years before I was arrested through a mutual friend, the actor Richard Dreyfuss. Dreyfuss had just had a breakout role as Curt in *American Graffiti* when we met in Los Angeles. I was in LA doing research for Mailer's book on Marilyn Monroe. Dreyfuss and Eisenberg played poker together in New York, and Eisenberg would occasionally hit me up for an ounce or two of the best reefer I had at any given time. He was a dentist to the stars, and even to the stars' dogs; he did dental work on *Penthouse* publisher Bob Guccione's Doberman pinscher.

There is virtually no dental care available for prisoners serving time in federal prison. You got a toothache, too bad. If it becomes abscessed, tough shit. They might set you up with some poor schmuck who got busted selling pain pills and is doing his community service bid by yanking out a convict's rotting teeth. I had already had my front teeth chipped and broken in a bicycle accident as a kid, with more damage later when I got punched in the mouth in a fistfight. My front teeth are in need of laminates to repair my smile. Eisenberg X-rays my teeth, he draws up a treatment plan, and then he turns me over to his lovely young assistant and dental hygienist for a thorough cleaning.

So it happens. The hygienist becomes the singular subject of my attention. How could it be otherwise? There she is, her face mere inches from mine, within kissing distance. She is a petite, striking young Colombian woman whose name I learn is Paloma. As I lie back in the chair with my mouth wide open, I'm thinking, *Paloma, hmm, the Spanish word for* dove. Paloma in my mind becomes a little bird, and she is like a lovely little dove whose delicate hands flutter like wings all up inside my wide-open mouth. I could eat her, this little bird, just gobble her up. All I can see is her big dark brown eyes peering into my head over the mask covering her mouth and nose. Yes, something is happening here beyond having my teeth cleaned. I'm having my senses reamed of all prior sentiments. A connection is being formed at a sensual and emotional level. The thought crosses my mind: Is there something sexy about going to the dentist? No, how could there be? Is it a turn-on? All this oral activity. . . . I recall a scene from Roger Corman's classic movie *Little Shop of Horrors.* Young Jack Nicholson is in the dentist's chair and he screams for more. More pain! More drilling! Obviously getting off on something. There is no question what I am getting off on—Paloma's gorgeous brown eyes, her delicate touch. . . . As I go deeper, I sense she feels it too—we are both feeling the invisible force, the yearning that built up inside me over eight years of enforced celibacy and internalized desire that still has not been depleted no matter how much fucking I have done. Paloma is curious; she asks why I have neglected my teeth. "Well, you see," I explain to her in my passable Spanish, "I was only recently released from *el cárcel*—prison."

If she's shocked, she doesn't show it. "So, you speak Spanish?"

A little, I say. I ask where she is from in Colombia.

"Medellin," she says.

"Ah, then you are a *paisa, una Antioquiania.*"

"You know Colombia?" she asks.

I let the question go unanswered as the doc returns with my treatment plan.

"It looks like we will be seeing a lot of each other," I say to Paloma as I am leaving.

"That's nice," she replies and smiles. "I like that."

A FEW DAYS and a couple more visits to Eisenberg's office, and Paloma and I make plans to meet after work. She asks me not to let Eisenberg know that she agreed to see me, as she is not allowed to date the patients.

"I'm good at keeping secrets," I tell her.

We dine at Victor's, a Cuban restaurant on Fifty-Second Street, and drink mojitos.

"How long were you in prison?" Paloma asks.

"Eight years."

"Oh." Her eyes widen. "That's a long time."

"Yes. Don't you want to know what I did?"

"Eisenberg told me."

She's thirty-seven but looks like she's in her twenties. Never been married. I suspect she may have had an affair with Eisenberg, but I do not probe. I'm curious about her life in Colombia before she came to the US, and her family, how she happened to settle in New York and take up dental hygiene. There is something about Colombian women that has always intrigued me. Of all the Latinas I have known, Colombians strike me as the most emancipated, the most independent and sophisticated. I am still so raw emotionally, so open and susceptible to the charms of a woman, that by the time the drinks and appetizers arrive, Paloma has told me enough about herself that

I am ready to get down on my knees right here in the restaurant and propose, carry her off to the nearest justice of the peace, and take her as my bride.

The relationship with Naomi has begun to falter, sad to say. She's a great lady. Had she never been married—if only by common law—and never had children, and were she ready to start a family, it may well have been different. And the adulterous affair with Nora, the Indian professor of sociology I met while taking courses at the MCC, great as the fucking turned out to be, that holds no future either. She has a husband and children living on Staten Island. She told me she had an open relationship with her husband, that he didn't mind her fucking me. But I do. I don't need any more guilt.

The attraction I feel for Paloma is different. It has a new sense of promise. Timing is everything in life. I don't want another affair; I want a wife. I want a family. I want to be a father. Time is running out. I'm forty-five years old. I've got my freedom, but I don't have much time, or so I believe. I feel like so much of life has already passed me by. I don't even know for sure if I can sire offspring; all these years, all these women, nobody ever got pregnant. Maybe I'm shooting blanks. Let's find out. Let's just elope, I'm thinking. Fuck supervised release. Fuck my job and my writing career. We'll flee to Colombia. Go live on the beach at Santa Marta and make babies. I'll pick up where I left off. Purchase huge loads of Colombian Gold pot. Dispatch freighters full of reefer back to the States and become a multimillionaire gringo drug lord in exile. Or not.

"Where do you live?" I ask as we step outside the restaurant after the meal.

"Queens," she says, "Jackson Heights."

"You're beautiful," I tell her. "You're a lovely person, Paloma." I take her hand; kiss her lightly on the cheek. "I hope we can see each other again, and not just in Eisenberg's office."

I hail a cab, give the driver her address, and hand him a twenty.

Good night, sweet lady. Such a chaste first date, I'm proud of my horny, promiscuous self.

AT FISHER'S OFFICE the next day, I busy myself reading proofs of the *Smack Goddess* galleys while I wait for Ivan to come in with a new case assignment. At lunch time, I walk over to the Birch Lane editorial offices to deliver the corrected galleys. I have to say, I'm not happy with all the cuts to the manuscript. My editor, Hillel Black, says he wants the book to read like a runaway train, whatever that means. I suppose he means pacing. So he and his editorial assistant have stripped out all of the asides, the internal dialogue, the descriptive passages. It's spare all right. The story has momentum; I'll give it that. But while hurtling along on that runaway train, it might be nice to look out the window occasionally and take in the passing countryside, muse on the journey, and think about what it means. This is my first novel. Hillel has been at this a long time. I suppose I should defer to his judgment.

I spend the rest of the afternoon at my desk drafting an affidavit in a new case, *United States v. Miguel Munoz* et al., an all-too-common story of a drug deal gone awry that resulted in kidnapping charges for a bunch of inept Dominican dope dealers. It's still early when I leave work to head downtown for a meeting with Steve Fishman, a journalist who writes for *Rolling Stone* as well as other publications. Fishman wants to pitch a story on me to coincide with the publication of *Smack Goddess*. We meet in the East Village. I'm impressed to see how many freaks still abound in the streets of New York City. They don't get up to Park Avenue in the sixties, nor do they migrate to Brooklyn Heights, but they are here in droves on St. Marks Place.

Fishman published a book called *A Bomb in the Brain: A Heroic Tale of Science, Surgery and Survival* about his experience as a neurosurgery patient after he developed a cerebral blood clot. I met him through John Hubbard, a fellow prisoner at FCI Ashland. Hubbard is a radical libertarian and failed mad bomber. Described as "a guerrilla fighter in his own mind," Hubbard made and planted some fourteen bombs in and around the city of Salem, Kentucky. None of the bombs went off. Fishman wrote a story on Hubbard for *Rolling Stone*. At a café on St. Marks Place, I give Fishman a copy of the *Smack Goddess* galleys.

He tells me he also wants to read my short story, "A Skyline Turkey." It's a good meeting; I like the guy. I expect he'll write a good piece.

On the way back to Mailer's, I stop by the gym in Brooklyn Heights and have a good long workout and steam bath. Nothing like physical exertion and a good sweat to dispel residual malaise. Some guy tries to hit on me in the showers. "Listen, pal," I tell him, "you don't know who you're dealing with. Better just back off."

After eight years in the can, the mere sight of a naked man is about as attractive to me as a prison cell.

So, IT'S OFFICIAL: I have the written notice from Lawless signed by her supervisor. My employment has been approved. I should feel vindicated, or at least relieved. The book is on track to come out in November. After working on an hourly basis, I presented Ivan with a salary proposal: $1,200 per week based on thirty dollars per hour for a full forty-hour week. He feels it's too high but says we're close.

With my employment secure, I feel encouraged to look at an apartment just down the block from the Mailers. It's one large front room and a small bedroom just big enough for a bed. Sure beats a jail cell. It has the same endlessly absorbing view of New York Harbor and the looming cityscape of Lower Manhattan backlit by luminous sunsets—a beautiful sight most nights. The Mailers are due to return from Cape Cod at the end of August. I need a place of my own before then, so I give the real estate agent a deposit to hold the apartment and make plans to meet with the landlord.

Back at Norman's, Ivan calls to tell me he spoke with Tom Puccio, John Mulheren's lawyer, a few minutes ago. He tells me that John was convicted. He faces five years at sentencing in front of US District Court Judge Miriam Goldman Cedarbaum. She's a Reagan appointee who may well give John the whole five. This is a man who, along with his wife, has adopted nine kids, all of whom were born with life-threatening medical conditions. John and Nancy nursed the children back to health and raised them as their own. The entire Boesky affair, and John's manic plan to murder Boesky, resulted from a government sting that rebounded on John when Boesky flipped. I call John, who is still out on bond pending sentencing and an appeal. He tells me he's frustrated with the whole jury process. He says his case is so complicated, with reams of documents from conflicting teams of accountants, and the various complex SEC regulations and statutory restrictions governing the market, to say nothing of the zeal of the Giuliani regime in 1989 with the Boesky case, and particularly given the prosecutor's closing argument comparing Mulheren to a heroin dealer, there is no way a lay jury could comprehend it all and reach an informed, open-minded verdict. The jurors were overwhelmed. They figure he must have done something wrong if the government is spending all this time and money to present their case and seek to send him to prison. So it's on to the appeal and, John says, "another several million dollars for the lawyers to continue to defend me against what is a noncrime."

I know the feeling. I tell him of my hard-fought victory over the federal government, the Bureau of Prisons, and now the parole commission. "I should have had you defending me," John says.

NAOMI CALLS FROM Vancouver; she'll be back next week. She is a wonderful woman. She's been so good to me, I really do love her, but it just doesn't feel right. Not now, not yet. I don't know how to tell her this, and I don't want to broach it over the phone. But she knows. She can sense it in my voice.

IT'S NOT EASY trying to restart your life in early middle age. Having been an outlaw my entire adult life and a juvenile delinquent before that, I've always been a troublemaker, a trouble seeker; it is how I defined myself. How am I ever going to reinvent Rick Stratton as an upright citizen and continue to obey the law? Where's the danger in that? Where's the excitement? And what difference does it make anyway? A life in prison or out here in the world, does it really matter? I want to believe it does—it must. But it matters only if I make something of it: a record, however incomplete, to convince myself that life has meaning. I know that's why I kept my journals all these years, and why I am now writing this book—to prove that it all really happened and hope that the writing, the putting down in words, might reveal some universal truth, and give me peace of mind.

That's the main reason I have come to love the law: the words have real meaning and consequence. Guilt, innocence, imprisonment, parole . . . the words mean something important. Ah, but how those fuckers know to deceive us with the simple substitution of different words: *parole* becomes *supervised release*.

And suddenly I know what's missing, why I still don't feel satisfied. Yes, I may have won the battle, but not the war. Perhaps I need to fuck with them some more, take the Parole Commission and the Bureau of Prisons to court and challenge this whole doublespeak concept of supervised release. Let a judge order them to explain how it's any different from parole, or, better yet, order them to cut me loose.

This is my dilemma: I'm really only happy and feel fully alive when I'm engaged in a life-or-liberty-affecting conflict with authority. What a sick fuck.

It's a beautiful midsummer night. I make myself a stiff drink of rum and tonic, take it out onto the balcony at Mailer's, and sit gazing at the harbor traffic and downtown skyline with pink-and-shades-of-blue skies in the background. How I love this city. Ever since I was a kid growing up in the staid suburbs of Boston. On my first visit to New York I fell in love with Manhattan, and while free I only wanted to live here. Right down there on the docks in Brooklyn we landed containers filled with contraband—cannabis, outlaw herb of mindfulness. New

York was and still is the center of the movement to change the culture of America through proliferation of this mysterious plant. Maybe I should just say "fuck it" and revert to my old ways as an outlaw. The temptation is great.

I feel like smoking some weed right now, doing some serious examining of my situation and dwelling on life in general from the various new perspectives open to the mind after ingesting tetrahydrocannabinol. Zapping the synapses with some fresh energy to figure this shit out. Norman must have a few buds stashed around here somewhere. . . . But no, with Lawless on the warpath, she is sure to pee me next time I report. She may even show up here unannounced with her little bottle to collect a sample of my piss. She has the right to order me to pee in a bottle at her whim to have my urine analyzed for traces of controlled substances. Ms. Lawless can show up at my place of employment or my dwelling unannounced whenever she pleases. I could sit here and drink a whole bottle of rum, get thoroughly shitfaced, and, though excessive alcohol consumption is frowned upon, it does not merit revocation of one's parole unless abstinence from booze is a specific condition of release. But smoke a joint, get a dirty urine for reefer, I'd be on the next bus back to Lewisburg.

Speaking of Lewisburg, I had a call from Danny Marino, a guy I met and became friendly with while in holdover there in K Unit. Danny is what's known as a knock-around guy, not a made member of a mob family—in fact, he told me he would have refused the "button" as the wiseguys call the official rank of inducted Mafia family member if it had been offered. "Too much heat," Danny'd said. "Organized crime means big time." He is an associate of a New Jersey branch of the Genovese Crime Family. A funny guy, Danny, and a nonstop raconteur of wacky, horrendous mob tales. We would walk around the small, enclosed recreation yard attached to K Unit at Lewisburg, and Danny would regale me with stories of *dis*organized crime: guys who were killed by mistake, brutal murders in retaliation for minor offenses. Danny reached me at Ivan's to say he wants to introduce me to a friend of actor Robert DeNiro, a guy named Clem Caserta who has had a role in every one of DeNiro's movies. We made plans to meet at the Tribeca Grill tomorrow evening.

I'm ready to go to bed when Ivan calls back. He says he's reading *Smack Goddess*, and he wants to know if the Frin X I name in the dedication is the same Frin he knows, whom I met when were both locked up in the MCC. "None other," I confess. And the lawyer, her attorney, Aaron Held, is that character based on anyone he might know? Ivan asks. I plead the fifth. I tell him he's not supposed to call me until he finishes the book, not while he's still on the first chapter. Fifteen minutes later he calls again. "And this Aaron Held fellow smokes English Ovals, Richard? But only five a day." I suggest he'll be ready to fire me by the time he finishes the book. "No," he says. "The one has nothing to do with the other. If I don't like your book, we'll settle it mano a mano."

Ivan tells me there is to be a meeting with co-counsel on the Munoz case tomorrow morning. He wants me there, as well as his investigator, Charlie Kelly.

I WAKE EARLY the next morning in a cold sweat from a prison nightmare. It's the same dream I used to have when I was locked up in the Hole at FCI Ray Brook waiting for the Bureau of Prisons puppet masters to figure out what to do with me. My release date was in limbo after I'd won the appeal in the Second Circuit Court of Appeals and was fighting with the bureau over good-time. This was easily the hardest time I did during the entire bid. The worst possible punishment is to be locked up in solitary confinement with no idea how long you'll be made to stay there, no discernable end to the isolation. It is a sure prescription for madness. In my dream, the prison has no walls, no fences strung with razor wire, no cellblocks or guards or even other prisoners. But it still feels so real, so oppressive, like being caught in a giant invisible machine. I can't get free. Unseen captors monitor my movements. They—whoever they are—are on to my every move. It's the thought police, and they know how I defy them. They know how I question, dispute, and ultimately flout their rules and regulations. They know I'm sitting on a huge cache of illegal plants I intend to use to alter the consciousness not only of America but of the world.

When I sit up and look around the small, cell-like room in Norman's writing studio I am hardly assured that it's a dream. This is a process, I remind myself—getting out, and then getting free. It takes time . . . and it takes patience.

I get a call from the guy Dick Goodwin turned me on to, the aspiring film producer Tony Suarez; he calls me at Ivan's office just as the Munoz meeting is wrapping up. When I call him back, he tells me I should leave the office and head over to a bar called Hemingway's on Fifty-Sixth between Madison and Park. I arrive at the bar, but there is no Tony Suarez. Instead a tall, gorgeous woman with long blond hair sidles up next to me at the bar.

"Richard?"

"Yes."

"I'm Susan Loring . . . from Tony Suarez's office."

She offers me her hand.

"Tony got held up in a meeting. He asked me to meet you and give you this." She hands me a copy of *Taxi: The Harry Chapin Story*, a biography of the singer/songwriter by Peter Coan.

"He asked me to get him a copy of your book," Susan Loring tells me.

If I'm supposed to be impressed, I am. Not only is Susan beautiful, her blouse is unbuttoned to her navel, and she's not wearing a bra. I try not to be rude and gawk at her boobs, but isn't that the point? Horny ex-con. Give him a glimpse of some succulent tits and he'll be smitten. This is obviously some sort of honey trap. Okay, I'll go along with it—at least for now. I explain to Ms. Loring that if I had been asked, I would have gladly brought her a copy of my book—or, actually, a copy of the bound galleys, as the book won't be out for a few more weeks. But I'm happy to give her a copy of the galleys if she's willing to come back to the office with me.

"Sure," she says. "But first let's have a drink."

Susan says she's an actress (Really? Imagine my surprise) and a friend of Dick Goodwin's son, Richard Junior, who she tells me now lives in New York. I learn she's originally from New Hampshire. No surprise there either. She's definitely got that willowy New England Yankee look. I can picture her on a field hockey pitch. Or on horseback. Susan and I have a couple of martinis. Why not? When with WASPs, do as WASPs do. The woman can hold her booze. She excuses herself to make a call to Suarez and tell him we're heading back to the office to pick up a copy of my book. She's not the least bit unsteady as we walk the few blocks to Park Avenue.

In my office, I give Susan a copy of the *Smack Goddess* bound galleys. She says she will be working with me on the Harry Chapin project.

"Really?" I say. "And what exactly will you do?"

"I'll be your research assistant. Help you organize the materials. Set up interviews. Take notes. Whatever you need . . ."

"That sounds great."

Fisher passes by. He looks in my office, sees Susan Loring, and does a double take. He circles back around and appears in the doorway to ask for an introduction. He's tall, well over six feet, an impressive figure in his tailored, pin-striped Brooks Brothers suit and fashionably long hair. I introduce him to Susan, who is decidedly more his type than mine, and tell him that she and I may be working together on a film project. Fisher encourages her to read *Smack Goddess*. He indicates the copy of the galleys on my desk, and he tells her she should be sure to pay special attention to one character in particular, a criminal defense attorney named Aaron Held. "You may note some resemblance," he says with a mock half bow. "I'm available to play the part."

And he excuses himself. "Do please come see us again."

I get a call from the receptionist. Tony Suarez is here. Send him in. Suarez appears wearing a western-cut, midthigh-length jacket (a *duster*, I think it's called), and he strides in like Wyatt Earp sauntering into a saloon, looking for a gunfight. He takes a seat beside Susan and asks if

she has explained that we will be working together on the Chapin project. He suggests Susan and I get to know each other, spend some time
together, talk over the story once I have had a chance to read the book,
and make plans as to how we might approach the writing.

"Sure," I say. "But let's talk money first."

Suarez agrees to pay me five grand to write a treatment, half up
front, and half upon delivery. "When can you get started?"

"As soon as you're ready to pay me."

"Don't worry," he assures me. "The money is no problem. I'll get
you the twenty-five hundred right away."

Susan hands him the copy of *Smack Goddess*.

"Are the film rights available?" he asks.

This guy is a trip. I'm sure he sees himself as a smooth operator,
a player. But to me he's so blatant, so obvious, it's not working. He
figures he'll dazzle me with the prospect of working in close contact
with a beautiful woman, the delectable Susan Loring, and hold out
the possibility of optioning the film rights to my book as an added
attraction. Susan is certainly enticing, but Suarez's whole come-on is
incompetent, so amateurish and inept that I have no real difficulty
reminding myself to stay focused on the goal—get paid. I may be fresh
out of prison, but I am hardly new to the scenario of the honey trap.
Perhaps Suarez fails to consider that I spent most of a good number of
years in the criminal underground where trust is earned, where cash
talks and bullshit walks. Pussy must take a backseat to business. That
is not to say that I am immune to the charms of Ms. Loring. I would
love to get to know her better. But even she looks uncomfortable with
how transparent Suarez has made his come-on. I sense she can see that
I see right through Suarez. And I believe she knows I am not about to
be snookered into working on this project for no money just because
I hope to get into her pants. If I do it—if I take the job and write the
treatment—it will be because I intend to get paid, and also because
it's something that I want to do. From what I know of Harry Chapin's
life, there is a movie here. And who knows, maybe Suarez will come up

with the money. Maybe I'll write a treatment, and then a screenplay. Maybe the movie will actually get made, and I'll have the beginnings of a new career in Hollywood.

"Okay," I say. "I'll read the book. Let me know as soon as you're ready to get started."

THE REST OF the week I work on the motion to suppress in the Munoz case. Ivan reads my draft and pronounces it, "Not bad." Not bad is his way of saying good. I join Ivan and his investigator, Charlie Kelly, in a follow-up meeting with the Munoz co-counsel, three of Manhattan's better-known criminal defense attorneys, after all the parties have received a copy of the motion. I'm the only one in the room who has done any research on the legal issues involved, possibly the only one who has read the indictment and discovery, so Ivan asks me to explain the merits of the suppression motion. I say that I also found what I believe to be a defect in the indictment; it is all explained in the motion. Ivan is pleased. As I make ready to leave for the day, he comes into my office, sits down, crosses his long legs, and asks about Tony Suarez's assistant, Susan Loring.

"Who was that, Richard? You're holding out on me."

"No, not holding out at all. I just met her myself. It has been proposed that we work together, but I'm not sure it will happen."

"Why not?" he wants to know. "When you meet a woman like that, you mustn't hesitate. They don't come along every day."

"Yes, I believe that. But I think this guy Suarez is hoping to lure me into a honey trap."

"Explain," Fisher says.

"Well, he wants me to believe that a fringe benefit of the job would include the opportunity to possibly seduce Susan when in fact I know he's trying to use her to seduce me into writing a treatment for him without paying me."

He considers for a moment, and then says, "In that case, by all means, play along. Allow this fellow to believe his lady friend can seduce you. In fact, let her seduce you . . . if she is so inclined. Don't hesitate. But never allow that to deter you from getting paid. Make her your ally in getting well compensated. Make the deal, and get the girl."

"Yes," I say, "that's good advice." And I remind him that I was educated in the Beirut school of business where one of the basic principles holds that everything is a negotiation.

"Indeed, you were," Ivan agrees. "And that is true. Everything is negotiable."

Ivan uses this to segue into a counteroffer to my proposal of $30 an hour. He offers me $22.50. He says he can't see his way clear to pay a nonlawyer sixty grand a year. So far, he continues, he's pleased with my work. I should expect a raise in four to six months. I thank him and say I'll think about it and get back to him. After all we went through to get my parole officer to approve this job, it hardly seems right to quit now. Perhaps, I say, what's needed is a less formal arrangement where I work from home and give up my office. That way, Ivan can rent the space out to another attorney and cut down on his overhead.

"Ah, but then I'll miss you," he says, "And possibly miss the opportunity of meeting other charming ladies with hidden agendas."

He stands, and we shake hands.

"By the way," he tells me, "I finished your book. It's good." He allows a definite improvement over his usual critique of not bad. "You're a good writer, Richard. I particularly enjoyed the courtroom scenes. I was impressed with the technical skills you displayed in pulling off the legal and law-enforcement aspects of the story."

"I should expect to have some understanding of what I write. Prison was my law school. And that's why I'm worth thirty bucks an hour."

"Point well taken," he says.

Ivan then informs me that he needs an emergency brief, a petition for certification to the New Jersey Supreme Court that must be submitted by the end of the day tomorrow. I tell him that I have a new name for him: "Eleventh-Hour Ivan."

"The name may be new," he says, "but the concept is not."

"You are hampering my abilities. If I had a week, I might be able to do a good job."

"Yes," he says. "And if I had tubes, I'd be a radio. Come on, Richard, show me you're worth thirty dollars an hour."

MY EDITOR, HILLEL Black, takes me to lunch at the cafeteria in the zoo at Central Park. I feel empathy for the animals in their cages, reminds me of from where I came. Hillel says that the publisher, Steven Schragis, might be willing to throw us a book launch party, and he wants to know if I would like that. I'm not sure. Much as I love a party, it may be better to spend the money on advertising. Hillel says word-of-mouth is the best advertising. A well-attended party of New York literati may have a bigger impact than paid advertising.

"Let me think about it," I say. "And talk it over with Norman."

"Relax," Hillel tells me. "Enjoy the moment. We don't need to decide anything today. This is just your editor taking you to lunch. It's a New York publishing rite of passage. You are on your way, Richard. But now you've got to write another book."

I tell him of the novel I'm thinking about and have been making notes on, which I call *Holy War*. It is to be set in Beirut and the Bekaa Valley of Lebanon at the height of the Lebanese Civil War and play out during the Iran hostage crisis and Iran-Contra scandal. Also, I have compiled a collection of my prison stories I call *American Gulag*. Hillel says he's eager to see both as soon as they are ready. Much will depend on how *Smack Goddess* is received.

Back at the Birch Lane offices after lunch, Hillel and I check in with Fern Edison in the publicity department. "Promotion, this is where you really must focus now," Hillel tells me. Fern says that Steve Fishman got an assignment to do a story for *GQ* magazine. He's doing his reporting now and will be in touch with me again soon to set up another interview.

I HAVE PLANS to meet with Tony Suarez this evening to pick up a check for the initial payment of $2,500, but he calls and begs off at the last minute, claims that he is "backed up on something."

Yeah, backed up on bullshit. This is hardly encouraging.

Then Norman calls. He's still on the cape. He says he spoke with a woman named Radha Battachargi who came to visit in Provincetown. She is a producer who works for the Guber-Peters Company. He told her about my novel, and she asked to meet me. I'm to call her. Then, just as I am about to leave, I get a call from a guy named Mike Marvel from *Interview* magazine. He's interested in doing a story, but says he has to clear it with his editor first.

Ah, yes, promotion . . . It's not enough to write the book, you've got to promote it as well.

AT THE TRIBECA Grill, Clem Caserta sits at the bar with another guy, Vinnie, who also appears to have been called in for an audition from central casting, New York mobster division. Soon a guy named Ron, Clem Caserta's factotum, joins us. He lays a "package" on me. I hand it back. I explain that when someone who looks like Clem and his friends wants to give me a "package," I'm wary of what it might contain. It takes a minute, but then they get it. Of course, not to worry, it's nothing illegal. It contains two of Clem's original screenplays and a video: Clem's reel of the scenes he's been in from *Once Upon a Time in America*, to *Goodfellas*, and *A Bronx Tale*. He indicates a table in the rear corner of the restaurant where Robert DeNiro sits in deep conversation with Al Pacino, both bearded and incognito. Clem tells me DeNiro always insists that his friends be cast in his movies, no matter how small the part.

LATER, BACK IN Brooklyn Heights, I meet with my new landlord. He's pleasant enough: a gay, aging bachelor who lives in a beautifully appointed apartment directly above where I will be living—hardly an ideal situation. He says he has a home in the Hamptons and is away a good deal of the time. We sit for an hour talking and drinking cranberry juice. He seems impressed that I am close to the Mailers. After our meeting, I walk over to Montague Street for Japanese. Flying solo tonight.

The Mailers have decided that they can no longer keep young Hubert, the pug canine that has become my charge and companion over the summer. Norman's wife, Barbara, also known as Norris, calls to ask if I know anyone who might like to have Hubert. I call Naomi, whose youngest son had expressed a desire to have a dog. Would they like Hubert? He needs a new home with a loving family. It's decided to have the dog go visit for the weekend and see if everyone is compatible. I'll miss my long walks with Hubert along the promenade, but he will no doubt be happier living in the country with a family that enjoys having him around.

I send my father, Emery, a check to help my parents with their rent. It feels good to be able to help them, though I admit I am beginning to experience some preliminary money anxieties of my own. This week alone my bill from Eisenberg is $1,250. Then there is the deposit and first month's rent on the new apartment. I eat out in restaurants practically every night—a foolish extravagance. I'm blowing through the advance from my publisher at an alarming rate. In prison I never had to worry about money—food, shelter, clothing, everything was provided—but out here, the basics are my primary concern.

The truth is, I've never been good with money. Good at making it, yes, just not good at saving it, not good at budgeting. Actually, the word "budget" is not part of my working vocabulary. I make money; I spend it. As Ivan advises, life is short. You never know when some crazy motherfucker may come along and club you on the head with a paving stone. No doubt this is one of the main reasons Ivan and I get along so well—he too spends money lavishly. A luncheon with Ivan at the Four Seasons can go for several hundred dollars. His extravagant lifestyle is what got him in trouble with the taxman.

I wrote myself out of prison, now I will write myself out of debt and into prosperity. I visualize large checks coming to me from various sources. This week I should make around eight hundred dollars cash working for Ivan. And then there is the Harry Chapin movie deal, an initial payment of twenty-five hundred if Suarez comes through with the cash. I still hold on to some hope that he will.

No sooner do I begin to fret over Suarez when the phone rings. It's the lovely Susan Loring, Suarez's ersatz assistant and my would-be seductress. She tells me she finished reading *Smack Goddess* and she loves it. Couldn't put it down. Stayed up reading until three in the morning. I hope this isn't just more of the Suarez shuffle. I decide to ask her outright if the guy is real. She says she's not sure; she doesn't really know him. I'm not surprised. Suarez does apparently have some kind of an arrangement with Harry Chapin's wife, Sandy, who Susan says she has met. But beyond that all she knows is that Suarez claims to have made money in Manhattan real estate, and now he wants to branch out into making movies. The fact that Suarez comes to me through Dick Goodwin is not encouraging. Dick once introduced me to another guy who turned out to be not only a fraud, but also an out-and-out crook.

Never mind. I'm not going to worry about Suarez. There are others with real credentials on the horizon. Norman's friend, Radha Battachargi from the Guber-Peters Company, sent a messenger to Birch Lane to pick up a copy of *Smack Goddess*. And Danny Marino's pal from the DeNiro camp, Clem Caserta, also sent his guy Ron Peterson by for a copy, though I have no clue what those guys are capable of beyond playing wiseguys in DeNiro's movies.

I had lunch with my former Empire College professor, Shirley Ariker. Shirley was helpful during my time in MCC. She gave me a copy of *Man's Search for Meaning* by Victor Frankl that chronicles his experiences in Auschwitz. That book more than anything else helped me during those early years to navigate the psychological pitfalls of imprisonment. Shirley has agreed to help me compile my college credits so I can get a BA from Empire State. And then, who knows—law school? I thought I had my mind made up not to pursue becoming a lawyer after my visit with Norman, but the lure of the law persists. I do enjoy it, and besides, it's a real job. Writing as a career may never be enough to sustain me.

Times have changed since Norman began writing and publishing novels. People aren't reading as much—particularly fiction, and particularly men. Unless you're Stephen King or some other megabest-selling writer, publishers are loath to spend money to promote novels. It's tough to make a living writing books. Screenwriting pays much better. I just read an article in the *Times* about how the studios are paying big bucks for spec scripts. We'll see what happens. Best to keep all options open and pay attention to what appears to be working. Guber-Peters is no fly-by-night operation. These guys are the real deal. Producers of *Rain Man*, *Batman*, and *Gorillas in the Mist*, among other films that were both critically acclaimed and made lots of money at the box office. Let's hope Radha Battachargi likes *Smack Goddess* as much as Susan Loring does.

I feel an acute need to get back to writing something other than legal briefs. So much of my future will depend on whether I can make a living doing what I love. I can't go back to smuggling pot. No, no, never, much as I loved that occupation, and the option remains open to me, the lure is still strong, very strong indeed. I have all the right connections. I could do one big trip, make several million in cash, and then retire. But if I get busted again, it's an automatic life sentence with no possibility of parole. And these days everybody gets busted. There is no honor anymore. Rats come out of the woodwork. No one stands up.

Forget that. I'll stay legit. And stay out of prison.

NAOMI COMES IN for the weekend and brings me a computer and a printer. She gives them to me as a gift, she says, to encourage me to get back to my writing. She explains that the computer belonged to her oldest son, but he has a new laptop, and he has gone off to college at Amherst, so they both agreed to give the computer and printer to me. I'm blown away. This woman is so thoughtful, so good to me. For years I've been writing in longhand on yellow legal pads. Then I type my manuscripts on a manual or electric typewriter. I make copies using carbon paper. I have to go back and retype the whole manuscript after a line edit. I do have access to a computer, and I am familiar with the word processing program on the system at Ivan's office. But to have my own computer, and my own printer, and once I have my own apartment, this will be a huge boon to my fledgling career as an author.

Friday evening, Naomi cooks dinner for us at the Mailers' apartment. She makes a salad and sautés fresh vegetables from her garden. It's delicious. We sit out on the balcony and drink wine. I confess my reservations about committing to an exclusive relationship. My life in the world is still so new, I'm trying to figure out who I am and what I want to do with my life. I do love her. She's a fantastic person. Amazing lover. Great cook. So good to me . . . I just don't know what I want to do with my life and whom I want to do it with. But I do know that I want a family eventually and children of my own. I know I want to be a father.

She says not to worry. She understands, and she appreciates my being open and honest with her. These past few weeks have been her way of welcoming me back into the world. After our steamy correspondence, we had to see where it might lead. She says she has not been disappointed, and she hopes that we can continue our friendship, and see where it goes.

But that night, after we make love, we both know that it's over, if not immediately, then soon. Hubert leaves with her on Sunday. He gives me a dismayed look as they drive away—where am I going? I immediately miss them both.

I sign a two-year lease for the apartment at 150 Columbia Heights, pay the landlord nearly four grand I can hardly afford. I'm set to move in August 1, a little over a week from today. Ivan takes me out to lunch at his favorite sushi place. He says he has a new case he wants me to focus all my attention on. It's a big heroin-trafficking case out of the Middle East being prosecuted in the Eastern District. It involves a DEA investigation code-named Operation Pyramid Overdrive. Ivan's client, said to be the ringleader, is an Israeli citizen named Chaim Levy.

"This is right up your alley, Richard," Ivan tells me.

Still no word from Radha Battachargi at Guber-Peters. And Tony Suarez has not been back in touch with the agreement or the down payment on the Chapin biopic treatment. I'm ready to begin writing. I read the Coan biography of Chapin, I made extensive notes for the script, and I spoke briefly with Chapin's widow, Sandy, who lives in Huntington, Long Island. I'm due to go out and meet her next week.

I'M DEEP INTO reading discovery and drafting a motion on Operation Pyramid Overdrive. Ivan wasn't kidding; it's a fascinating case. There is a novel here. Ivan's client, an Israeli junk dealer, was lured out of Israel. He arrived in Cairo expecting to rendezvous with a temptress, a plump odalisque named Sari Angel. Instead of the expected assignation, Levy was captured by Egyptian cops. He was beaten, tortured by the Egyptians with DEA agents in attendance. He was then bundled onto a plane and delivered onto US soil, where he was formally arrested. This resulted in multiple violations of his Fourth Amendment right against unreasonable search and seizure. The government wishes to justify the agents' actions all in the name of America's holy war on drugs. When Levy appeared in court looking like he'd been in a prizefight, the agents claimed he'd injured himself in a suicide attempt while in the bathroom on board the airplane.

Fisher is certainly getting his money's worth out of me. I'm writing a brief a week, and not a word of fiction—nothing since my release from prison. I sit in my new apartment and stare at the screen on my new computer, which I am still trying to figure out how to operate. It doesn't really make the actual act of writing any easier. Norman calls writing "the spooky art." I recall his advice on how to deal with writer's block. Just before you go to bed at night, tell yourself that in the morning you will get up and go to work writing. You must keep your word to yourself and follow through in the morning. Then, as you sleep, your subconscious will be at work preparing you for the next day's writing. But if you tell yourself you are going to write, and then you don't follow through the next day, soon your subconscious will tune out, and the words won't come. He also advises against talking to others about what one is working on, cautioning that many a novel has gone the way of barroom blather.

I am not so much blocked as I am stymied, drained by the demands of earning a living. I am writing for several hours most every day, and there's the rub. My work for Ivan is so close to writing fiction—taking the elements of a story/case and crafting them into a narrative/statement of facts—that, after however many hours spent writing legal pleadings, I'm fried. I find my creative energies are exhausted. At the end of the day, all I want to do is have a couple of drinks and quiet the voices yammering in my head.

At last I have a brand-new smile. It may be only temporary while the permanent veneers are made, but it still makes all the difference. No more snaggle-tooth. After the doc finishes installing the temporary veneers, he leaves the room while Paloma instructs me in the proper method of cleaning my new teeth. It's all I can do to keep from taking her gently by the hips and easing her down onto my lap.

"*Hermosita*," I whisper, "when am I going to see you again?"

"Shhhh," she cautions. "Soon."

"Promise?"

"Of course. I want to see you, too."

Another week goes by, and Tony Suarez still has me hung up on the Harry Chapin deal. I would love to tell him to forget it. As much as I like the story, as much as I would be happy to write it, I hate being jerked around. All this talk and no real action on his part pisses me off.

I'm beginning to dislike the guy. His secretary (someone else, not Susan Loring) calls and asks for the fax number at Ivan's office. She says she is going to fax over an agreement. Hours later, by the time I am ready to leave for the day it still hasn't arrived. And there has been no word from Radha Battachargi at Guber-Peters.

AFTER A WORKOUT at the gym in Brooklyn Heights, I am at the Mailers' apartment making my dinner, drinking margaritas, when Fisher calls. He asks if I have had dinner.

"Something has come up," he says. "I need to speak with you right away."

In fact, he tells me, he's in the car on his way over to pick me up.

Jesus! What could it be? Have I done something else I should not have done without first getting his permission? No, nothing I can think of, and he didn't seem angry.

Ivan picks me up in front of the Mailers' brownstone, and we dine at Norman's favorite Japanese restaurant on Joralemon Street. I'm already half buzzed from the margaritas I drank at Norman's. Ivan orders drinks and scans the wine list, looking for the most expensive bottle.

"I've had a Richard Stratton weekend," he tells me. He's excited. The long locks usually tucked behind his large ears with pendulous lobes (said to be a sign of intelligence) have come unstuck and frame his flushed face. "This afternoon I met with Chamon Efradi, who you will recognize is the Israeli attorney representing our client, Chiam Levy of Operation Pyramid Overdrive renown. Just an hour ago I dropped Efradi off at the airport; he's on his way back to Israel. Now, listen to this, Richard. It turns out that Mr. Efradi, who was a cop in Tel Aviv before he became a lawyer, represents a certain Lebanese drug merchant who is in custody somewhere in Israel and—"

"Don't tell me," I interrupt. "Mohamed Bero."

"Yes! How did you know?"

"Lucky guess."

It's not really a guess. I learned while in holdover at K Unit in Lewisburg penitentiary; I was told by another Lebanese heroin dealer that Mohamed Bero had been busted on a big junk case in Israel and that he was trying to negotiate his way out of a life sentence by ratting on everyone he knows. Bero, who is the former Chief of Customs in Beirut, was my connection for moving large loads of hashish from the Bekaa Valley up near the Syrian border in Lebanon over the Chouf Mountains and then to pass the load through perhaps half a dozen roadblocks manned by troops from any number of the different factions of the warring tribes in the Lebanese Civil War. It was Bero's job to assure that the loads arrived safely at the port in Beirut. There, while still under Bero's protection, the hash would be hidden in a shipment of legal goods, packed into containers, loaded onto freighters, and shipped to the US with no red flags to alert American customs. We made a small fortune together, Bero, my partners, and I. But then Mohamed and his son Nasif got greedy and decided to go into the heroin business. We parted company. Inevitably, Nasif was busted in New York as he tried to sell ten kilos of heroin to an undercover DEA agent. In a deal to free himself and return to Lebanon, Nasif, along with his father, Mohammed, set me up to be captured by federal agents at the airport in Los Angeles.

Ivan tells me that Efradi approached him on behalf of Bero. Efradi wants Ivan to represent Bero gratis and have Bero brought to this country. The proposal is that once Bero arrives in New York, we would set up an operation in cooperation with the State Department to free American hostages being held in Beirut and, more recently at locations in the Bekaa Valley.

"What 'we'?" I ask. "Who? How do I fit into all this?"

"Who . . . that would be Efradi's contacts in the State Department. And you, of course. . . . Richard, what American knows Lebanon, and the Lebanese, and the Bekaa Valley, the various warlords and drug czars better than you? You would, let's say, contribute your expertise, and your connections, your influence to see that whatever Bero is able to come up with is in fact legitimate and viable—"

I shake my head. "Hold on, Ivan," I interrupt. "We went through this once before. Remember? When I was being held in the county jail in Portland, I was approached by Senator Mitchell's people through my lawyer, Marshal Stern, and—"

"Yes, yes, I know. Of course I remember. And it fell through. Okay. But keep in mind you were in custody then. And facing multiple indictments in several jurisdictions. You bargained hard, but it was a much more complicated negotiation. And this time . . . well, you're out."

"So what's the point? Why would I get involved? And what would I expect to get out if it besides—if this is even feasible—of course I would like to help free the hostages. But my guess is Mohammed is just blowing smoke up their asses. He's doing a life sentence in Israel. He turned on and ratted out any number of people—not only me. He's run out of people to set up and rat on. He's desperate, Ivan. He'll say anything to get his fat ass out of jail. You can't believe anything the man says. And besides, it's dangerous as hell over there. Look what happened to Terry Waite."

"Precisely! That is why they need you. First, to find out if in fact Bero has the ability and the relationships to make this happen. Second, to use your considerable connections in the Bekaa Valley, and your reputation for keeping your mouth shut, with the drug lords to make sure it goes according to the agreement."

"And?"

"And . . . Well, first of all, we know your parole officer will never go along with it." He laughs. "I can just see Lawless now. We'd like permission for Mr. Stratton to return to Lebanon. Oh, sure, why not? So, therefore, boobie, I would suggest the first order of business ought to be that your parole is terminated immediately. After that, we'll see what happens."

This is all reminiscent of an evening before my second arrest, while I was out on bail, and before I decided to go on the lam. I stood on the promenade after leaving Mailer's in Brooklyn Heights. I had recently returned from Lebanon and I had the distinct feeling I was being followed. Moments later I was approached by my DEA nemesis, Special Agent Bernard Wolfshein, who was the lead agent in the investigation that ultimately resulted in my arrest. Wolfshein made me an offer that still to this day intrigues me. In so many words, the DEA Special Agent told me that there is a variety of criminal who works both sides of the law, and he alluded to Jimmy Bulger, a.k.a. Whitey, the infamous South Boston Irish gangster who was a longtime secret FBI asset. Whitey was allowed to continue committing crimes as long as he provided valuable information to his FBI handler. Wolfshein told me that this was an option open to me as well. I could continue doing what I did, smuggling large loads of hashish and marijuana, and I could remain free, keep the money I made, and make even more money so long as I continued to provide the government with intelligence that would ultimately result in the arrest of others in the dope trade. I passed. Later I would come to know this rarefied criminal specimen is what federal law enforcement terms a Top Echelon Criminal Informant.

And then again, after I was arrested and in custody, housed in the county jail in Portland, Maine, awaiting trial in my first federal case, the government came to me through my attorney with yet another offer. This one I was willing to accept, though not right away. My Maine lawyer, Marshall Stern, was close to Maine senator George Mitchell. A Lebanese family had adopted Mitchell's father when he was orphaned in Lebanon. Mitchell's mother was Lebanese. Her maiden name was Saad; her family came from Bkassine, Lebanon. Several American hostages were held by Hizballah in Beirut, and later moved to the Bekaa Valley near the ancient village of Baalbek, close by the border with Syria. Government agents knew that I had close ties with the major hashish producing clans in the Bekaa Valley. The offer was simple. If I were willing to return to Lebanon and use my connections to arrange back-channel negotiations to free American hostages, all the outstanding charges against me would be dropped. Ross Perot was willing to put up $10 million ransom money.

What they were offering was not exactly a vacation hike in the cedar forest of Lebanon's Chuf Mountains. The civil war in Lebanon was still raging. I was reminded of a statement made by Pablo Escobar: "Better a grave in Colombia than a jail cell in America." For me that translated as "Better a jail cell in America than a grave in Lebanon." Hadn't the Anglican envoy Terry Waite been captured and held hostage in Lebanon after several successful efforts to negotiate the release of hostages held in Iran? I had narrowly escaped Beirut during the Israeli invasion in 1982. But, confirmed action junkie that I am, I countered the government's offer: if my wife, who was being held on money laundering charges in Canada, were set free, and if I were guaranteed that no future charges would ever be brought against me for my various cannabis-related exploits, I would consider going. One thing I was sure of: the hashish trade is the lifeblood of Lebanon. If anyone has the connections to negotiate the release of hostages being held in the Bekaa, I believe it could well be the warlords whose armies are financed and armed by proceeds from the drug trade. I had close relations with members of one of the major hashish barons' family, and I was still respected by them for not having cooperated with DEA and federal prosecutors after my arrest. After the initial approach in Maine, a few weeks went by and we heard nothing. My trial date loomed. The government ended up going with another prisoner, a Lebanese heroin dealer who ripped them off and disappeared with Ross Perot's money.

I'm still intrigued by the idea of high adventure in the Middle East. The antipathy between the opposing factions in my psyche—artist and criminal—escalates to a pitched battle. After drinks and wine with dinner, I would sign on to just about any parlous enterprise. Good to be in a position to bargain with the US government. Who knows what might develop out of this? I could agree to go to Lebanon, and then insist that only by moving a massive load of hashish out of the Bekaa Valley along with the hostages and shipping it to North America can we expect safe passage, which is not unrealistic. It wouldn't be the first time or the last that American officials facilitated an illegal drug transaction for a supposed greater good; that's how business is done in certain parts of the world. There is no question in my mind that the drug lords in the Bekaa have the sway, the imprimatur to make this happen . . . if the deal is right. And such a deal could be carried out. We are talking about huge amounts of cash money. And money changes everything. But Mohammed Bero, after what he did—ratting out and setting up not only me but others well placed in the business—from what I've heard this resulted in Bero being considered persona non grata in the world of Lebanese drug trafficking. Hence, he was busted in Israel. Still, it's the Middle East, after all, where alliances, treaties, deals, formal and informal agreements are as transitory and shifting as the desert sands.

WHEN IVAN DROPS me off back at Mailer's I'm too hyped up to sleep. I rummage around looking for pot but find none. I wander into the bathroom and grin at myself in the mirror. Why settle for a life of quiet desperation? I ask myself. Why not live life on the edge, where anything is possible? Especially in Lebanon. Not long ago, I was in the belly of the beast with broken teeth staring down the long dark tunnel of a twenty-five-year nonparoleable sentence. Now that I'm out, I could be on my way to Beirut with a brand-new passport in a brand-new name. My addled brain is alive with the possibility of new high-stakes escapades and/or quasi-official criminal machinations in foreign lands.

"You could do this, Stratton," I tell my reflection. "You could make a phone call and see if there is any move to be made here."

The madman in the mirror leers back at me with a dazzling mouthful of new, white choppers.

Chapter Five

AMOR A LA COLOMBIANA

It's Ivan's birthday. The office staff throws him a surprise party. Just as I am about to leave for the day, feeling restless and oddly out of place, Paloma walks in. What a lovely surprise! We go out for a drink, dinner, and then to the movies to see *The Freshman* with Marlon Brando. The movie does nothing for me, but Paloma's sweet kisses make it worthwhile. We're like two kids on a date smooching in the theater. Again, after the movie, she bids me goodnight and takes a cab home. But a lingering hope survives: she has invited me to dinner at her apartment this Saturday night.

Later in the week, Ivan leaves for LA on the Menendez brothers murder case, a referral I brought him through John Mulheren. I get a call from a woman named Jan Yee at Davis Entertainment in LA. She wants to read *Smack Goddess* and asks if I'd be interested in doing a movie of the week based on my story. Meanwhile, this dildo Suarez is still jerking me off.

Saturday evening I arrive at Paloma's apartment for dinner, and I bring her flowers and a bottle of wine. This really appears to be turning into a traditional courtship. Early in the evening, over dinner of *pollo a la Colombiana* and a bottle of chardonnay, Paloma tells me that although she likes me very much and finds me attractive, she hopes I will understand that she is not ready to sleep with me, not yet . . .

"That's fine," I tell her. "Of course I understand. You'll let me know when you feel you're ready."

We make love all night long. First on the sofa, then again on the living room floor, and finally in her bed. In the morning we shower together, she lathers and washes my cock and balls, and she instructs me in the proper way to floss my teeth. At 6:00 a.m. she hustles me out the door and admonishes me once more, "Don't tell Eisenberg!"

She kisses me, pats me on the cock, "Take care of my little friend," she says, imitating Al Pacino in *Scarface*, and closes the door.

I'm dazed. What just happened? I feel like I'm nineteen years old as I step out onto the sidewalk in front of Paloma's apartment building in Jackson Heights. What am I doing here? Is this okay? Am I allowed to feel this good? Am I allowed to have so much love? What a little bundle of intense Latin passion that woman is! And more. There is something so open about her, so giving in the act of making love; she holds nothing back. She's so ready and willing to take me and love me for all I'm worth, I've never known that kind of uninhibited desire before.

Calm down, Dickless, I tell myself. Yes, it's true; I do appear to have become some sort of pussy magnet. This is a new experience. Never before have women seemed so eager to fuck me. Amazing what eight years in prison will do for you. But can it last? Or will I have to go back to the joint for another jolt to have this mysterious attraction recharged?

The morning air is as fresh as it gets in New York City, the pavement on the sidewalks still damp with morning dew, and the trees and shrubs and plants show the first colorful traces of fall. My body and soul are sated, rejuvenated, revivified with the deft loving touch and embrace of a woman. It's as though I were a whole new creation, as though I'd shed years of pain and loneliness in one night. I take a deep breath and look up at the sky and thank God that I am alive . . . and free.

SUAREZ DID FINALLY fax me an agreement to write the treatment, but he still hasn't come up with the $2,500 initial payment. Dealing with this guy has become a real pain in the ass. He makes appointments, and then he cancels them at the last minute. He tells me he is going to do something right away; days go by and he still hasn't come through. But of course, now I'm hooked. I've begun the research—my favorite phase of the work—and I'm into the story of Chapin's life.

While reading his biography and compiling my notes, I conceive what I believe to be a viable concept for the biopic I'm calling *Listen to America: The Harry Chapin Story*. Harry may have been one of the first commercially successful pop music artists who was also a socially conscious activist. He made his music and his life stand for a higher cause than fame and fortune. He was a dedicated humanitarian, and a key organizer and participant in the Presidential Commission on World Hunger. Until his tragic death in a freak automobile accident on the Long Island Expressway, Harry continually sought deeper personal commitment to aiding the arts and helping the less fortunate. More than half of his concerts were benefit performances. So I have a theme, a concept to build the story around: Harry as a voice and an embodiment of the emerging idealism coming out of the youth movement of the sixties and seventies that was abruptly cut short. His life could be symbolic of a positive cultural upheaval that seemed to die before its time. I want to meet his wife, Sandy, in person, and hear her story of life with Harry. I'm ready to write a treatment and then a screenplay that will hopefully get made into a movie.

MEANWHILE, CLEM CASERTA and his pal Ron Peterson want to get together and talk business—film industry business. Lots of talk, drinks, meetings . . . but no one is coming up with any money, or even any ideas as to how we might raise some money. I've heard nothing from Radha Battachargi at Guber-Peters. It occurs to me that if the illegal marijuana business operated like the movie business, no one in this country would be getting high.

Efradi calls Ivan and asks him for a photograph of me to prove that

I am who Ivan claims I am. This strikes me as weird: who else would I be? I find a photo of me sitting at a table in Beirut with Mohammed and two of his sons, and I fax it to Efradi's office in Tel Aviv. I complete a draft of the motion to have Levy's indictment in the Operation Pyramid Overdrive case dismissed on the grounds of the several egregious violations of his Fourth Amendment rights. Ivan reads it, he has his associate Ken Tuscillo read it, and when they are both happy with the edits, the motion is printed up, and I take it with me on my way home to file with the clerk at the Eastern District Federal Court in Brooklyn—the same courthouse where, nearly fifteen years ago, I beat my first hashish importation case.

I think we all know that this motion is a loser. Courts have held that it doesn't matter to what lengths the agents go in their efforts to bring a defendant to trial. Constitutional rights don't apply until the defendant is on US soil. The brief is aimed at trying to get the judge to order an evidentiary hearing, and to then force the government to reveal the sordid details of Levy's abduction and torture, as well as to uncover the facts of the rogue DEA Special Operations Group we have identified as Group 33, and to use all this material as a bargaining chip to urge the prosecutor to make a better offer should Ivan's client agree to plead guilty. We have a good judge, the Honorable Jack B. Weinstein. When presiding, Judge Weinstein eschews the judicial robes. He dresses in a business suit and chooses not to perch above the proceedings and rule from the bench, but rather he takes a seat at a conference table in the well of the court with the representatives from both sides. It was in a ruling by Judge Weinstein that I found the language that resulted in my sentence being vacated.

There is an ugly underbelly to the Operation Pyramid Overdrive case, and several related international heroin investigations that I suspect the government would prefer to keep hidden from a judge like Jack Weinstein. Charlie Kelly and I meet with a former agent who tells us about a rogue DEA Special Operations Group that calls itself Redrum—*murder* spelled backwards from the movie *The Shining*.

Once again, this resonates with a story I heard from a young Lebanese prisoner I met while in holdover at USP Lewisburg. He was busted in a controlled delivery setup while working with DEA agents in the Middle East. Multikilo shipments of heroin from Lebanon's Bekaa Valley were packed into suitcases, placed on prearranged commercial flights into Detroit and other US cities where they were allowed to clear customs. The heroin was then turned over to wholesale distributors in a law enforcement scheme known as "allowing the drugs to walk." Once a significant amount of the junk hit the streets, federal narcotics agents would swoop in and make any number of arrests of mid-to-low-level distributors, to much local media fanfare. Most of the money and drugs was never accounted for. In our brief, I compare this narcotics agents' enforcement tactic of "walking" the drugs to firemen setting fires so they can keep busy and be heralded for bravery by putting them out, and then partner with the real estate owners to collect on the insurance.

The Special Operations Group Redrum is in fact Group 33—somehow Mohammed Bero fits into all this, though I haven't figured out how as yet. It's life imitating art. So much of Operation Pyramid Overdrive resembles aspects of the plot of *Smack Goddess*. In the hopes of finding out more, I put in a call to a real estate office in southern New Hampshire, and I leave a payphone number and a callback time.

I WRITE UP a draft of my degree program for Shirley Ariker to submit to Empire State College. Once I have a BA, if I still have any inclination to pursue a career as a lawyer, I could go to law school for one year, work for two more years for Ivan, which, if approved, would qualify me to take the bar exam and, possibly, after further consideration of my criminal convictions, allow me to be admitted. Something else to think about as the *Smack Goddess* publication date draws near. If I can't be a criminal, why not a criminal defense attorney? Or a crime novelist? Or both? The principal goal must always be to write, otherwise none of this makes any sense, and there's no telling what aberrant urge may hold sway.

SUSAN LORING SHOWS up at my office unannounced to present me with Tony Suarez's check for $2,500. Ivan, to his misfortune, is not around to ogle her. She suggests we go out for a drink to celebrate. Much as I would like to join her for a drink, perhaps even spend the evening with her, I must beg off. I have an appointment to meet for dinner with the journalist Steve Fishman. As soon as Susan leaves the office, once I allow her time to clear the building, I rush out to the bank to deposit the check before the ink disappears.

So, it's really happening. I have been hired to write a treatment for a film about Harry Chapin. Apparently, Suarez reached an agreement with Harry's wife, Sandy. This is exciting, my first gig in the entertainment business—actually, it's not my first. While I was still locked up I was hired by Dustin Hoffman, through Mailer, to critique a prison-based novel called *Green River Rising*. An English psychiatrist who I suspect never set foot in an American penitentiary wrote the book. Hoffman had starred in the classic prison movie, *Papillion*. He also worked with crime novelist Eddie Bunker, and starred in the film *Straight Time*, an adaptation of Bunker's great postprison/parole novel *No Beast So Fierce*. Norman told me that Hoffman was fascinated by prison stories. Hoffman believed he had been a prisoner in a former lifetime. He was considering optioning and making a film based on *Green River Rising*.

It's a good thing Suarez finally came through with the initial payment, since, while doing my research, I already wrote a rough draft of the treatment. The movie business, as I am learning, may be an occupation that attracts a lot of charlatans and scam artists who hope that by becoming movie producers, they might also get laid. Still, I'm serious about pursuing the entertainment business and feel drawn to the work not only because I want those big pay checks that are so hard to come by as a novelist these days but also because the form appeals to me. It's the communal waking dream, the shared journey of watching a movie. Myths are evoked. Heroes, antiheros, heroines, and femme fatales are all ten feet tall. They speak to us. I remember once going to see *Last Tango in Paris* in LA with two young actresses, sisters I was hoping to fuck, and being so stimulated by the film that, once we left the theater, without saying a word the three of just ran for several blocks to release the energy provoked by Brando's incredible performance. A great movie can change the way you feel about yourself, the way you experience your own life, and the way you see the world at large.

Much of Harry Chapin's life was spent in and around the Brooklyn Heights neighborhood where I now reside. I visit a playground just down the street from my apartment that is dedicated to, and named for, Harry. And I walk by 45A Hicks Street, also nearby, where Harry spent some of the happiest years of his life from age eleven to seventeen.

I've been watching similar biopics about musicians and rock stars: *The Buddy Holly Story*, starring Gary Busey, directed by Steve Rash, and *La Bamba*, directed by Luis Valdez about Chicano rock star Richie Valens, starring Lou Diamond Phillips and Esai Morales. Like Chapin, both Buddy Holly and Richie Valens died young, at the height of their careers. They were killed in a plane crash along with the Big Bopper. For contrast, I also watch *The Rose*, starring Bette Midler and Alan Bates, and *Sid and Nancy*, directed by Alex Cox and with an unforgettable performance by a young actor named Gary Oldman as Sid. I was living at the Hotel Chelsea off and on around the time when Sid Vicious's girlfriend, Nancy Spungen, died in their rooms at the famous hotel. These folks were heavily into the junkie life/death downward spiral. *Sid and Nancy* may well be the polar opposite of what I intend to do with the Harry Chapin story; still, it's a powerful film.

I JOIN JOURNALIST Steve Fishman downtown for dinner and to do an interview. He records much of our conversation about writing, and, specifically about writing in prison. We talk about drugs, the international illegal drug trade, and the politics of the drug war, particularly when it comes to cannabis. Over the weekend, Steve comes by the apartment in Brooklyn Heights to complete the interview. I let him borrow Mailer's letters to me in prison.

Radha Battachargi finally calls. We make plans to have lunch next week. My prison pal, the inimitable defrocked psychiatrist, Doctor David Buckley, shows up in town and invites me to join him at an informal dinner party at the Bromley Building on West Eighty-Third. On the way home, I am stranded in a stalled subway car somewhere under the streets of Manhattan and have to struggle to keep from having a claustrophobic panic attack. I remind myself that this is a subway car, not a prison cell in an isolation unit, not a bullpen filled with angry prisoners. Being stuck in the subway is not the same as being locked in a prison cell doing twenty-five years with no parole. The train will soon move on, the doors will open at my stop, and I will be able to get off and move about freely once more.

Doc Buckley is engaged in some sort of contentious situation over parental visiting rights with a former paramour, Judith Regan, with whom he has a child, a boy named Patrick. The Doc is always up to some shenanigans, but Judith Regan is not one to be trifled with. Judith edited the tabloid *National Enquirer*, and she is a producer for *The Geraldo Rivera Show*. I let the Doc talk me into writing Judith a letter on Fisher's stationary, and I fax it to her.

Big mistake. When am I gonna learn? Or, as Neil Young would sing: "Why do I keep fucking up?" Judith promptly calls Fisher and threatens to have him disbarred for hiring "a notorious criminal." Notorious goofball would be more like it.

Guber-Peters passes on *Smack Goddess* sight unseen. When Radha Battachargi tells Peter Guber that the book is about a woman drug dealer, he says there is no way they will have anything to do with a story about drugs or drug dealers as both he and his partner, Jon Peters, have been depicted in the media as illegal drug users themselves, and they do not wish to appear soft on the subject. Radha tells me this over lunch at the Trump Plaza Bistro. She says that although she found the novel absorbing, in the end she was disappointed because she "didn't know who to root for," a statement that strikes me as ludicrous in this day and age. I explain that to me a novel is not a football game or a boxing match; there doesn't necessarily have to be someone to root for, although I would argue that one could root for Rickie Rude, the punk rock star who is falsely implicated in the main character's drug enterprise. "Who do you root for in *Sid and Nancy*?" I ask her. To which she answers the book may be ahead of its time, and that she believes it will eventually be made into a movie, "but not by Guber-Peters."

As Ivan would say, "Next."

I HAVE A meeting with poet, novelist, and short story writer Fielding Dawson at his apartment in the West Village. Fielding is chairman of the PEN Prison Writing Program. Founded in 1971, the program fosters the restorative, rehabilitative power of writing for prisoners; PEN also sponsors an annual prison writing contest. My short story, "A Skyline Turkey," was selected as the first prizewinner in 1989 while I was still locked up. "A Skyline Turkey" will be published in *Fortune News*, a publication of the New York Fortune Society that offers assistance to ex-prisoners upon release. It is also scheduled appear in an anthology of prison writing, *Doing Time: 25 Years of Prison Writing*, edited by Bell Gale Chevigny. Sometime later, it will also be published in *Story* magazine.

Fielding invites me to his home to talk about writing in prison, and to ask if I'm willing to speak on the subject and read at this year's PEN Prison Writing Awards ceremony. Of course I will; I'm passionate about the restorative value of writing for prisoners. Even as it does out here in the world, writing sustained me while I was in prison and in danger of losing hope. The act of taking raw experience and emotion and crafting them into a story to be shared with, and possibly move or inspire, others kept me sane during the years of my imprisonment. It kept me from becoming murderous, picking up a new case, and possibly never getting released. Writing gave me a purpose to get up every day. It gave me confidence in my competence to compose and submit legal briefs that ultimately moved courts to give me back my freedom. Writing in prison is power for the powerless. And it gave me hope, always hope, hope of release, and hope of a new life after prison. Writing—all art—is the highest form of hope.

It was never easy—no, writing in prison was always hard, a clandestine activity because the authorities discouraged anything they felt they couldn't control. And writing is still hard out here, even given the marvelous accoutrements of a computer, a printer, and a desk in a clean, well-lit, quiet place of my own with no prison guards to harass me. Now it is the exigencies of earning a living and the inner demons of doubt and self-sabotage conjured to stand around my desk mocking me that give me pause. But, as I learned in prison, there is only one way to deal with impediments to doing the work, be they human or psychological, personal or universal: put ass in chair and write. The first word, and then the next, then a paragraph, and a whole page as you follow your dream, find your inspiration, and make it reality. Out here, as well as in there, the act of writing is a way to find and give purpose to your time here on earth.

I tell Fielding I am happy to share my experience in the hope that it might inspire some other prisoner or ex-con to seek new meaning in his or her life through writing. Fielding signs me up to speak at the coming event; he invites me back to meet with the other speakers as we draw closer to the date. He asks if I know Kim Wozencraft, author of the novel *Rush*, who is also scheduled to read at the PEN event. "No," I say, "I've not met her. But I do know her book."

Tonight I am to see my sweet Paloma. I will sleep in her arms. Tomorrow I must report to my parole officer.

•

I AWAKE IN Paloma's loving embrace. She clings to me all night long like a frightened child. And when we wake, she rolls over and sticks her ass up in my face, and I enter her from the rear. She is so lovely, so passionate, and already devoted to me. She's ready to have our child.

I leave Paloma's at 6:30 and take the train to Brooklyn for my meeting with Ms. Lawless. I prefer riding the train to above ground transportation even after my panic attack. Ivan can't understand why I choose the subway rather than taxis or a car service. Well, there's the expense for one thing; but beyond that there is also something about mingling with the hordes of commuters, the hoi poloi, the great unwashed that humbles me and reminds me how grateful I am to be out of prison. It helps me to feel that I am part of a greater humanity. When I chided Ivan about his preference for traveling in a hired car, he said, "Do you know how lonely it gets in the back of a limousine?"

At the parole offices, I have to wait for over half an hour, but when Lawless finally shows up and we meet, it turns out to be the most relaxed and friendliest visit we have had to date. Something about her attitude toward me has changed, it's as though she has finally come to terms with who I am. She understands that I will not be bullied by authority, that at some level I simply don't give a fuck, I'll fight, I'll even go back to prison if need be. But I think she has also come to believe that I am sincere about my work for Ivan, it's not a bullshit job, and that I am determined to fulfill my obligations and abide by the reasonable conditions of my supervised release in an effort to turn my life around; and, more important, to get out from under government control. This has given Lawless new comfort in our relationship. I offer to give her a signed copy of *Smack Goddess*, which she declines, says she is not allowed to accept gifts from her parolees, but that she will buy a copy. Still, before I leave, she remembers to hand me the little plastic container and motions me off to the men's room.

I HURRY BACK to Columbia Heights and out onto the promenade to meet with a man who I refer to as Uncle Georges. He's Lebanese, related to the man I spoke to in the real estate office in Southern New Hampshire, and well connected in Lebanon and in New England organized crime circles, specifically with the Patriarca Crime Family out of Providence, Rhode Island. We embrace, kiss three times Arab style, and walk.

"They have these microphones," Georges says and waves an arm at the surrounding buildings. "Parabolic . . . or something like that. They can sit in a room somewhere a block or two away and pick up conversations."

Even as we hugged, I could feel him frisk me to make certain I wasn't wired. His caution, call it paranoia, is why he's still out here walking around after a lifetime in the underworld. Georges looks well, tan and fit. He's in his sixties and has a full head of iron-gray hair, thick black moustache, and bushy black eyebrows. He's dressed in a tweed jacket, tan slacks, and a mock turtleneck sweater. He looks like a Middle Eastern version of Burt Lancaster and has the same masculine vitality.

"Pig!" Georges practically spits out the word when I mention Mohammed Bero. "It's a trap. *Don't do it!* They will lure you to Beirut and make you a hostage. They want the seven million they say you owe them. They will keep you until you pay the seven million, and then they will kill you. I know . . . I know; it's that thief Alain who stole their load who owes them the money, not you. But they will always blame you because he used your name. You must find me that money, Richard. Or give me an address where I can locate this Alain whatever his name is. And your other friend, Ayla. He was a snake! Working for the DEA all along! You must be very careful, Richard. *Trust no one.* They have not finished with you."

Georges goes on to say that the Middle East is overrun with under-cover agents, narcotics merchants, CIA agents, professional informers, terrorists, former terrorists, and prisoners hoping to get out of jail, all claiming to have the connections to free American hostages. "For a price! But it's all bullshit. The Americans know who has the power and how it has to be done. It's all politics, Richard, and big business, bigger than you or I know. It will only happen when your lying government wants it to happen, and not before, and definitely not because of anything that fat meatball says or does. Let him rot in an Israeli prison."

Georges hands me a business card with a company name, address, and phone number in Paris. "Have this Israeli lawyer call me. I will tell him what to do with Mohammed Bero. Skewer the fat fuck, and roast him on a spit like the pig he is!" He laughs. "And you! When do we get back to business?"

If Gloria Lawless could only see me now.

I HEAD TO the Mailers' to meet with Norman and Norris for breakfast. Norman is my great, good, and helpful friend, full of cogent advice about my writing, about writing in general, and just as warm and intimate after all these years of our friendship, and even after being my friend brought him serious federal law enforcement heat. He suggests I read poetry to improve my prose style, to give new resonance to my sensibilities so long suppressed, beat down, and flattened of nuance by years of imprisonment. Norris comments that she loved *Smack Goddess*. Norman, perhaps recalling his own meteoric success upon publication of his first novel, *The Naked and the Dead*, at the tender age of twenty-five, warns me of the perils of public exposure that come with the published novelist's life, particularly after such a long time as a polymorphous underground criminal, and then having endured the anonymous numbered half-life of the prisoner. He cautions that it may all be overwhelming. He speaks of the reviews that will upset and even anger me. And he encourages me never to sell out, not that anyone's making me offers.

The Mailers are in town for a few days. Norman has at last delivered the edited manuscript of his long-anticipated CIA novel *Harlot's*

Ghost. He says that they will be back in time for the *Smack Goddess* book launch party in November.

"You've paid a dear price for this, Rick," he says. "You deserve all you have coming with this book, and more."

THE DAY TURNS into perhaps the happiest day of my life thus far—even happier than the day I walked out of the prison gates. I get a call from Fern at Birch Lane to tell me that they have received advance copies of the hardcover edition of *Smack Goddess.* I go by the office and pick up three copies. And what a beautiful sight it is! I present Ivan with my first autographed copy. Ivan hugs me, gives me a big kiss; he immediately sends out for bottles of Dom Pérignon and calls for a celebration. He gathers all the office personnel in his office to toast the author. Charlie Kelly, Ken Tuscillo, Ivan's *of counsel* associate, Melissa, the receptionist, and Carmen, Ivan's paralegal and Spanish interpreter. To make the day even better, Paloma shows up and joins the party.

TONY SUAREZ CALLS to tell me that he loves the treatment I wrote for the Chapin film, *Listen to America.* Better yet, he sent the treatment to Harry's wife, Sandy Chapin, and she also liked it enough to want to meet me and discuss the treatment. I tell Suarez that Sandy and I have already spoken and made plans to meet. Suarez says he's ready to pay me the $2,500 balance of the fee for the treatment, and, if all goes well with Sandy, to hire me to write the screenplay for an additional ten grand.

I take the train out to Huntington, Long Island. Sandy Chapin meets me at the station, and we go to dinner at a local restaurant. Sandy impresses me as one of the most intelligent, gracious women I have ever met. I am so taken by her, and so interested in all she has to tell me about her life with Harry, that I often find myself at a loss for words—something, I will learn over the coming years, that is an attribute in an interviewer. Allow the interviewee to talk. Prod them with the occasional observation, but never dominate the dialogue. People generally love to talk about themselves; all they need is to be asked the right questions. Sandy tells me that Harry often referred to himself as "a third-rate rock star" based on his record sales, and yet he sold millions of records. His favorite sayings were "No problem" and "Onwards and upwards." He was, she says, perhaps the most positive person she ever knew, but hard on himself, constantly pushing himself to do more. It wasn't ambition so much as a genuine desire to help others less fortunate. They met and fell in love when she hired Harry to teach her to play guitar. Later they collaborated on the lyrics of some of Harry's most memorable songs, such as *Cat's in the Cradle*. Harry was conflicted about the demands of his career and his commitment as a husband and father, which inspired the song. We sit talking until the restaurant staff tells us they want to go home. It's nearly midnight when Sandy drops me at the train station. I thank her and head back to the city convinced that, with Sandy's help, I have all I need to write a screenplay worthy of being produced.

Chapter Six

YOUR WHOLE TRIBE EATS DONUTS

IF EVER THERE were an unlikely client to be represented by my employer and dear friend, criminal defense attorney Ivan S. Fisher, it is none other than the infamous, imprisoned crack cocaine kingpin Howard "Pappy" Mason. Ivan shows up in my office and hands me the Mason file. "Richard," he says, "please read this and give it your unique perspective. It's . . . shall we say, it's a challenge worthy of your expertise."

Pappy's attorney of record is a criminal defense lawyer named Harry Batchelder Jr., who came to represent Pappy under the Criminal Justice Act, whereby criminal defense attorneys are assigned a certain number of federal criminal cases and paid by the court to represent indigent defendants. How Batchelder managed to lure Ivan into the case is not immediately clear. It's not about money, certainly not if Batchelder is paid by the court. Reading the file, I see where Pappy may have been a street drug boss at one time, and with of a crew of dealers called the Bebos that were said to be making upwards of $200,000 a week slinging crack in the Jamaica, Queens, neighborhood he ruled with his alleged former partner Lorenzo "Fat Cat" Nichols. But both Pappy and Fat Cat have been locked up for years by the time we get the case, and their drug enterprise is long since defunct, or it was taken over by a new crew. Ivan may have agreed to come into the case to garner some of the extensive publicity it has attracted since Pappy, who was in prison at the time on gun charges, was charged and convicted of having ordered the brutal assassination of a twenty-two-year-old rookie New York City police officer named Edward Byrne.

I read how Officer Byrne was assigned to guard a witness to neighborhood drug activity whom the police were supposed to be protecting. On February 26, 1988, Byrne was shot in the head five times as he sat alone in a patrol car outside the witness's home in Queens. Pappy is due in court to be sentenced after he was convicted in 1989 of racketeering and ordering the murder of Officer Byrne in furtherance of a racketeering enterprise. He's facing life in prison with no possibility of parole. The lengthy delay in the sentencing phase is due mainly to issues of Pappy's mental competency at the time of his trial.

Clearly Ivan did not join the defense to win favor with the Police Benevolent Association. Knowing Ivan as I do, I believe there has to be some legal conundrum, some cause or issue he believes in, or fascination with the client that attracts him and sparks his combative nature. Ivan is like an intellectual gladiator who thrives on the drama in a heated battle of wits and verbal warfare in the arena of the courtroom during a fiercely contested case. He shines on his feet in the heat of cross-examination. The rest is up to me: reading all the discovery; devising some workable theory of defense; doing the legal research on the issues; composing the motions, briefs, and tables of authorities and compiling the exhibits; and even finding issues the lawyers may have overlooked.

"Well," Ivan asks when I return the file, "what's your verdict?"

"Not guilty."

"Why?"

"Because I don't think he did it. I don't believe he gave the order to kill Officer Byrne."

"No? Why not?"

"Because I don't think Pappy had the presence of mind or even the position of leadership in the gang to order anything—at least, not at that time. He'd been off the street for too long, he was out of touch with what was going on in the street, and there is every indication that the man is, and was then also, out of touch with reality—completely out of his mind. The government's theory as to what supposedly motivated Pappy to order the killing also seems weak to me. They claim he ordered the killing to retaliate against the cops for his prior conviction in the weapons case. That strikes me as pretty far-fetched.

"The witness the police were supposed to be protecting was going to testify about ongoing drug-dealing activity in the neighborhood; that would have a direct impact on the crew's current drug operation. To me, this looks like a classic instance of ratting down. He's a fall guy. Pappy's partner, Fat Cat Nichols, had a lot more to lose as a result of the witness's information reaching the cops than Pappy did. So Fat Cat makes a deal to implicate Pappy for giving the order to kill Officer Byrne, knowing Pappy is so crazy he's the ideal scapegoat. Fat Cat then uses this maneuver as a bargaining chip to manipulate the prosecutor and make a deal in his own case. During Pappy's trial, his lawyer, Batchelder, told Judge Korman that Pappy refused to cooperate in his own defense. He said that Pappy was suffering from hallucinations, that he believed his mother was performing voodoo exercises on his head—which, given what I've been reading about Pappy's mother, may not be incredible. She may have been the mastermind behind the whole operation. We should see if we can arrange to get Pappy a psychiatric evaluation, and, if he's found to be as crazy as he appears to be, then move to get the conviction thrown out on the grounds that he was mentally incompetent to participate in his defense."

"Very good." Ivan has been nodding throughout my interpretation of the case. "I agree. Done," he says. "Draft the motion. Find the forensic psychiatrist you want to use, and write him or her a letter. Let's get the evaluation. Do it right away. The government is anxious to sentence Mr. Mason and get him out of MCC, where, apparently, he is hardly an ideal inmate. This is your case, Richard. I'm depending on you to run with it. Keep it up, you'll be getting your thirty dollars an hour sooner than we imagined."

INDEED, WE ARE on a roll. In the Operation Pyramid Overdrive case, Levy is offered ten years for a guilty plea after the prosecutor gets a look at our motion for an evidentiary hearing on the Group 33 matter. I reported on my meeting with Georges, and Ivan forwarded the information to the lawyer in Israel. All this encourages me to enroll in a class that will prepare me for the LSAT test. Shirley Ariker submits my degree program to the Empire State College degree evaluation board, and I am awarded a bachelor's degree based on my credits from Arizona State University, the writing course I took at Harvard Summer School, credits I earned in classes I took at MCC, and through additional credits awarded for life experience, that is, my efforts and successes as a jailhouse lawyer.

I compose a letter to Dr. Abraham Halpern, a professor emeritus of psychiatry at New York Medical College and president at the American Academy of Psychiatry and the Law. Dr. Halpern is a champion of human rights, especially in matters of law and mental health, and he is one of the founding leaders of the psychiatric subspecialty of forensic psychiatry. Dr. Halpern agrees to consult on the case and examine Pappy. He visits with Pappy and presents us with his opinion.

Pappy, Dr. Halpern writes, suffers from paranoid schizophrenia with pronounced delusions of grandeur. In Halpern's opinion, Pappy was at the time of his trial and is now mentally incompetent to assist in his own defense. Judge Korman orders a hearing. After weeks of reading about Pappy and the case, conferring with Dr. Halpern, and with co-counsel Harry Batchelder and Ivan, all of whom have met Pappy, at last I will have the opportunity to see him and witness his behavior in person.

I am not to be disappointed.

THROUGHOUT MY WORK on this case, I have come to view Pappy Mason as a living personification of the madness that is the government's declared war on drugs. Just as crack cocaine was created as a product in response to the war, so Pappy is an embodiment of the damage the drug war is doing to communities all across America. Pappy, Fat Cat Nichols, and their entire street crew of dealers are financed, armed, emboldened, and called to battle by our government's demand for a violent street war on what is clearly a medical problem. None of this would have happened: Officer Byrne would still be alive, and God only knows how many other souls might have been saved, had our politicians been honest in their approach to the issue of drugs and addiction.

Further, I see the way this case has played out up to this point, and the way it has been orchestrated both by the defense and by the prosecution as a clear picture of how the war on drugs is corrupting and perverting the criminal justice system from the streets to the upper echelons of the Justice Department. In the race to the witness stand to rat out others and save their own asses, savvy criminals and criminal defense lawyers are able to manipulate ambitious, naive prosecutors into making deals that have little to nothing to do with justice and everything to do with public perception, expenditure of tax dollars, prosecutorial overzealousness, expedience, and careerism.

On the day of the hearing, twenty-eight-year-old Pappy appears in the courtroom as the nightmare version of the spawn this insane war has birthed in our inner cities and in the outlaw nations financed by the illegal drug trade. Hustled into the courtroom in shackles and chains by a contingent of beefy deputy US marshals, Pappy reminds me physically of Bob Marley, with his waist-length dreadlocks and lithe, rail-thin body that seems to be in constant motion, animated by some inner rhythm that is part dance, part self-defense moves as well a need to release trapped manic energies. As soon as his restraints are removed, Pappy drops to the floor before Judge Korman's bench and does twenty rapid-fire push-ups. The deputy marshals don't even attempt to stop him. He leaps to his feet, hyperalert, his dreadlocks swirling, waving about his body like a cape. Pappy has the otherworldly presence of a mystic mad genius. Finished with his quick warm-up exercises, he faces the bench, then he looks around the courtroom warily, and shouts, "What is this, a Klan meeting?"

When the court clerk asks him to state his name for the record, Pappy responds, "I'm the mayor of Brooklyn!" Judge Korman attempts to bring order to the court. Pappy chastises him. "You shut up!" he says. "I'll kill you! You may be a boss, but I'm the boss of all bosses!"

The prosecutor, a young white woman assistant United States attorney who appears utterly bewildered, attempts to address the court. Pappy turns on her. "I'll kill you too!" he says. "All you motherfuckers!" and he waves around the room, glaring at the spellbound audience. "Who are you? I didn't ask for no Klan meeting up in here! I'm leaving."

"Mr. Mason—" the judge says, trying to quiet Pappy down.

Pappy turns on him viciously. "I told you to shut up! No one wants to hear what you have to say!"

He drops to the floor and does another quick set of push-ups, then he announces he's had enough. "I said take me away from this evil place!"

Judge Korman, however, is determined to get in the last word. He denies our motion to have the verdict thrown out and declares, "I believe he is competent to be sentenced at this time." He then turns to Pappy. "Mr. Mason, I hereby commit you to the custody of the attorney general or his designated representative for a period of life without the possibility of parole."

"I told you to go fuck yourself, motherfucker! You can't touch me! I have all the power in this place," Pappy says, and then he swings his long arm around and points it at the terrified prosecutor. "You! I'll kill you, too." Then back at Judge Korman, "All you punkass motherfuckers!"

And then Pappy delivers his final statement to the shocked court: "Your whole tribe eats donuts!"

IF PAPPY ISN'T mad, he's one hell of an actor. He had everyone in the courtroom on the edge of his or her seat, including Judge Korman. A shame to think of all that manic creative energy going to waste.

The motion may have failed, but it not only provides ample material should there be an appeal, it also convinces me of Pappy's mad genius. I leave the court with an image of the judge, the court officers, the marshals and cops, and the lawyers and agents all sitting around a campfire congratulating themselves as they nosh on donuts.

A few days later I read in the *Post* that Fat Cat has disappeared into the Witness Protection Program—no doubt as his reward for implicating Pappy.

Chapter Seven

MAILER PAL WRITES DRUGGIE NOVEL*

The early reviews of *Smack Goddess* are in, and on the whole they are encouraging. My agent, Jack Scovil, is elated. He calls me at the office and reads me the *Publishers Weekly* review. "*Smack Goddess* is a striking, documentary style novel teeming with manic drug world characters. An exciting prison break is detailed with dreamlike lyricism. While the author's account of a degraded, manipulative justice system may be biased, he conveys it with a passionate authority." And from *Booklist,* another publishing trade journal: "For its convincing depiction of a circle of hard core, high-living drug dealers with their contingent of lawyers, and for its fast-moving plot, readers will 'just say yes' to *Smack Goddess.*"

The *Kirkus* review is mixed, calling the novel "a lumpish, intermittently energetic mulligan soup of a novel . . . (read: great sex in the prison conference room). . . . A.G.'s powerfully jaundiced view of the drug industry helps smooth out the bumps."

I get a call from a writer in Toronto who is doing a piece on the book for *Maclean's* magazine. And writer Anthony Haden-Guest calls to tell me he is doing a piece for *Vanity Fair.* We meet for a drink after

---

* Story title in the New York *Daily News.*

work. Anthony intimates that he is working on a book he's calling *Zigzag* about a character he says I may know called John Donahue. That name means nothing to me until Haden-Guest mentions that Donahue is also known as "The Wizard of ID." Of course I know Donahue. He's the conniving motherfucker who stole my briefcase from the rear of my locked car (expertly, I might add), and then ran off to Lebanon to do a huge hash deal with Mohammed Bero while using my name as his introduction. I had a confrontation with Donahue at a dinner in Beirut, and I hit him hard across his mouth with an open hand, bitch-slapped him. He ended up ripping the Lebanese off for their share on seven tons of hash his people landed safely in the US; this is the money, the seven million dollars, that the Lebanese claim I owe them. Haden-Guest, who had some sort of book collaboration deal with Donahue that also went bad, tells me that his experience with the Wizard has caused him to redefine evil as "a sickness of the soul for which there is no known cure."

I go to see Barbara Kopple's new documentary *American Dream*, about a strike at a meat-packing plant in Minnesota, with Shane, my Iranian friend from jail, and Shane's friend Charlie Minnig, and Charlie's wife, Sarah, a.k.a. Maddy. We go to dinner after the film, and I wonder how Gloria Lawless would react if she could see me now. These folks are all former, semiretired, fully retired, or still active international drug smugglers. Maddy was Smack Goddess Frin Mullin's cellmate at the women's prison in West Virginia before Frin escaped. She tells me she heard from Frin recently; she's back in England living the fugitive life. The conversation at the table is all about the current state of "the business." It's not good. Too many rats. Even people you know and trust from the old days, they get busted now with these heavy mandatory sentences, and they flip and give up everyone they ever did business with, including family. It's depressing, enough to make someone want to go straight; it certainly has that effect on me.

Shane says Barbara Kopple, who is a close friend of his, may have a new project, a documentary about the former heavyweight champ

Mike Tyson and his fall from grace after being convicted of rape. She is looking for someone who knows about boxing to write the proposal. He asks if I'd be interested. Yes, sure, I'd be happy to work on it with Barbara.

Suarez calls to tell me that Sandy Chapin has given the project her blessing. He says he will messenger a check for five grand to my office to get me started on the screenplay.

Good. I can pay my rent. Things are definitely looking up.

AT LAST THE eve of November 14, 1990, is upon us. I ride over to the Century Club in a car with Norman and Norris. On the way, Norman advises me that these events tend to get off to a slow start. He says people don't usually begin to arrive until the last hour, and he says that I should not be disappointed even if the party is sparsely attended. The New York literary crowd, he cautions, is a fickle and unpredictable lot. You never know what will bring them out in numbers.

We arrive at quarter of six and are directed to a cavernous, empty room on the ground floor. Indeed, it will take a sizable crowd to fill this space. By 6:15 the room is half full, and by 6:30 the place is jammed. It's an eclectic mix of literary types and cops, lawyers, and crooks who have come out to celebrate the publication of *Smack Goddess* and drink free booze. Writers Gay Talese, George Plimpton, William Styron, Jay McInerney, and Hunter Thompson, to name a few; editors and publishers from Birch Lane and Random House; literary agents; perhaps even a few undercover federal agents; and more than a few representatives of the criminal bar, including Michael Kennedy, Ira London, Marshall Stern, Bob Leighton, and Ivan, of course. There are former cops and current private investigators: Charlie Kelley and Bill Majeski, the NYPD homicide detective who tracked down and arrested Jack Abbott. And there are a fair number of former and perhaps a few still active criminals in the crowd: Shane Zarintash, Charlie and Sarah Minnig, and former lawyer and ex-con

Alan Frank, whom I was friendly with during my final year at FCI Ashland.

My mother, Mary, has taken the train down from Boston and is enjoying the night as much if not more than I—it's her wish come true as well as it is mine. Her son has finally done something she can be proud of. The old man, as expected, stays home. Paloma comes as my date and brings her niece, Tiffany, who is strikingly beautiful. Everyone from Doc Eisenberg's office is there now that it is no longer a secret that Paloma and I are seeing each other. Tony Suarez and the lovely Susan Loring come with Sandy Chapin. Naomi has come down from Upstate. My nephew Robert is there with his girlfriend, Lisa. John Mulheren stops in after his sentencing. He tells me he got a year and a day and a $1.6 million fine. He remains out on bond pending an appeal.

Steven Schragis, the Birch Lane publisher, and Norman both speak. Norman, drink in hand, opines that there are writers who have rich experience and mediocre talent, and then there are writers who have much talent and little experience. He says I am one of the few writers he knows who has vast experience and a talent to equal it. I hope he's right.

After the party breaks up, a group of us head uptown to Elaine's, the literary hangout on the Upper East Side, for a late dinner and fitting finish to a New York literary evening. I sit with the lovely Paloma on one side and her gorgeous niece on the other as in some prison fantasy become reality. Ivan orders bottles of Dom Pérignon. My mother sits with Norman and Norris. It is well past midnight when Elaine finally shoos us out so she can close the place.

This is a night to remember for the rest of my days, a culmination of dreams and ambitions, of efforts, and of prodigious resources of will and determination at a time when all seemed hopeless. And it is the beginning of a new phase in a life that still seems alien to me—not quite real or somehow not truly mine—a life belonging to someone I am pretending to be.

Back at the apartment in Brooklyn, lying in bed beside Paloma, I'm way too hyped up to sleep. I think back to a very different night—the night I spent in a county jail in Lowell, Massachusetts, the town named for my forebears. I had just been convicted of smuggling pot and sentenced in Federal District Court in Portland, Maine, to the maximum, fifteen years in the penitentiary. I was on my way to New York City, in the custody of deputy US marshals, and there I would be tried again, charged under the kingpin statute with operating a continuing criminal enterprise, be convicted once more, and pick up another ten years running wild for a total sentence of twenty-five years and six months.

The wing where they housed me in the county jail in Lowell had been condemned, which struck me as appropriate. They locked me up for the night in a damp, cold, filthy cell that had no bed and only a stinking bucket full of piss and shit in which to relieve myself. Good, I thought, this is perfect. This is where I belong. Instead of feeling sorry for myself, I felt content, gratified that I was finally getting what I deserved, finally had arrived where I'd been headed all my life, fulfilling everyone's worst expectations, including my own. It had nothing to do with my so-called crimes, the illegal activity for which I had been sentenced. No, rather it had only to do with who I believed they—the authorities—determined I was: a bad kid, the kid the mothers of the other kids said stay away from, don't play with that Rickie Stratton, he'll get you in trouble, he's a wayward child doomed to end up—exactly where I was, in a filthy, dank dungeon. From that night to this night, in a place of my own with a beautiful woman lying by my side, and all the nights and days in between, I have tried to discover who I really am beneath all the names—dope smuggler, prisoner, ex-con, novelist, forensic specialist—why I am here, and why, wherever I am besides perhaps in a jail cell, I never feel as though I belong, I always feel I'm a fraud, a pretender, and basically full of shit.

I roll over and sniff between Paloma's legs. Ah, now this makes sense. Here is something a man can feel clear about. . . .

Come to papa, *mamita*.

THE *NEW YORK Times Book Review* features *Smack Goddess* as the lead fiction review, a full page in the December 9, 1990, edition, under the title "Still Bored, Still Dealing Dope" by a guy named James Atlas. Norman is upset; he tells me this is a hit job; he and Atlas despise each other. Atlas wrote a nasty piece about Norman for the *Times Sunday Magazine*. Predictably, in the review, Atlas can't resist attacking Mailer by revisiting the Jack Henry Abbott debacle.

> Thirteen years ago Mr. Mailer discovered another promising author who had come out of that unlikely writers' workshop, the Federal prison system. Jack Henry Abbott, a convicted murderer who had been in jail for nearly 25 years, had initiated a correspondence with Mr. Mailer, who was so enthralled by the charged rhetoric of Mr. Abbott's prose that he got him a book contract and sponsored him for parole. Six weeks after being released from prison, in 1981, Mr. Abbott provoked a dispute over use of the men's room in a Lower East Side restaurant and stabbed to death a young actor and playwright who worked there as a waiter. Mr. Mailer was philosophical: "It's a tragedy all around."

Mailer, it seems, will never live down the Jack Henry Abbott disaster. And apparently, I am destined to be compared to a man with whom I bear no resemblance except for the fact that we both served time in prison. Yes, the Abbott story is a tragedy all around, certainly it is, particularly for the family of the young man Abbott killed; but it has nothing to do with my story or who I am. Abbott's life is a tragedy. He was the bastard child of a prostitute, a state-raised convict in and out of jails and prisons all his life. By the time he was released from prison, Abbott was a fully formed product of the brutal, inhumane American penal system, where there is not even a pretense of reform or rehabilitation, where there is only dehumanizing dog-eat-dog survival, guard-on-prisoner violence, institutional malevolence, and gang warfare.

Mailer was credited and damned for supposedly helping to get Abbott released on parole. Anyone who knows anything about how the parole board and prison system work understands that this is nonsense. Nothing Mailer or anyone else except the governor or the president could have done would have enabled Jack Abbott to get out on parole. In fact, having someone famous like Mailer lobbying on your behalf could have the opposite effect. The people who sit on parole boards in both the state and federal system have their own way of doing things. The real story is that Abbott got parole because he became what he railed against in his own book: a jailhouse snitch, a rat, the lowest form of prison life.

A convict named Garrett Trapnell, who had done time with Abbott, wrote a letter to novelist Peter Matthiessen and revealed the truth about Abbott. Abbott had given up the names of strike leaders at the US penitentiary in Marion, Illinois—an unforgivable transgression of the convict code fervently espoused by Abbott in his book. In a 116-page affidavit Abbott provided to an assistant United States attorney, he also gave the names of lawyers who were smuggling drugs into the penitentiary and passing them to prisoners. The prison officials knew Abbott was vulnerable. His book was about to be published. He had every reason to want to get out and bask in the glory of his unlikely success as a writer. The fix was in.

I have done some things in my life that I am not proud of, and a few that still haunt me to this day, mostly to do with the way I treated women who loved me. But refusing to cooperate with the government—refusing to provide evidence and testify against Mailer, Hunter Thompson, my lawyers, and other friends and enemies, and refusing to become a jailhouse snitch—that will never be something I regret. Accepting the punishment and doing the time has actually worked to my benefit. I have respect and acceptance in both the criminal world and from those in law enforcement. And I can look in the mirror without feeling ashamed of who I see looking back at me.

For James Atlas or anyone else to compare me and my long and close friendship with Mailer to his brief, unfortunate, no, tragic convergence with the life of Jack Abbott may be inevitable, but it is also bogus, and a cheap shot. I smuggled and distributed cannabis. That, and laundering the money I made, is the extent of my criminal activity. Abbott was a low-level thief who turned a short bid into a revolving prison sentence that then became self-murder. And for all the hoopla, *In the Belly of the Beast* does not hold up to the best prison novels like Dostoyevsky's *House of the Dead*, Edward Bunker's *Animal Factory*, or *On the Yard* by Malcolm Braly, to name just a few examples of great prison literature. Of course, I'm disgusted with Abbott, not only for what he did to Adnan, which is unforgivable, but also for what he has done to Mailer's reputation, and to the hopes of other prisoner writers.

STEVE FISHMAN'S PIECE in *GQ* is out. God bless my mother, Mary Stratton. As much as she loves her only son, and I know she does, she goes on record in her interview with Fishman to call me an asshole. And she's right, I was and no doubt still am an asshole. My mother refers to when I was an unabashed drug kingpin making way too much cash money to keep my needy ego in check. Money will do that to a man, particularly one who grows up in a household where his parents are always fighting about money. I remember those fights. They were bitter, nasty, and upsetting to me as a young boy. One time at breakfast my mother threw a frying pan full of sunny-side-up fried eggs at my father. He ducked and the eggs ended up all over my mother's new green curtains.

It wasn't as though we were broke. My father was never a big earner. My mother pretty much always had a job outside the home when we were kids, and that was not as common at that time as it is now. I think Mary enjoyed working; she was not content to be a homemaker. She certainly enjoyed spending money, though never on frivolities. She had an eye for real estate as well as for good quality antique furniture. She bought homes, furnished them tastefully, and often sold them at a profit. The money usually came from my grandmother on my mother's side, who was a descendant of the Boston Brahmin Lowell family.

The old man enjoyed playing golf, that was his true love, and he was very good at it. He was an amateur New England champion. Golf celebrities from all over the world would come to play golf with Emery Stratton at the exclusive Charles River Country Club. Had he been born a decade or two later, he would have been on the pro circuit and probably made a lot of money. When he wasn't playing golf, Emery played cards: bridge and gin rummy and later cribbage. He was good at cards also. But he was never much good at making money which, I suspect, is because he didn't care about money. And he wasn't particularly good at being a father. Both my parents came from relatively well-off blue-blood New England Yankee families. I like to say that our family was at the vanguard in the decline of the WASP.

I rebelled against all of that. Growing up, I wanted to be a tough guy, to be the opposite of my taciturn, withdrawn father. I aspired to be a criminal. "What do you want to be when you grow up, kid?" A gangster. Getting in trouble was a sure way to attract my father's otherwise self-absorbed attention. And being tough was my way of distinguishing myself from what I saw as my father's passive manhood. The man played golf; I wrestled and played football. While still in elementary school, I formed perhaps the one and only kids' gang ever to emerge from the suburban, tree-shaded streets of Wellesley Hills, Massachusetts. Our gang was called the Pink Rats, named after a teenage gang of motorcycle-jacket-wearing hoods depicted in an episode of the TV cop show *Dragnet*. We specialized in shoplifting, vandalism, protection, and extorting lunch money from other kids at recess.

Smuggling pot from Mexico in my late teens, by my twenties I was making and spending crazy amounts of cash money, living like an outlaw rock star, and certainly at times behaving like a total asshole. If I were out to dinner with, say Mailer, Dick Goodwin, his wife Doris Kearns Goodwin, Hunter S. Thompson (who was always broke), Jann Wenner of *Rolling Stone* magazine, and assorted girlfriends and hangers-on, when the check came and there was that sometimes awkward moment as the men in the party looked at each other waiting to see if someone was going to make a move to pick up the check, or if it would be one of those group payments with some proffering cash, others putting up their credit cards, and Hunter reaching for all the cash, saying to put it on his credit card, which ultimately Wenner would have to pay, in my assholeishness I relished the moment as I picked up the check and paid it not with a credit card, but from the fat roll of bills in my pocket. Was there any doubt what Rick Stratton did for a living? He certainly wasn't making that kind of money writing for *Rolling Stone*. More like working at *High Times*.

Frances "Frin" Mullin, the woman who was the basis for the heroine of *Smack Goddess*, understands how much fun the outlaw life was. She has an attitude, an insouciance, and may have been one of the first women ever to be charged under the dreaded kingpin statute. She and I were introduced in the attorney visiting room at the MCC, which was always my preferred stop on the Bureau of Prisons national tour—naturally, if for no other reason, there were women prisoners at MCC.

Frin's reputation, indeed her infamy, preceded her arrival at the federal jail. She was busted while living in an apartment owned by writer Nik Cohn, who wrote the magazine article on which the movie *Saturday Night Fever* is based. In the TV room at the MCC, we saw Frin on the local news, this lovely doe caught in the headlights as she was led from an Upper West Side apartment building in handcuffs surrounded by DEA agents. The following morning, while Frin sat in a bullpen waiting to be processed into the jail, a picture of her arrest was on the cover of all the New York tabloids under bold headlines calling her, among other things, SMACK GODDESS and DEALER TO THE STARS. According to the news reports, limos bearing rock stars and movie idols would line up and cause traffic jams outside Frin's apartment building.

The woman has what I call British aplomb; very little fazes her. When asked by a reporter what she thought of her life as a prisoner in the MCC, she compared it favorably to life in an English boarding school. Frin got a job in the kitchen while at MCC, and she used to smuggle bags of swag, special meals, and other contraband to me on the ninth floor. After she pled guilty and was sentenced to the minimum, ten years in a federal women's penitentiary with no possibility of parole, one day before she was shipped out of MCC she took me aside and told me she had no intention of going for ten years without heterosexual sex. When I asked her how she intended to remedy that, she said she planned to escape. And she did, from the women's maximum-security prison, at the time located somewhere in the boonies of West Virginia. No small feat: first you need to escape from the prison, and then you need to get out of West Virginia. All of which became the story I based my novel on. I got a postcard from Frin after she escaped. It had a picture of the Rockettes on the front high-legging it, and, on the back, well wishes. The feds got it in their heads that I had somehow assisted Frin in her flight even as I was still locked up in the MCC. They sent an FBI agent in to interview me, but I declined to speak with him. And Frin, bless her, was still in the wind, still a fugitive at the time of the *Smack Goddess* publication.

Chapter Eight

I WAS HUNGRY, AND IT WAS YOUR WORLD

THE NOVELIST KIM WOZENCRAFT is seated cross-legged on the floor in the living room at Fielding Dawson's apartment among the other PEN Prison Writing Awards presenters when I enter. Fielding looks from her to me, and then back to Kim, and he says, "At last you two meet," as though it had been preordained.

Indeed, it is a meeting of destinies. There are several other people in the room—writers, poets who will speak or read at the PEN Prison Writing Awards ceremony. All have notable histories; but none other than Kim and I have served time in federal prison. None have been active players in the government's war on drugs. There is an instant, unspoken affinity between Kim and me based on shared experience; we both sense it. There is a whole range of knowledge about and emotions engendered by imprisonment, and a life and the situations and experiences one goes through as a prisoner that we will never have to try to explain simply because we've both been there and experienced all of it firsthand.

Kim worked undercover as a narcotics cop in East Texas when she was in her early twenties. She got strung out on coke and was shot by one of the dealers she and her partner set up and busted. Sometime after all the arrests came down, Kim and her partner were arrested by the feds, charged and convicted of violation of civil rights for doing what they were ordered by their superiors to do: set up and bust low-level drug dealers. Kim served time at the federal prison in Lexington, Kentucky. When she got out, she came to New York, enrolled in college, first at Hunter and then Columbia, where she graduated from the esteemed master's writing program under the tutelage of Gordon Lish, who dubbed himself Captain Fiction. Kim's master's thesis based on her experiences as a narcotics cop became her bestselling novel *Rush*. I read *Rush* while I was still in prison. I remember thinking that finally someone from law enforcement is writing truthfully about this war on the American people and the harm it's causing not only to the users and dealers of illegal drugs, but also to the cops and agents who are sent undercover and onto the front lines and ordered to make arrests at any cost.

Kim may be the only person at the PEN Prison Writing Awards ceremony who gets my lame jailhouse joke about how to do a long prison sentence that I tell as an introduction to the story I read. How do you do a long prison sentence? Winter/summer. Winter/summer. Skip spring and fall. We speak before, during, and after the reading. I notice that she wears sensible shoes. I find her attractive in a sexy, Texas law woman way; I can picture her with a gun on her hip and a badge on her breast as she sashays into a roomful of bad hombres and says, "Put 'em up!" So I give her one of my Ivan S. Fisher Forensic Specialist business cards in the hope that I will see her again.

A few days after the reading, Kim shows up at my office with her copy of *Smack Goddess*, which I inscribe for her. We make a date, but she cancels on the day, says she's down with a stomach virus. I assume she's had second thoughts about dating a former criminal. But then a week later, we try again and go to the Ninety-Second Street Y to hear Norman read from his new novel, *Harlot's Ghost*.

At a reception after the reading, I introduce Kim to Norman and Norris. Kim wears a gray wool skirt. I can't help but notice when she squats down to speak to a small child that she has a great ass and an apparent fondness for kids. Later, at dinner at Elaine's, Kim tells me she doesn't drink. I answer without thinking, "Well I do," and order a drink. Here's where our similarities begin to diverge. She smokes cigarettes. Typical pothead, I can't abide cigarette smoke. She orders sausage. I haven't eaten beef or pork except during extended stays in Lebanon since my early twenties. But we have much in common. Besides both having served federal prison time and both having played active roles in the war on drugs, we are both writers, both crime novelists who actually lived the lives we write about. And this like-mindedness can be either an affinity that draws us together in mutual pursuit and respect and becomes a bond, or, in time, it can devolve into a negative force driving us apart, even turning us against each other as our separate careers rise and fall. In some ways, we are too much alike, in others opposites.

When I drop Kim back at her apartment building in the East 30s after our date, we share a brief, passionless kiss in the back of the cab, and I carry on home thinking that we will probably never see each other again.

But God has other plans.

NORMAN CALLS TO tell me that his friend Buzz Farbar killed himself. After he was released from prison, Buzz was living in Amagansett and trying to write a book, for which he had been paid an advance, about his experience as part of the hashish smuggling conspiracy that had brought about his arrest and subsequent cooperation with the government. On the last day of his life, he went to the gym and worked out. He said goodbye to all his workout buddies at the gym, took a shower, and then went home. He attached a vacuum cleaner hose to the exhaust pipe of his car and asphyxiated himself. Norman says it was like Buzz to go to the gym and work out so he would leave a good-looking corpse. Norman tells me that he was aware Buzz had been seriously depressed. Norman went out to Long Island to visit Buzz, but he couldn't seem to find anything to say to him that penetrated his deep, hopeless despair. Norman forgave him for agreeing to wear a wire and arrange a lunch meeting in an attempt to get Norman to say something on tape that the feds could use to indict him. I never could forgive Buzz. There was a time when I seriously considered killing Buzz myself. Norman talked me out of it. When I tell Ivan that Buzz killed himself, he throws open the window in his office, takes a deep breath and says, "Ah! The air in New York smells better already."

PALOMA TELLS ME she quit her job at Dr. Eisenberg's dental offices, and she has decided to move to Miami. She's heartbroken; we both are. And yet we know that what's missing and what's not working in our relationship can't be fixed. If she were to get pregnant, I would marry her. That's a given for me. And perhaps that shared fantasy of having a big family and living happily in a finca somewhere near Cartagena might have come true. But it's not to be.

I see her one last time at the café outside FAO Schwartz in Rockefeller Plaza. She's carrying a copy of *Moby Dick* she says she's reading to expand her knowledge of American literature. Then she cries and tells me that she loves me, and that she always will, but that she knows we must part and go our separate ways, look for and hopefully find happiness elsewhere. I know it's my doing, my apparent restless dissatisfaction not only with her but also with myself, with my work, and with my place in the world. I walk away from our meeting with what feels like a deep gouge ripped out of my chest, a bloody gaping hole where once there had been nothing but tender feelings for a woman who had only love for me.

NORRIS MAILER AND I attend a session at the Actor's Studio, and then we go to a cocktail party for Kurt Vonnegut. I immediately start pounding back shots of vodka. What the fuck am I doing here? I'm miserable over the split with Paloma. Norris tells me that, as much as she likes Paloma, she never felt she was right for me. What is right for me? Who? Certainly not anyone or anything I might find here among this gaggle of pompous, self-satisfied fops and sharp-eyed, sharp-tongued Manhattan career women. The feeling of being an outsider in this world, of never being accepted by the likes of James Atlas or Jay McInerney, the sad-eyed guy who's standing talking to me now, the feeling of alienation is deep, as it should be, for I will always be an outlaw in their eyes, a criminal, an ex-convict, and no partisan of the literary establishment. If I could run from this party now, run from my new life, and catch Paloma before she boards her plane, violate the terms of my supervised release and just—what? Disappear? Become somebody else? Become a criminal again? I'm still floundering, trying to find my way.

As PART OF my ongoing research on the Harry Chapin story, on a whim, I call Kim and invite her to go with me to see *The Buddy Holly Story* musical on Broadway. I think we are both surprised there is a second date, and yet it feels good. The show is upbeat and fun. Music I grew up listening to, and though a little before Kim's time, she digs it. *Peggy Sue. Everyday. That'll Be the Day. Rave on.* C'mon, she's a Texas girl at heart. What's not to like? You can't tell me it's not getting to her. I can see it in her smile, in the glow suffusing her lovely face. We hold hands and snuggle closer. Now I'm feeling this woman in a way that eluded me before. She's a gal with a big heart, but it's been seared, scarred, and it's men who did that to her. After the show, we go to a bar, and end up making out heavily until someone tells us to get a room. We go back to her place, make intense love, soul-exposing love. I stagger out the next day deliriously well fucked.

From the beginning our romance is a rocky one, at once giddy, passionate, tumultuous, fun, painful, hurtful, and ultimately glorious. Yes, glorious, for it's the fruits of such mating that will go on long after our brief time together. We are having dinner at the Red Inn in

Provincetown on our first trip out of town together when I say to Kim, "If you are serious about this, then let's forego all means of contraception." Then again while on vacation in St. John when I ask her to marry me, Kim wants a reciprocal vow: that I promise to leave the outlaw life behind once and for all.

It has been a struggle for us to reach this point. Several times I have left her, walked out, and thought, *No, no way, Stratton, this will never work; we are all wrong for each other.* One night we sit in her car outside my apartment in Brooklyn when she tells me that in the past she has only been attracted to men who abused her either physically or emotionally. That, I say, is something I never want to do. I don't want to be that guy. So let's just leave this now where it is and go our separate ways. Walking across the street and back to my apartment I think, *Good, let it go; forget about her.* This is not for you—not for her, either. We may end up doing more damage to each other than good. There may be few differences between us, but those differences are enormous.

First, there is the disparity in where we are in our respective careers and bank account balances. My career as a novelist appears to have stalled. I can't survive without my income from the legal writing I do for Ivan. I have a job, but I'm broke, struggling to get paid, teetering on the verge of resorting to my previous source of income. Kim is riding a financial windfall and international acclaim as a bestselling novelist. The film rights to *Rush* have been bought by a major Hollywood producer and the novel is in the process of being made into a movie starring Jennifer Jason Leigh and Jason Patrick. *Smack Goddess* appears to have attracted a cult following of dedicated doper readers. (The fact-checker from *Vanity Fair* tells me that the novel has attained an underground reputation as one of the best novels to come out of the drug subculture.) Kim has a contract and is at work on a new novel about women in prison to be called *Notes from the Country Club.* Kim shows up at my office and says, "C'mon, let's go out and play." I'm too busy, too preoccupied trying to rebuild my life at forty-five to go out and play, but I go anyway.

And there is a deeper divide. We are both lying to each other. Kim is still involved with a former lover, a married man who is the editor of *Rush* and of her new book. She makes up an affair with an Italian musician she says is over. I am still married to my first wife who went to prison in Canada for money laundering, and whom I have not seen for a decade. We are divorced psychically, physically, and emotionally, if not yet legally. But I tell Kim the marriage was not legal to begin with, another lie. It's as though Kim and I both wish to reinvent ourselves in order to embrace the inevitability of this new relationship unfettered with our past attachments and subterfuges—a clean slate. It feels like a karmic necessity, a sense that it must be, and that it must do deep character work for each of us, be founded upon honesty, bring us to a new level of growth in our journeys no matter how painful, no matter how hurtful to each other if we are to transcend our old disingenuous selves and become truthful as to who we were, who we are now, and who we are striving to become. But first we will have to confront the old selves living their duplicitous lives—undercover cop, outlaw drug smuggler—so we can come clean with each other, and then start over.

IT HAPPENS IN a tent in a campground in the wilds of Maine under a night sky emblazoned with stars that appear close enough to reach out and touch. We're on the loose, I've left the five boroughs of New York without my parole officer's permission, and we've been munching on magic mushrooms like a couple of hungry chipmunks. Kim confesses. Not only is the Italian musician a fictional character (ah, the mind of the novelist) but she has also continued to meet with her real lover, the editor, while telling me she hasn't seen him. So there is a lie on top of another lie. I accept all that. There is no stopping where this is going. I allow that my marriage is long over all but for the paperwork. There is no one else for me. My dear, sweet Paloma flew the coop. I miss her, but I'm ready to commit to a monogamous relationship with Kim. She and I have decamped from the workaday world and taken up carnal residence in Fuck City. Moved in just down the street from Cunnilingus Corner, and around the block from Blowjob Boulevard. Do they have a piss test for psilocybin in Fuck City? Never mind. Who cares? Get naked. Take off all your clothes, smear your body with mud and gobs of green moss, stick slabs of tree bark and twigs in your hair, shed all pretense of civilization, and dance around the campfire like a couple of aborigines. Nature Boy and Earth Goddess delight in the campfire light.

And then I leave Mother Earth. Oh, yes, I am way out there. Other entities gather in the cosmos looking for the right circumstance to reincarnate. Hold on tight, for there is no going back. This is the beginning of a great adventure. I enter deep space during an exquisite orgasm that is timeless, boundless, extraterrestrial—a revelation!—and I drift out among the planets and stars. I have become a disembodied consciousness, a heavenly body to float beyond the known universe, where I meet—what? My karma . . . and my son. Yes, a child is conceived. I see him as a giant embryo in orbit around our fused entities, as he seeks to merge with a cosmic flow of earth-bound energy and incarnate.

It comes as no surprise when a few weeks later Kim tells me she is pregnant. I knew it the moment our child was conceived. We are both blissfully happy. When I tell Norman, he says his only concern is that, if the writing doesn't work out, Kim and I will resort to robbing banks.

Chapter Nine

HEAVYWEIGHTS

AT SHANE'S SUGGESTION, Barbara Kopple hires me to write the treatment for her film about Mike Tyson to be called *Fallen Champ: The Untold Story of Mike Tyson*. She gets the gig, a ninety-minute documentary to air on TV, and she brings me on as a producer. Here I get lucky. In an interview with the woman who ran the home where Tyson's mentor, Cus D'Amato, lodged the young fighters he was training, she tells me that she has footage from some of Tyson's earliest fights at the Junior Olympics Games in 1981 when he was just sixteen. She gives me the tape, and the footage ends up being a crucial element in the story of Tyson's early years under Cus's tutelage.

I quickly become absorbed in the whole process of making the documentary. My job involves running around from pay phone to pay phone (cell phones are still a few years away), setting up the interviews, finding and arranging locations, arranging to have a crew on set, often conducting the interviews, and then getting the footage developed and delivered to the editors, sitting with the editors and with Barbara to review the footage and make selects and to take phone calls from Barbara at all hours. The process of making the documentary reminds me of nothing so much as my previous business as a drug smuggler, although with one important distinction: it's not illegal. They can't lock me up for this even if no one likes the film.

I'm hooked. This is my new calling. Maybe it's not as lucrative, but it's much more satisfying than smuggling pot.

Through Leon Gast, the editor on the Tyson film, I secure a second documentary film gig producing Norman Mailer's interview for the Academy Award–winning feature documentary *When We Were Kings*, about the 1974 Heavyweight Championship fight between Muhammad Ali and George Foreman in Zaire.

I move from the apartment in Brooklyn. Kim and I move into a larger apartment in her building on East Thirty-First Street. We spend a glorious week on St. John in the US Virgin Islands scuba diving, hiking, making love, and drinking. One evening at dinner, I ask Kim to marry me and she agrees, but again on the condition that I continue to abstain from all illegal activity. She says she does not want to bring up our child having to visit a father who is in prison. When I inform Ms. Lawless that I have moved to Manhattan and that I plan to marry, she appears relieved to have me off her caseload. My case is transferred to the Southern District of New York office.

THE SOUTHERN DISTRICT parole offices are located in a top floor of the stately old Thurgood Marshall courthouse in Foley Square. My new parole officer, whom I call Rocky Raccoon because he reminds me of Rocky Graziano, the Middleweight World Champion, and because he has dark circles around his eyes, informs me during our first meeting that he knows all about me and my kind of criminal. He says I may have got one over on Gloria Lawless and the Brooklyn Eastern District office, but I'm in Manhattan now, the Southern District, and here they know how to deal with big shot offenders like me.

"Sophisticated criminal activity," Rocky says and looks up from my file, "continuing criminal enterprise. Lots of media coverage . . . Guys like you, you don't quit. You're a career criminal. I give you a month, or two, six at the most under my supervision, and you'll be right back at it, doing whatever it is you do." He looks down at the file again. "Importing drugs. Bringing in that poison and selling it to our kids—you're probably back at it already. But this time . . . this time is gonna be different. You know why? Because this time I'll be right there to catch you and send you back to prison."

Thanks, Rocky, for the vote of confidence. Sure helps to know you're on my case.

EVERY TIME I leave the five boroughs to do an interview for the Tyson film I am supposed to get prior approval from Rocky. Fuck that.

"What about the job with Ivan Fisher?" Rocky wants to know. Is this movie business supposed to be my new employment? Because if it is, Rocky says, he's probably not going to approve it since it's only a temporary gig until the film is completed. Next he tries to block my planned marriage to Kim. He says we will not be approved to marry on the grounds that she is also a former convicted felon who served prison time, and therefore I am not allowed to associate with her, let alone marry her, so long as I am still on supervised release.

"Well," I tell Rocky, "then we're going to have a real problem. Because she's pregnant with my child, and we are going to get married. So do whatever it is you've got to do, and I'll see you in court."

These *federales* just don't quit.

I AM STILL working for Ivan but on a part-time, case-by-case basis. I've also taken a job at the Fortune Society editing *Fortune News*, a magazine that is distributed to prisoners throughout the country and written largely by prisoners or ex-offenders—the preferred term for ex-convicts in the criminal justice system reform movement. And I have entered into talks to take over as the editor and publisher of a struggling new publication called *Prison Life* magazine.

KIM AND I marry at the Religious Society of Friends Meeting House near Gramercy Park. The ceremony is presided over by the justice of the supreme court of New York, Shirley Fingerhood. Norman Mailer is my best man. Kim's close friend and now editor at Houghton Mifflin, Betsy Lerner, is Kim's maid of honor. We have a festive reception at the nearby New York Arts Club. Our tiered wedding cake is topped by a miniature bride and groom joined wearing handcuffs. The reception might be the largest group parole violation in history.

On our honeymoon in the mountains of New Mexico, Kim is spooked. The landscape, the people . . . perhaps it is all too reminiscent of her time in Texas. I receive word that my short story, "A Skyline Turkey," is to be published in *Story* magazine. *Story* is also where Mailer published his first story. This strikes me as auspicious. Kim comments, "When you're hot, you're hot."

Back in New York, Kim takes it upon herself to catch me up on all the independent films I missed during my imprisonment. Most nights we stay in and watch crime movies. One film in particular, the Coen brothers' *Raising Arizona*, starring Nicholas Cage and Holly Hunter, about an ex-con and a former cop, strikes a resonant chord, particularly when one morning we get a visit from a jailhouse pal who shows up at the apartment with two suitcases full of ivory. He says he needs a place to leave the suitcases just for a couple of hours while he determines if the buyer he is to meet is on the level or merely trying to rip him off. He seems frazzled and may also be high on coke. Before I can refuse to take possession of the suitcases, he excuses himself to use the bathroom, and then splits, leaving the suitcases behind.

No sooner is he gone than we get a call from the doorman to say that there is a Mr. Rocky Raccoon here to visit.

Holy shit! It's my parole officer, he's making his first home visit, and we are sitting on two suitcases of what is most likely stolen ivory. Quick, stash the suitcases. Kim and I both look at each other and wonder aloud if this is a set up. How could it be? Kim is eight months pregnant. This is all we need, to get busted with a stash of—whatever it is,

I assume it must be stolen ivory—and my parole violated, a new case, and back to prison with the baby due, and proving Rocky's prediction.

Kim stashes the suitcases under the bed. Rocky shows up. Kim welcomes him, offers him coffee, which we know he'll refuse. He does a cursory inspection of our living arrangement, takes a heart-stopping peek in the bedroom, and then he sits down to visit and to let us know that he's troubled by the relationship. One ex-con in a marriage is already one too many, according to Rocky. We may both be published authors, but that in and of itself is no guarantee that we have foresworn our lives of crime. Rocky does appear enchanted by Kim. It's the fraternal law enforcement bond that prevails no matter that she was accused of having crossed the line. Once a cop, always a cop, Rocky seems to say, and he hopes that she will be able to keep me on the straight and narrow, but in all honesty, he doubts it. Once an outlaw, always an outlaw.

Guys like me, Rocky tells Kim, do not respect the law, and therein lies the fundamental issue—the difference between a confirmed criminal and someone who makes a mistake, and then is able to reform. The confirmed criminal blames law enforcement for having caught him rather than admitting that he was wrong in the first place. Yes, yes, we know all that, Rocky; we are both steeped in the psychology of the criminal miscreant. But the offender in question is about to become that most exalted member of the male component of the human family—a father, goddamnit—and that, it is believed, at least by your parolee, that will finally, or has already, convinced him to embrace a life of upright citizenship and adherence to the laws and mores of civilized society. Now, please, get the fuck out of here, Rocky Graziano before that coked-up whacko comes back looking for his suitcases full of stolen ivory. One look at that guy and Rocky will know something is up.

And what, I'm wondering, what is it with me and ivory? I abhor and want nothing to do with the brutal, horrendous practice of hunting and stripping elephants, these magnificent beasts, of their elegant and formidable tusks, and yet I seem fated to be connected however tangentially to the crime. While living in Lebanon preparing to smuggle the fifteen-thousand-pound load of hashish out of the country, I was billeted in a West Beirut penthouse apartment that had one room decorated with wall panels engraved with ivory, and a menagerie of ivory statuettes cluttering a huge display case. I was appalled and demanded to be moved. Now the ghosts of slaughtered elephants and extinct mastodons are once again impinging on my peace of mind and possibly my freedom.

Rocky seems satisfied, even a bit impressed that I have managed to find and marry a woman as remarkable as former narcotics officer and bestselling author Kim Wozencraft, and at last he departs.

Days go by and we hear nothing from the ostensible owner of the ivory. He's probably back in the slammer, or on a coke binge and forgot all about the suitcases. I am so distressed by even having the cache in our apartment that I make some calls looking for someone to take it off our hands.

THE HARRY CHAPIN biopic project founders and then dies in a sad, slow demise. Kim works with me on the screenplay, but it soon becomes apparent that Suarez can't raise the money. He never optioned the rights to the Chapin biography, and that's a fundamental problem. He tries to stiff me on the balance of the ten grand once I deliver my draft of the script. He tells me he won't pay me until Sandy Chapin agrees to sign over the rights to Harry's music. This, I remind him, was never part of our deal. It takes a call from Sandy to tell Suarez that until he pays me, there will be no further negotiations on the music rights. Suarez does eventually make good on the contract and he pays me the remainder of my fee. But from there the project goes nowhere.

LISTEN TO AMERICA: The Harry Chapin Story, based on my script, is to be the first of several films I write over the next several years that will never get made. Other film projects, however, are about to come together in such an apparently serendipitous and yet somehow finely plotted manner that even I must sometimes step back and wonder if I am making all this up.

While out for a walk one afternoon, Kim and I spot a poster advertising a film called *Blowback* about the CIA and drugs that somehow managed to get made. We go see the film in a theater with three other ticket holders. The movie is suitably bizarre, given the subject matter. As we leave the theater, I say to Kim, regarding the director and writer of *Blowback*, "I've got to meet that guy."

A week later we go to see Oliver Stone's *JFK*. I'm enthralled. This is the most intense cinematic experience I have ever had. However long the film is, I'm so mesmerized, so caught up in the story playing out on the screen that it seems to happen in a time warp. As a child of the sixties, I came of age under the guilty, miasmal dread of the Kennedy killings and the murder of Martin Luther King. I was never able to recover my faith in our government, so convinced was I that these murders, as well as the killing of Kennedy assassin Lee Harvey Oswald, were not isolated events as the government would have us believe, not the work of lone deranged assassins, which struck me as too convenient, too contrived. Rather, these murders were the result of something much more sinister, much more conspiratorial. The brazen, seemingly staged killing of Oswald by Jack Ruby had to be a prearranged hit. Even as an eighteen-year-old, sitting in the den of my girlfriend's home glued to the TV in the aftermath of the Kennedy assassination, when I saw Ruby in the basement of police headquarters in Dallas, Texas, walk up to the man who had allegedly just killed the president of the United States, pull out a gun, and shoot the suspected assassin right there in the police station while surrounded by cops, it seemed all wrong, impossible, clearly a setup intended to forever silence a man who was already claiming to be "a patsy."

Like so many of my generation, I came of age believing that we live in a nation that is inherently no better than other empires past and present. America is, or has been, simply better at covering up the truth, more sophisticated in disguising its leaders' malfeasance and criminality, more adept at creating propaganda to pass off American democracy as pure and above reproach, when in fact this country's history is as dirty and manipulated by bad actors as any other's. We are simply better at creating a false narrative, better at public relations. I love this country, and I believe in the concept of American democracy. But I want to see America become what it was created by its founders to be: a land of liberty and justice for all. The hits on both Jack and Bobby Kennedy, as well the murder of Martin Luther King, and to this list I would add the killing of John Lennon, to my mind these assassinations were the work of a cabal of intelligence agents, high- and low-level organized crime figures, professional hitmen, and an even more sinister mutation: Manchurian candidates programmed to kill. Call me a paranoid conspiracy theorist, but there is ample evidence that a conspiracy exists. And why not, why should America be any different from other empires riddled and ultimately undermined by conspiracy, when human nature and the lust for power have not changed?

I lived a good part of my life in the criminal underground where conspiracies abound. As a result, I have come to trust that very little happens that is random in the milieu where organized crime and government meet; very little is the result of freak events carried out by losers and fall guys. High-profile murders of men like the Kennedy brothers, King, and Lennon, men who represented a threat to the entrenched power elite that secretly rules America, all reek of conspiracy.

I was made to be moved by Stone's *JFK*. And when Kim and I hear that Oliver Stone is going to be present at a town hall meeting to discuss his film and the Kennedy assassination and defend his use of documentary footage in a feature film, we decide to go. Stone is impressive. He marshals his facts, has made notes, and is articulate in his defense. It's my belief that, like most assassination investigators, Stone is naive when it comes to the role of organized crime in the Kennedy hits. He dismisses the mob as a bunch of old-time Italian mobsters and fails to appreciate the long and complex relationship between the master killers of organized crime and certain elements within the ranks and the upper echelons of federal law enforcement—Hoover's FBI, Allen Dulles's CIA, and the Federal Bureau of Narcotics (FBN), now renamed DEA.

After the town hall meeting, Kim and I go across the street for dinner. As we are leaving the restaurant, a guy seated at the bar stops us. "Aren't you Richard Stratton?" he inquires. Yes, I admit that I am. It's Danny Schechter, also known as "the News Dissector," formally of Boston, a radio personality, human rights activist, and television producer whom I'd met through Barbara Kopple while working on the Tyson film.

Danny is sitting with another man who, he says, shares similar interests and, yes, we have all just been to the town hall meeting to hear Stone discuss his film. I mention that Kim and I recently saw a wild underground film called *Blowback*, which I thought had some thematic similarities with Stone's film.

"*What?*" the man with Danny asks, "You saw *Blowback*? You must be the other two of the four people in New York who actually bought tickets and went to see that movie."

Danny introduces us to Marc Levin, the auteur who wrote, produced, and directed *Blowback*.

YOU SEE, IT's true, at least for me, and here is proof: this is all predestined; nothing in life is random. You cannot cheat life, you pay for every last thing you get out of life, and you are rewarded for every good thing you bring to life because there are repercussions that are not subject to the space-time continuum but that happen in another dimension beyond the world we know and will manifest where and when we may never know. There is no such thing as coincidence or luck, not if you believe otherwise. It wasn't just chance that brought Kim and me together in Fielding Dawson's living room any more than luck brought me and Marc Levin to meet in a bar after going to hear Oliver Stone speak about his masterpiece, *JFK*. No, no such thing as chance encounters like running into Joe Stassi on the subway for those who live according to the belief in a master plan. It is as inconceivable as to believe that the planets are ruled by chaos. There is method, and even meaning to all this seemingly haphazard experience. It is all worked out, all part of a grand, vast cosmic creative conspiracy, a master plan that is the very mind and divided consciousness of the Creator. We are only allowed to glimpse nanoseconds in the scheme of the master plan, for to fathom the mind of God we must become gods ourselves. If we believe, then we can achieve our given divine destiny. Faith is the essential element. Belief makes it all come true. If you don't believe, then it's not true for you.

I PETITION THE parole commission to cut me loose from this nonparole supervised release bullshit on the grounds that it has been over two years since my release from prison, and I am fucking sick of it; it's cramping my style as a documentary filmmaker. I want to burn some herb without the threat of a piss test. I want to travel when and where I choose. I want to hang out with criminals and ex-criminals and write about grand criminal enterprises, arrests and trials, imprisonment. Of course I couch all this in different terms in my petition, and it is incorporated as part of a larger argument to the effect that I cannot engage effectively in my new occupation—that of documentary film producer—while under the yoke of governmental supervision that, at best, is questionable in its legitimacy and, at worst is a violation of my rights as one who has fulfilled his obligations to the government under the requirements of my nonparoleable motherfucking sentence for doing something that should never have been illegal in the first place.

It's a strong argument, seeing that we are close to the termination date of this foolishness. Also, given that I am willing to take them to court if need be, and they know that, and given that I think they know

I have solid grounds for relief, those in authority seem obliged to release me. But Rocky Raccoon is still not convinced that I am reformed, and, as my designated parole officer, he is required to review my case and sign off on any decision having to do with my status unless I choose to, and am successful at, going above his level of authority.

Rocky confronts me one afternoon as I sit in his cramped office for my scheduled report. Earlier, while sitting in the outer waiting room with all the other unhappy ex-offenders summoned to be grilled by their parole officers, I had the inspiration for a TV drama to be set in the world of parole. Here we have this room, a room that is filled with male and female ex-offenders, ex-convicts, allegedly former criminals, and now parolees. By and large, they are interesting characters, many with colorful histories, and they are prohibited from associating with one another under the terms of their release on parole. Yet here they all are, gathered together in this room on their given report days as though at a reform school reunion where and when they will surely meet one another, possibly revive old friendships, old rivalries, and even possibly hatch new criminal conspiracies. I observe them as they behave like a classroom full of elementary school children—chattering, greeting one another, laughing, goofing around, and making plans to get together later and play—all while the teacher is out of the classroom. And then, as soon as the door opens and one of the parole officers sticks his or her head in to call the next parolee, like kids in a classroom they immediately shut up, sit up straight, eyes straight ahead and attention focused on behaving themselves and certainly not associating with one another.

It's ludicrous. And when you put it all together with the degree of invasive authority the parole officers have over their parolees' lives, it's almost familial; they become like unwanted relatives who show up on the doorstep and beg intrusion; you must let them in; that, given the challenges parolees face trying to readjust to living in so-called free society while in fact under close scrutiny after however many years of confinement; and the parole officers' powerful, complex relationship with his or her parolees; how they in fact might be influenced by their charges: it makes for an inherently complicated and fascinating dynamic rife with potential drama.

For example, Rocky and I adjourn to his office and he instructs me to fill out the standard report form. Have I moved? No. Have I changed jobs? No. Have I met with any agents or police officers? No. Have I been in contact with anyone who was or still is engaged in criminal activity? No—a lie, clearly, but one I have managed to get way with so far. Again, I remind him that I am due to be terminated.

While reviewing the form, when Rocky gets to the question concerning contact with other criminals, he stops. He looks up at me with an expression that seems to say: Aha! *Caught you!* No contact, huh, Stratton? Well, what about this? And he produces a letter written by me to none other than one Frances Mullin, a.k.a. Frin, also known as the Smack Goddess, a fugitive wanted by the FBI, living under an alias in London, and ratted out by her disgruntled, rejected boyfriend. She was recently arrested by British police and is now being held in England on a warrant pending extradition to the United States, where she is wanted for having escaped from federal prison. This letter from me was discovered in her property.

"You wrote this letter, did you not?" Rocky demands.

"Yeah, so?"

"So? So it's a violation of the terms of your supervised release! That's *so*. I can have you violated."

"Okay," I tell him, "go ahead and try. But I beg to differ. The letter, as you will see when you read it, advises Ms. Mullin to seek an arrangement, a deal with the authorities where she does not fight extradition back to the US under prearranged terms that assure her she will not be prosecuted for the escape but merely be required to complete her sentence in the United States. This, in my capacity as a forensic specialist working for Ivan S. Fisher, is no violation of the terms of my release, since I was not in contact with Ms. Mullin for the purpose of engaging in criminal activity but rather to advise her on how best to come to equitable terms upon her surrender to US authorities."

Rocky may be loath to admit it, but he's all done—finished, at least with this ex-offender. Over his objection, I am cut loose. A few weeks later I receive written notice that I have satisfactorily fulfilled the terms of my supervised release. I have discharged my obligation to the United States attorney's designated representative, the Bureau of Prisons, and the US Parole Commission. Therefore, my two-year-plus supervision that never should have been required in the first place is finally officially terminated.

Hallelujah! Praise God and pass the doobie. I am one step farther from the prison gate, one degree of liberation beyond government infringement upon my freedom, past all official demands for asshole scrutiny or urine analysis. So much for Rocky's prognostication that this ex-offender would soon be back in the marijuana trade and that when he was, old Rocky Raccoon would be there to bust the ingrate and send him back behind prison walls where he belongs.

Adios, muchachos! I'm outta here. . . .

PART TWO
HOLLYWOOD:
ADVENTURES IN THE SKIN TRADE

PART TWO

HOLLYWOOD:
ADVENTURES IN THE SKIN TRADE

Chapter Ten

BLOWBACK, PROJECT MK-ULTRA, AND BEYOND

A FEW DAYS after our meeting following the Oliver Stone town hall event, Marc Levin calls to invite me over to his studio. He asks if I still smoke pot. Yes, of course, light it up. What am I working on? I show him early issues of *Prison Life* magazine I edited. Marc asks if he can keep them. Sure, I brought them for him. He tells me that he is currently working with his father, Al Levin, on a documentary for HBO called *Mob Stories* about various wiseguys, most of whom are still locked up or only recently released from prison. I offer to put him in touch with some of the organized crime characters I know who might make good subjects for the film.

This night, and my meeting with Marc Levin, turns out to be the beginning of a rich creative collaboration that has lasted years and changed both Marc's and my life and the lives of several others, as well as resulting in some award-winning film and TV productions. Marc shows the issues of *Prison Life* to Sheila Nevins, his executive producer at HBO. Sheila says she wants to meet me. Marc and I go to Sheila's office at HBO's corporate headquarters. Sheila is the doyenne of documentary film executives, and HBO has begun to distinguish itself as the premier television exhibitor of quality documentaries. Soon the cable network will dominate the entertainment industry with some of the best movies and scripted TV series ever produced.

As I take a seat in Sheila's office, she pulls out a pair of antique leg shackles and tells me that she is going to chain me to the chair until we make a deal. What do we want to do? Sheila says she would like us to make prison-based films as part of HBO's America Undercover documentary series on subjects that will also be covered in issues of the magazine and published in tandem when they air on HBO. Okay, that's a great idea. We love it. Sheila asks what subject we want to explore as the first HBO and *Prison Life* Presents production.

Marc and I suggest that the most important prison-related subject at present is the war on drugs. The government's drug war is responsible for America's alarming incarceration rate—the highest in the world. The drug war is the engine driving the criminal justice system, overwhelming our criminal courts, over-populating our prisons and jails, and fueling the expansion of the prison industrial complex with new prisons being built at an unprecedented rate, and yet still not fast enough to house all the new prisoners locked up for using or dealing illegal drugs.

And, I say, the irony in all this is that illegal drugs are even more available in prison than they are on the street. What? Yes, it's true, and why not? What would you expect is going to happen when you lock up a bunch of experienced, creative, and well-connected drug traffickers and ingenious smugglers and put them in close quarters with a captive market of confirmed drug users? Business is booming both on the streets and behind the walls. And there is not even a pretense of rehabilitation, no real drug treatment for addicts in the system. Families are being ripped apart. Inner-city neighborhoods have become war zones. The so-called war on drugs has become a war on American citizens; it is being waged at home and in third-world drug-producing nations around the world but has only made the situation worse by increasing the profit incentive to smuggle and distribute illegal drugs and by enriching and empowering gang bangers and ruthless drug lords. It's all become a big business supporting armies of agents and cops, judges, lawyers, and prosecutors, propping up politicians' careers, and creating hotspots around the globe teeming with heavily armed insurgents who buy American-made weapons with profits from drug trafficking. There is way too much money being made in the illegal drug business and financing the criminal justice system and the prison-industrial complex for anyone in authority to get serious about stopping this fraudulent but highly profitable and insidiously destructive war. Marc and I are both passionate about the subject.

Great. Done. The series is to be produced by Marc's company, Blowback Productions, and we'll begin with HBO and *Prison Life* magazine presents *Prisoners of the War on Drugs*. Sheila says she is ready to get started as soon as the contracts can be drawn up. As we get up to leave, Sheila says, "Don't forget your leg irons," and she hands me the antique shackles.

"That went well," Marc says as we leave HBO.

PRISON LIFE MAGAZINE, like many other print publications, is struggling to stay afloat. Kim and I buy out the original publishers and move the magazine from its Manhattan offices to the basement of our home in the Hudson River Valley to cut down on overhead. It's a gamble, of course, and hardly a sure bet. The HBO deal looks like it could provide the financial shot in the arm we need to keep the magazine alive, and possibly help boost circulation, but it's definitely a day-to-day struggle.

My history in the magazine business dates back to the founding of *High Times* in the early 1970s. *High Times* was a phenomenon, profitable after its first few issues for the very good reason that it offered a unique opportunity for manufacturers and distributors in the burgeoning drug paraphernalia industry to advertise their wares in the only magazine devoted to the illegal marijuana trade. Rolling papers, various pot grinders and joint rolling machines, bongs, roach clips, hemp products, and on and on: *High Times* drew advertisers in droves. Not so

Prison Life. It is 1995 and yes, the US prison population is exploding; we have a captive—actually a captured—market. But for the most part our readers have very little disposable income, and often do not have ready access. They can't get to the newsstands to buy our magazine, and prison authorities around the country have already mounted a campaign to keep *Prison Life* out of prison.

So the purchase of the magazine is quickly perceived by its new publishers—Kim and me—as a failure in good business planning. Add to that the fact that the magazine industry as a whole is about to go into a nosedive as the internet comes online and eventually decimates print media, threatening the survival of even the most profitable and established publications. For me, it was never about the money. It never is. Even my criminal enterprise was always about more, about the cultural struggle. It is always about the issues, the subject matter, the human stories, and the larger social and political story of the drug war and the massive build-up of the criminal justice system juggernaut and its impact on American society. My goal for the magazine is to have it act as what we call the Voice of the Convict, to give voice to the voiceless. The stories, poems, and essays are all written by prisoners or ex-convicts. The artwork also is created by prison artists; we run an annual Art Behind Bars contest that draws dozens of submissions and provides us with exceptional prisoner art to illustrate stories in the magazine and to exhibit in galleries.

Prison Life soon becomes a succès d'estime, if not a financial success. We win awards, including a prestigious *Utne Reader* independent magazine award. We are written up in *Time* and *Newsweek* magazines and in the *New York Times*. Simultaneously, the magazine is seen as a security threat and banned in different prisons around the country and in the entire California prison system, which only adds to its credibility and allure. I am invited to appear on TV and radio shows to talk about the magazine as well as topical issues in the criminal justice system. I am invited to give talks at colleges, including Harvard Law School, where I discuss how the emerging World Wide Web is changing the way people receive and consume information. I become known in criminal justice circles as an expert on prison culture and prison violence. Soon I am hired to appear as an expert witness for the defense in federal and state courts in prison homicide cases and at sentencing hearings. But we are rapidly going broke trying to keep the magazine afloat—and it's Kim's money that is supporting my magazine habit.

Prison Life Magazine Presents *Prisoners of the War on Drugs* airs on HBO in January 1996. Marc meanwhile has teamed up with an aspiring producer, a former club promoter named Henri Kessler, also known as Henry from Brooklyn. Marc and Henri hire me to do research and then to write a screenplay based on the long-rumored but little-known story of the CIA's secret testing of LSD on unwitting human guinea pigs in a covert Cold War program code-named Project MK-ULTRA. Henri has an angel investor, David Piepers, who puts up the money for me to write the script.

While researching Project MK-ULTRA, I take a trip to Washington, DC, to visit the National Archives. There, I am directed to a room in which I'm told what remains of the CIA's records on MK-ULTRA are stored, along with files related to other secret Cold War drug experiments. Most MK-ULTRA records were destroyed on orders from CIA director Richard Helms when the project was first exposed, but what endures resides in this room.

"Those boxes there," the clerk in charge of the archives tells me, "you are free to examine." He then points to several cartons stored on a higher shelf. "But those are not for public viewing."

As soon as he leaves the room, I take down the prohibited cartons and begin rifling through the enclosed documents.

FOR ANYONE STILL naive enough to doubt or dispute that elements within our government have conspired to carry out anything as nefarious as political assassination, I challenge them to look into the history of Project MK-ULTRA and its several secret mutations, Midnight Climax, Project MK-NAOMI, and ZRRIFLE to name a few. It began in the early 1950s as the brainchild of CIA director Allen Dulles and under the direction of Dr. Sidney Gottlieb, the head of CIA's chemical division for the Technical Services Staff (TSS), as the CIA set about to purchase and control the entire world supply of a new drug, lysergic acid diethylamide (LSD-25). Discovered during the war by Dr. Albert Hofmann, a scientist at the Swiss pharmaceutical company Sandoz Laboratories in Basel, Switzerland, LSD was hailed by CIA officials as the most powerful mind-altering drug known to man. Infinitesimal amounts of the odorless, colorless, and tasteless chemical could alter a person's consciousness for hours, possibly forever. Dulles had received a memo from an agent in Europe reporting that the Soviet agents had purchased ten kilos of LSD. The CIA director was alarmed. Ten kilos of pure acid would be enough to dump into the water supply and dose the inhabitants of an entire city the size of New York or Washington, DC.

This was at the height of the Cold War. Dulles and other CIA officials believed that the Soviets and Communist North Koreans had already developed insidious mind-control techniques using psychedelic drugs and brainwashing procedures. Dulles was determined that the United States would not be left behind in the race to control men's minds. He dispatched CIA agents to Switzerland with a briefcase full of cash and orders to purchase the entire current and future output of Sandoz LSD.

In reality, the KGB had purchased ten grams of LSD, not ten kilos. Sandoz had in fact only produced a total of forty grams of acid since its discovery. It turns out the agent who reported to Dulles did not know the difference between kilos and grams. Ironically, the entire CIA/LSD escapade that was to have a totally unexpected and lasting effect on Western civilization was based on dumb intelligence.

Once in possession of Sandoz's entire supply of acid, and with a deal to purchase all future LSD output (and later an arrangement with Eli Lilly and Company in the United States to acquire LSD in "tonnage" quantities), the CIA strategists needed to figure out what to do with it, how it could be used, whether as a truth serum or chemical weapon. To test its properties, they determined to use a cutout, someone who was not actually in the intelligence agency so as to circumvent the prohibition against domestic activities by CIA. The cutout had to be an experienced and discrete operative who could be trusted to keep his mouth shut and protect the agency if things got out of hand, which, given the nature of the project, was of real concern. They turned to a hard-drinking, rough-and-tumble undercover FBN agent named George Hunter White.

George was already a legendary figure in the world of covert drug testing. During the war, while with the Office of Strategic Services (OSS), George had been an organizer and even a willing test subject for a number of different drugs in an attempt to develop a truth serum that the army could use while interrogating enemy prisoners. To his credit, George would not test any drug on others without first testing it on himself. Once LSD was discovered, agency officials believed it might just be the panacea they had been looking for, a drug that could be slipped to enemy agents as well as used in interrogations. They brought George into the agency fold under Sidney Gottlieb and George's wartime friend and OSS controller, now CIA's counterintelligence chief, spymaster James Jesus Angleton. They had no idea what they were about to unleash on America and the rest of the world by supplying George White with an unlimited quantity of pure Sandoz and Lilly acid and sending him out to test it on unwitting human guinea pigs.

Most Project MK-ULTRA LSD field tests on civilians were carried out by White while he was employed by the narcotics bureau and moonlighting as a contract agent for the CIA. For his agency assignment, George adopted an alternative identity as a risqué world traveler, sexual deviant, and struggling writer, for which he used the alias Morgan Hall. At 81 Bedford Street in New York's Greenwich Village, he established a CIA-financed safe-house apartment and drug den with a hidden surveillance lair in an adjoining studio apartment. The apartment was made to resemble a playboy's pad, circa 1955. Walls were decorated with Toulouse-Lautrec posters of cancan dancers; cabinets were stocked with S and M sex toys, pornography, and photos of manacled women in black fishnet stockings and studded leather halters. White had CIA's technical services division install state-of-the-art bugging equipment, including microphones disguised as electrical outlets that were connected to tape recorders hidden behind a false wall. A framed, full-length, one-way mirror was installed in the wall separating the apartment and White's observation post in the adjoining studio. This allowed him to view the action as an unseen voyeur while he recorded the results and compiled written notes of his observations for his CIA masters. George would sit behind the one-way mirror and sip martinis, his favorite refreshment, from a chilled pitcher. He perched his portly body on a portable toilet so he could relieve himself without having to leave his station. From that post he observed and made notes on the effects of massive doses of LSD slipped to unsuspecting hookers, pimps, and johns, as well as other criminals, unsuspecting denizens of the Village, and others, including CIA colleagues.

"Gloria gets the horrors . . . Janet sky high," White dutifully recorded in notes sent to Dulles and Gottlieb. In another document, he wrote, "Lashbrook at 81 Bedford Street—Owen Winkle and the LSD surprise—can wash," apparently referring to visits to the pad and LSD tests conducted on CIA employees. White assigned LSD the code-name "stormy," by way of noting the often bizarre behavior brought on by the drug. According to an agency memo I found in the restricted files, the CIA feared Soviet agents might use psychedelics "to produce anxiety or terror in medically unsophisticated subjects unable to distinguish drug-induced psychosis from actual insanity." In an effort to school "enlightened operatives" for that eventuality, Dulles and Gottlieb instructed high-ranking agency personnel, including

Gottlieb's entire staff at TSS, to take LSD themselves and administer it to their colleagues with and without their knowledge.

"There was an extensive amount of self-experimentation for the reason that we felt that a firsthand knowledge of the subjective effects of these drugs [was] important to those of us who were involved in the program," Gottlieb explained at a Senate subcommittee hearing years later, as recorded in a CIA memo. Apparently, CIA spooks and scientists were tripping their brains out. "I didn't want to leave it," one CIA agent reported of his first LSD trip. "I felt I would be going back to a place where I wouldn't be able to hold on to this kind of beauty." The intelligence community, indeed the world, would never be the same.

GEORGE WHITE IS dead; he died of a diseased liver due to his heavy consumption of gin, some say up to a quart a day. But while rifling through the prohibited MK-ULTRA files, I find the name of White's right-hand man, a fellow named Ira "Ike" Feldman, who also worked undercover with the narcotics bureau. As George's CIA procurer, while posing as a Mafia gangster named Joe Capone, Feldman would prowl New York and later San Francisco bars, strip joints, and massage parlors, pick up hookers, johns, and sometimes criminals George was hoping to debrief while they were tripping on acid and lure them back to the CIA's safe house, where they would be given drinks spiked with massive doses of LSD.

As I read through the files, I suspect that Ike Feldman may still be alive since I can find no record of his death. If so, Ike might well be the only participant at the operational level of Project MK-ULTRA who is still living. Back in New York, I corner Charlie Kelley, who worked narcotics for the New York police department, and I ask him if he ever had any contact with a couple of federal drug agents named George White and Ike Feldman.

"Oh, Jesus, yeah," Charlie says. "Those guys, they were both fucking nuts—particularly George. And balls? George didn't give a fuck.

He'd walk into a room full of heavily armed Corsican dope smugglers and tell 'em all to line up against the wall and empty their pockets. Then, if he didn't find anything, he'd plant 'em and haul them all in for questioning. George was fearless. Ike was not as crazy. But George, that guy makes Popeye Doyle look like a Boy Scout. He had more stoolpigeons on his pad than any agent in New York."

Does he think Ike might still be alive, I ask Charlie, and, if Ike is still among us, could Charlie see if he can locate him, get his address and phone number, and possibly reach out to Ike on my behalf?

"Yeah," Charlie says, "I'll check it out. But what d'you want to talk to Ike about?"

"LSD," I say.

WHILE AT WORK on the screenplay, I meet and have lunch with Elizabeth Mitchell, the editor of Bob Guccione Jr.'s *Spin* magazine. When I tell her about the research I'm doing on the MK-ULTRA project, she's intrigued and puts me in touch with Guccione. There has long been a rumor, most famously postulated by acid guru Timothy Leary and Beat poet Allen Ginsberg, that it was the CIA who introduced LSD to America. Guccione says that, if I am able to locate Ike Feldman or someone else who has firsthand information to prove that in fact it was the CIA that turned America on to acid, he would be happy to give me the assignment to write a feature article about MK-ULTRA for his magazine.

Through Charlie Kelley, I contact Ike Feldman and set up a meeting. We meet at a hotel on Long Island. The interview turns out to be more than I could ever have imagined. Ike waddles in looking like the Penguin from the Batman movies. Not only does he go into detail about the acid tests, he proffers a handful of football shaped ampoules containing pure Sandoz LSD-25, and demonstrates how he and George would snap off the top of the ampoule and squirt a mega-dose of acid into some unsuspecting test subjects' drink.

"I always wanted to be a gangster," Feldman tells me. "So I was good at it. Before long, I had half a dozen girls working for me. One day, White calls me into his office. 'Ike,' he says, 'you've been doing one hell of a job as an undercover man. Now I'm gonna give you another assignment. We want you to test these mind-bending drugs.' I said, 'Why the hell do you want to test mind-bending drugs?' He said, 'Have you ever heard of *The Manchurian Candidate*?' I know about *The Manchurian Candidate*. In fact, I read the book. 'Well,' White said, 'that's why we have to test these drugs, to find out if they can be used to brainwash people.' He says, 'If we can find out just how good this stuff works, you'll be doing a great deal for your country.'"

As COVERT LSD experiments proliferated, things down at CIA headquarters began to get out of hand. "LSD favors the prepared mind," wrote Dr. Oscar Janiger, a Los Angeles psychiatrist and early LSD devotee. Nondrug factors such as set and setting—a person's mental state going into the experience and the surroundings in which the drug is taken—can make all the difference in reactions to a dose of LSD. It can be, as in the words of one agent on acid, a beautiful experience one never wants to end, or it can be the opposite, the classic bad trip one fears will never end.

Frank Olson was a civilian biochemist working for the Army Chemical Corps' Special Operations Division (SOD) at Fort Detrick in Frederick, Maryland. In a subproject of MK-ULTRA code-named MK-NAOMI, the CIA had bankrolled SOD to produce and maintain vicious mutant germ strains capable of killing or incapacitating victims. Olson's specialty at Fort Detrick was delivering deadly diseases in sprays and aerosol emulsions.

Just before Thanksgiving in 1953, at a CIA retreat for a conference on biological warfare, Sidney Gottlieb slipped Frank Olson and the other scientists a huge dose of LSD in an after-dinner liqueur. When Gottlieb revealed to the uproarious group of scientists now tripping their brains out that he'd laced the Cointreau, Olson suffered a psychotic snap. "You're all a bunch of thespians!" Olson shouted at his fellow acid trippers, then spent a long night wandering around babbling to himself. Back at Fort Detrick, Olson lapsed in and out of depression, he began to have grave misgivings about his work, and he believed the agency was out to get him for indiscreet comments he had made to nonagency civilians about his work for the CIA. Ten days after he was dosed, Olson crashed through a closed tenth-floor window of the Statler Hotel in New York and plummeted to his death on the sidewalk below.

"White had been testing the stuff in New York when that guy Olson went out the window and died," Feldman said. "I don't know if he jumped or he was pushed. They say he jumped, but I heard he was thrown out. Anyway, that's when they shut down the New York operation and moved it to San Francisco."

The CIA successfully covered up the Olson affair for more than twenty years. White, who had been instrumental in the cover-up, was promoted to West Coast District Supervisor, and transferred to San Francisco.

Unfazed by the death of their colleague, the CIA's acid enthusiasts were, in fact, more convinced of the value of their experiments. They would now focus on LSD as a potent new agent for offensive unconventional warfare. The drug-testing program resumed in the Bay Area under the cryptonym Operation Midnight Climax.

Ike takes offense at how his work has been characterized by former cops who knew him. "I was no pimp," Feldman insists. Yet he freely admits that his role in Midnight Climax was to supply whores. "These cunts all thought I was a racketeer," Feldman explains. He paid the girls fifty to one hundred dollars a night to lure johns to a safe house apartment White set up on Telegraph Hill with funds provided by the CIA. Unsuspecting clients were served cocktails laced with doses of LSD and other concoctions the CIA sent out to be tested.

"As George White once told me, 'Ike, your best information outside comes from the whores and the junkies. If you treat a whore nice, she'll treat you nice. If you treat a junkie nice, he'll treat you nice.' But sometimes, when people had information, there was only one way you could get it. If it was a girl, you put her tits in a drawer and slammed the drawer. If it was a guy, you took his cock and you hit it with a hammer. And they would talk to you. Now, with these drugs, you could get information without having to abuse people."

It wasn't just acid the CIA wanted White to test. "We tested this stuff they called the Sextender," Feldman says. "There was this Russian ship in the harbor at San Francisco. I had a couple of my girls pick up these Russian sailors and bring 'em back to the pad. White wanted to know all kinds of crap, but they weren't talking. So we had the girls slip 'em this sex drug. It gets your dick up like a rat. Stays up for two hours. These guys went crazy. They fucked these poor girls until they couldn't walk straight. The girls were complaining they couldn't take any more screwing. But White found out what he wanted to know. Now this drug, what they call the Sextender, I understand it's being sold as Viagra to guys who can't get a hard-on."

Feldman claims we have the CIA to thank for these and other medical breakthroughs.

"White always wanted to try everything himself," Feldman remembers. "Whatever drugs they sent out, it didn't matter, he wanted to see how they worked on him before he tried them on anyone else. He always said he never felt a goddamn thing. He thought it was all bullshit. White drank so much, he couldn't feel his own cock.

"This thing"—Feldman holds up a fountain pen gas gun—"the boys in Washington sent it out and told us to test the gas. White says to me, 'C'mon, Ike. Let's go outside. I'll shoot you with it, then you shoot me.' 'Fuck that,' I said. 'You ain't gonna shoot me with that crap.' So we went outside and I shot George White with the gas. He coughed, his face turned red, his eyes started watering. He was choking. Turned out, that stuff was the prototype for Mace."

I ask Feldman if he ever met Sidney Gottlieb, the elusive scientist who was the brains behind MK-ULTRA. "Yeah, I knew Sidney. Several times Gottlieb came out to Frisco," Feldman assures me. "I met Gottlieb at the pad, and at White's office. White used to send me to the airport to pick up Sidney and this other wacko, John Gittinger, the psychologist. Sidney was a nice guy. He was a fuckin' nut. They were all nuts. I say, 'You're a good Jewish boy from Brooklyn, like me. What are you doing with these crazy cocksuckers?' He had this black bag with him. He says, 'This is my bag of dirty tricks.' He had all kinds of crap in that bag. We took a drive to Muir Woods out by Stinson Beach. Sidney says, 'Stop the car.' He pulls out a dart gun and shoots this big eucalyptus tree with a dart. Then he tells me, 'Come back in two days and check this tree.' So we go back in two days, the tree was completely dead. Not a leaf left on it. Now that was the forerunner of Agent Orange.

"I went back and I saw White, and he says to me, 'What do you think of Sidney?' I said, 'I think he's a fuckin' nut.' White says, 'Well, he may be a nut, but this is the program. This is what we do.' White thought they were all assholes. He said, 'These guys are running our intelligence? They're all crazy.' But they sent George two thousand dollars a month for the pad, and as long as they paid the bills, we went along with the program.

"Another time, I come back to the pad and the whole joint is littered with these pipe cleaners," Feldman goes on. "I said, 'Who's smokin' a pipe?' Gittinger, one of those CIA nuts, was there with two of my girls, my whores. He had 'em explaining all these different sex acts, the different positions they knew for humping. Now he has them making these little figurines out of the pipe cleaners—men and women screwing in all these different positions. He was taking pictures of the figurines and writing a history of each one. These pipe cleaner histories were sent back to Washington."

A stated goal of Project MK-ULTRA and its offshoots, MK-NAOMI, ZRRIFLE, and other top secret CIA projects was to determine "if an individual can be trained to perform an act of attempted assassination involuntarily" while under the influence of various mind-control techniques and then have no memory of the event later. Feldman tells me that in the early 1960s, after the MK-ULTRA program had been around for over a decade, he was summoned to George White's office. White and CIA director Allen Dulles were there.

"They wanted George to arrange to hit Fidel Castro," Feldman said. "They were gonna soak his cigars with LSD and drive him crazy. George called me in because I had this whore, a Cuban girl, and we were gonna send her down to see Castro with a box of LSD-soaked cigars."

Dick Russell, author of a book on the Kennedy assassination titled *The Man Who Knew Too Much*, uncovered evidence to support the theory that Lee Harvey Oswald was a product of MK-ULTRA. One of the CIA's overseas locations for LSD and mind-control experiments was Atsugi naval air base in Japan, where Oswald served as a marine radar technician. Russell says that after his book was published, a former CIA counterintelligence expert called him and said Oswald had been "viewed by the CIA as fitting the psychological profile of someone they were looking for in their MK-ULTRA program" and that he had been mind-conditioned to defect to the USSR.

Robert Kennedy's assassin, Sirhan Sirhan, while working as a horse trainer at the Santa Anita racetrack near Los Angeles, was introduced to hypnosis and the occult by a fellow groom with shadowy connections. Sirhan has always maintained he has no memory of the night he shot Kennedy.

One of the CIA's mob contacts long suspected of involvement in John Kennedy's assassination was the Los Angeles–based Mafioso John Roselli. Roselli had risen to prominence in the mob by taking over the Annenberg-Ragen wire service at Santa Anita where Oswald's killer, Jack Ruby, sold a handicapper's tip sheet with information for horse race bettors. Ike Feldman tells me that Roselli was one of George White's many informants.

"On more than one occasion, White sent me to the airport to pick up Johnny Roselli and bring him to the office or to the pad," says Feldman. Roselli and White were close. Roselli had lived for most of his life in Chicago, where White had served as district supervisor of the Federal Bureau of Narcotics from 1945 through 1947. Following a big opium bust in 1947, Jack Ruby was picked up and hauled in for interrogation, then later let off the hook by none other than George White. Federal Bureau of Narcotics files indicate that Ruby was yet another of White's legion of stool pigeons.

The connection between MK-ULTRA mind-control experiments, the proliferation of the drug subculture, Mob/CIA assassination plots, and the emergence of new, lethal viruses goes on and on. Fort Detrick in Maryland where Frank Olson worked experimenting with viral strains (such as the deadly microbes Sidney Gottlieb personally carried to Africa in an unsuccessful attempt to assassinate Patrice Lumumba) was the locale of a near disaster involving an outbreak of a newly emerged virus. The event was chronicled in a lengthy article, "Going Viral," by David E. Hoffman, published in the January 23, 2011, issue of *The New Yorker*.

Though the *New Yorker* writer did not make the connection between Fort Detrick, the army SOD, Frank Olson, and MK-NAOMI, he told of a number of monkeys who had all died of a highly infectious virus known as Ebola that first appeared in fifty-five African villages in 1976, killing nine out of ten of its victims. Some epidemiologists believe AIDS originated in Africa. Feldman claims the CIA used Africa as a staging ground to test germ warfare because "nobody gave a goddamn about any of this crap over there."

The MK-ULTRA program, then the largest domestic operation mounted by the CIA, went on well into the seventies under its various new codenames. According to Feldman and other CIA experts, it still continues today under an alphabet soup of different cryptonyms. Indeed, one ex-agent told me it would be foolish to think that a program as successful and fruitful as MK-ULTRA would be discontinued. When an agency operation comes under scrutiny, it simply changes the name of the program and continues unabated.

The public first learned of MK-ULTRA in 1977 with the disclosure of thousands of classified documents and CIA testimony before a Senate subcommittee on health and scientific research chaired by Senator Edward Kennedy. Previously, CIA director Richard Helms had ordered Sidney Gottlieb to destroy all of the MK-ULTRA files in his possession. What was ultimately declassified and made public revealed only a portion of the record. Ike Feldman was subpoenaed and appeared on a panel of witnesses, but the senators failed to ask him a single question. Sidney Gottlieb, complaining of a heart condition, testified at a special semipublic session. He delivered a prepared statement and admitted to having destroyed MK-ULTRA files. The full extent of the CIA's activities under the rubric of MK-ULTRA, MK-NAOMI, and a host of other covert domestic and foreign operations may never be known.

George White retired from the narcotics bureau and from his role as a CIA contract agent in 1965. The last ten years of his life he lived in Stinson Beach, California, where, known as Colonel White, he became chief of the volunteer fire department and regaled fellow drinkers in his favorite watering holes with his tales of derring-do as a secret agent for the government. Local residents remember George for turning in kids for smoking pot, for spraying a preacher and his congregation with water at a beach picnic, and for terrorizing his neighbors by driving his jeep across their lawns when he'd had too much to drink. After White's death, his widow donated his papers, including his diaries, to an electronic surveillance museum. As information on MK-ULTRA entered the public domain, people who had known White only in his official FBN capacity were stunned to learn of his undercover role as Morgan Hall, his long employment as a CIA contract agent, and his close association with mafiosi and intelligence agents suspected of involvement in political assassinations.

According to George Belk, a former head of the Drug Enforcement Agency in New York, Ike Feldman quit the drug agency in the mid-1960s after a probe by the internal security division. "Feldman was the sort of guy who didn't have too many scruples," said Dan Casey, a retired FBN agent who worked with Feldman in San Francisco. "For him, the ends justified the means." A DEA flack confirmed Feldman "resigned under a cloud" at a time when a number of agents came under suspicion of a variety of offenses, none having to do with secret drug-testing programs. When I interview him, Feldman asserts that he still works for the CIA on a contract basis, mostly in the Far East and Korea.

On the day of our last interview, over lunch at a restaurant in Little Italy, Feldman tells me the CIA had contacted him and asked him why he was talking to me.

"Fuck them." Feldman says. "I do what I want. I never signed any goddamn secrecy agreement."

I ask him why he decided to tell his story after so many years of silence. "There's too much bullshit in the world." Feldman says. "The world runs on bullshit.

"To make a long story short," he sums up, using one of his favorite verbal segues, "I want the truth of this to be known so that people understand that what we did was for the good of the country." We amble down the street to a Chinese grocer, where Feldman carries on a lengthy conversation with the owner in Chinese. A couple of young girls, tourists, want to have their picture taken with Feldman. "Are you a gangster?" they ask.

"No," Feldman replies with a wave of his cigar, "I'm a goddamn CIA agent."

As we walk on, I ask Feldman to explain how his and George White's work for the CIA had been helpful to the country.

"I learned that most of this stuff was necessary for the United States," he says, "and even though it may have hurt somebody in the beginning, in the long run it was important. As long as it did good for the country."

I press him. "How so? How was it good for the country?"

"Well, look," Feldman gestures with his cigar at the throng of citizens in the streets of New York City. "We're goddamn free, aren't we?"

THE ARTICLE, "ALTERED States of America," published in the March 1994 issue of *Spin* magazine, immediately ignites heated controversy that still simmers and occasionally flares up all these years later over the exposure of details in Project MK-ULTRA and the CIA's acid tests first reported in my interview with Ike Feldman. Bob Guccione calls for a news conference at the Waldorf Astoria Hotel and asks me if Ike would agree to appear. Ike shows up dressed like a 1950s gangster and brandishing a large, unlit cigar. He tells the room full of assembled reporters that "everything in that article is all bullshit. This guy (me, sinking lower in my seat) doesn't know shit from shinola." And then he not only confirms the most provocative statements he made in the interview, but he elaborates and makes even more detailed and outrageous assertions about George White, the CIA's LSD tests in New York, and later when the project was shut down after Frank Olson's death and relocated to San Francisco under the new code-name Project Midnight Climax.

I include the *Spin* article as the title piece in a collection of my magazine journalism published by Nation Books in September 2005 as *Altered States of America: Outlaws and Icons, Hitmakers and Hitmen*. The screenplay I write for Marc Levin and Henri Kessler, which is alternately titled *MK-ULTRA* and *Acid Test*, is said by some of the producers who read it to be the best unproduced script making the rounds of Hollywood studios and production companies. At the time, the CIA/ LSD story appeared too farfetched, too bizarre and unbelievable for movie executives to wrap their heads around, more like an acid-induced fantasy dreamed up by the outlaw author and his equally conspiracy-minded partner, *Blowback* director Marc Levin. Since then, with the publication of a number of books on the subject, and the 2017 Netflix docudrama series *Wormwood*, directed by Errol Morris, MK-ULTRA and the CIA's involvement in domestic operations involving US citizens has undergone new scrutiny.

One statement in particular made by Ike Feldman during the interview, and that I reported in the *Spin* article, remains to this day the impetus for and the focus of much of the ongoing controversy. Though ruled a suicide, Olson's death has been reexamined as a possible CIA sanctioned murder. Ike was the first person to question the suicide verdict in print and suggest that Olson may have been thrown out of the hotel window, possibly murdered to shut him up as a security risk. Soon after the article appears in *Spin*, I get a phone call from the editor, Elizabeth Mitchell, to ask if I am willing to speak with Frank Olson's son, Eric Olson. Eric read the article, and he wants to speak to me.

Eric confides that the Olson family has long disbelieved the suicide story and lived with the haunting suspicion that men working for the government murdered their father. He asks me to put him in touch with Ike Feldman, which I do. Ike repeats his statement to Eric and elaborates, making the claim that the word at the time was that Olson had been thrown out the window to shut him up. Ike implies that none other than George Hunter White might have had something to do with Frank Olson's demise. George had a reputation from his days with OSS as having been proficient at what is known as "wet work," killing people for the agency.

Eric Olson has his father's body exhumed and arranges for a second autopsy, performed by James Starrs, professor of law and forensic science at the George Washington University National Law Center. Starrs and his forensic team examine Olson's body for cuts and abrasions that would have been consistent with a crash through the window and find none. They do, however, discover a large hematoma on the left side of Olson's head and a large injury to his chest. Starrs's team concludes that the blunt-force trauma to the head and chest injury were not sustained during the fall but most likely as the result of injuries inflicted in the hotel room before Olson went out the window. Starrs pronounces the evidence "rankly and starkly suggestive of homicide."

Two years after the *Spin* article appears, in 1996 Eric Olson approaches Manhattan District Attorney Robert Morgenthau's office to see if they would be willing to open a new investigation. I am deposed and repeat what Ike told me to investigators from the district attorney office's cold case unit. Investigators collect additional evidence, including the deposition of Robert Lashbrook, a squirrelly CIA scientist who worked on the MK-ULTRA program under Sidney Gottlieb and who was in the hotel room with Olson when he went out the window. The forensic evidence surrounding Olson's death suggests defenestration, the act of throwing someone or something out of a window, which was a favorite method used by the CIA. The CIA's first manual on assassination describes the procedure as "the most efficient accident, in simple assassination, is a fall of 75 feet or more onto a hard surface."

Ultimately, the New York City district attorney's office determined that there is no compelling new evidence to bring to a grand jury, and the investigation into the Olson case is closed. But the story of MK-ULTRA and the doubts about the circumstances of Frank Olson's mysterious death refuse to die. Eric Olson sustains an all-consuming effort to bring light and truth to the facts of his father's death. As recently as 2018, I am interviewed for a series of short documentaries on MK-ULTRA to air on the internet-based ATTN.

WHILE I WAS working on the HBO *Prison Life* series, Sheila Nevins asked me to read and comment on the verisimilitude of the pilot for a dramatic series HBO was developing for TV called *Oz*. Set in a fictional experimental prison, *Oz* is to be HBO's first production of a scripted TV series. Sheila and her boss, Chris Albrecht, had reservations about the script, given the reality of prison life as depicted in the magazine and in our documentaries. I read the script written by Tom Fontana, the creator of *St. Elsewhere* and one of the executive producers of *Homicide*, and delivered my notes.

Prison may be one of the most difficult subjects for writers who have never experienced it to write about convincingly. In films and TV shows, prison life has largely been portrayed in lurid clichés and one-dimensional stereotypes. To begin with, it's hard for someone who hasn't been incarcerated to capture the universal human drama of being deprived of one's freedom. It's like trying to imagine what it's like to live in New York City if you've never lived there and know it only through what you've seen on TV or in the movies. Also, so much of the prison experience is unique and depends on the character of the person forced to live in captivity. The essential adversarial relationship is not necessarily prisoner to prisoner but more often keeper to kept. The essential emotion is loneliness. Fear strikes in the hard, clanking sounds of steel bars slamming shut, and in the smell of so many men herded together in a confined space. The US prison population is overwhelmingly made up of men and women of color from impoverished inner-city neighborhoods. Whites are a distinct minority. And yet most prisons are located in rural areas where the guards are predominantly white.

As a result of my comments, HBO hired me to work on *Oz* as a technical consultant. In the beginning, Fontana complained that I was trying to rewrite his scripts rather than just give him notes. But over the course of the series, Tom became less concerned with trying to shock the audience with garish clichés and more engaged in dramatizing the social issues of imprisonment in America. I was enthralled by the experience of working on a scripted TV series. It struck me as the modern-day equivalent of the nineteenth-century novel, where one is able to create a wide cast of characters and develop their stories over many years and through changes that have a deep impact on their lives.

WHILE WORKING ON *Oz*, I was hired as an expert witness by the defense to consult on a case involving a particularly brutal prison homicide that took place in a lockdown control unit at the maximum-security Gunnison Penitentiary in Utah. A young white prisoner, Troy Kell, was accused of stabbing to death a black gang member named Lonnie Blackmon. As a new arrival in the control unit, Blackmon apparently didn't fit in. He upset the daily rhythm in the unit by playing his radio too loud, yelling and complaining to the guards, and generally upsetting the other prisoners, many of whom had been classified as violent offenders and were doing life or long prison sentences. They weren't happy to have their routines disrupted. Routine is everything in prison, particularly when one is serving a long or terminal prison sentence. Prisoners spend months and even years developing a routine as a means of *doing time*. Upsetting that is tantamount to some new arrival in a sedate, middle-class neighborhood suddenly turning their home into a crack house. Blackmon wasn't showing the proper respect to his neighbors. So the white boys decided to go to the head shot-caller among the white convicts, the charismatic and calculating Troy Kell, and implore Troy as the unofficial mayor of the control unit to take care of the Blackmon disruption. Troy was at that time a handsome twenty-six-year-old who looked like a muscled-up version of James Dean. He was doing life for a senseless murder.

Troy's whole history is a tragic story of a young life gone horribly wrong. He grew up in a broken home outside Las Vegas. His high school girlfriend answered an ad in a local newspaper for models. When she sat for the photo shoot, she was assaulted and then stalked by the pervert who claimed to be a photographer. When she told Troy what had happened, he and some friends decided to give the guy a beating. Someone brought along a gun. The kids shot the photographer and left his body out in the desert. For days after the killing, they told their friends what they had done and took the other kids out to show them the decomposing corpse.

Troy was eighteen when he was sentenced to life in the Nevada State Penitentiary. As a good-looking white boy, his best chance of survival as a man was to get down with the Aryan clique for protection. By the time he arrived in Gunnison on a prisoner-exchange program, Troy was a full-on tattooed convict badass, though still soft-spoken, gentlemanly, and even seemingly shy. In my meeting with the prose-cutor on Troy's case, he said he couldn't understand why Troy and his lawyer would bother to go to trial on the murder since the entire event was captured on the prison video recorder.

"You mean there's video of the actual killing?" I asked.

"Yes," he said, "I have it right here." And he took a VCR tape from his desk drawer.

Even at this early stage in my career as a documentary film producer, after the success with the Mike Tyson film, I have already adopted the default position of asking for videotape whenever it is mentioned.

"Can I have it?" I asked.

"It's my only copy," he replied.

"Just for a few hours," I said. "I'll get a copy made and return it."

The tape of Troy Kell's killing of Lonnie Blackmon is evidence of everything I had been writing about prison violence in *Prison Life* magazine, and what I have been saying on the witness stand in the courtroom when called to testify. It's horrendous. There is a kind of macabre beauty to the choreography, often sheer brilliance in the plan-ning and execution, as it is never random, never senseless, always the result of some real or perceived serious infraction of what is known as the convict code: an unwritten regimen of giving and getting respect. The convict code is a self-imposed dogma to control violent, caged men who have been further brutalized by their environment. Troy lived by the code: give and get respect. Respect is the currency of prison life. You fuck up, you refuse to live by the code, you refuse to respect your fellow prisoners, you disrupt the day-to-day rhythm of prison life in close confinement, and you must die. Troy stabbed Blackmon something like sixty-seven times while Blackmon was held down by another white convict, who also just happened to be out of his cell with no restraints. When I asked Troy why he stabbed Blackmon so many times, he answered, "Because I was so mad at him for putting me in a position where I had to kill him." Perfect convict logic.

The killing seemed to go on for a good fifteen minutes. Meanwhile the guards, who were watching it all take place on the closed-circuit video system that is recording the killing, did nothing; they merely commented that something was apparently going down in the control unit. Troy kneeled on Blackmon and stabbed him with a prison-made shank in the torso, throat, and head. At one point the shank got stuck in Blackmon's skull and Troy has to yank it out to go on stabbing. When he finished, his jumpsuit and arms covered with blood, this usu-ally mild-mannered, seemingly sweet young man stood up, raised his arms in a victory salute, and declared for the camera and for the other prisoners watching the killing, "Got some white power going off in here!"

A killing like the prolonged butchering of Lonnie Blackmon in a supposedly locked-down control unit could not take place without staff complicity. I would venture to say that most prison homicides involve varying degrees of staff awareness and even assistance in set-ting up the killing. Certainly, that is the case in the Blackmon homi-cide. Bear in mind that the prisoners in the control unit where Troy and Blackmon were held are all supposed to be locked down twen-ty-three and a half hours a day in single-man cells. They are never to be let out of their cells unless they are handcuffed behind their backs and escorted by guards. There is never to be more than one prisoner out of his cell at a time. Those are the rules governing prisoners who are confined in segregation units. These guys are already known to be dangerous; often, they have killed before while in custody. So how does it happen that Troy manages to get out of his cell, get free of the handcuffs, get a hold of the shank, and have another convict released from his cell to help attack Blackmon, who, conveniently, also hap-pens to be out of his cell at the same time? Ingenious planning, yes, and well-coordinated jailhouse moves by savvy convicts who are still able to wield power even when supposedly incapacitated: all that is true. But also, it couldn't happen without a little help from the guards, who may have had their own reasons for wanting to get rid of Lonnie Blackmon.

It's prison life in America, and the guards and administrators have adapted as well as the convicts. In a maximum-security prison in California, guards arranged gladiator fights between members of rival gangs and then bet on the results. I reported on the California gladiator fights case in an article for *Esquire* called "The Making of Bone Crusher," published in September 1999.

Witness the recent killing of infamous government rat James Whitey Bulger, another adroitly planned and executed prison murder that could not possibly have taken place without coordination at high levels within the Federal Bureau of Prisons. I have much more to say about Whitey in a later chapter, but to illustrate my point about prison killings it's worth noting that as a high-level informant with organized crime connections, Whitey should have been in protective custody. He should have been under a separation order to make certain he never ended up in a prison where there were known organized crime killers waiting for him. He never should have been transferred to this particular prison in the first place, and he definitely never should have been left unattended in a wheelchair where he could be attacked.

But Whitey had an attitude, he thought he was special, and he was a pain in the ass wherever they sent him, always fucking with staff, trying to run his scams, and pissing off the administration. So the bureau saw fit to transfer the eighty-nine-year-old snitch to a prison where there had already been two recent killings; and, within hours of his arrival, guards left him alone in a wheelchair and in his diaper in an unlocked cell, where convicts using a padlock in a sock beat him to death, his eyes were gouged out, and his tongue was cut off. That's convict-administered justice in the Big House.

When Sheila Nevins at HBO saw the Troy Kell tape, even though she was unable to watch it all, she was sold. We used clips from the video of the Blackmon killing as the basis for *Gladiator Days: Anatomy of a Prison Murder*, a film that looks in depth at the issue of prison violence in America. Troy was convicted of Blackmon's murder and sentenced to die by a firing squad. As of this writing, some twenty years later, he is still on death row.

THUG LIFE IN DC (1998), the fourth HBO documentary in the *Prison Life* series, about youth gang culture and wholesale incarceration in our nation's capital, wins the Primetime Emmy Award for Outstanding Documentary or Nonfiction Special. During the making of the documentary, we are able to gain unprecedented access to the DC jail, primarily because the warden is so frustrated with what is going on both in the streets of our nation's capital and in her jail that she hopes to bring public awareness to the problem.

At the same time, I have been given an assignment to write an article for John Kennedy Junior's short-lived *George* magazine about the resurrection of DC mayor Marion Barry. (*George* would cease publication in 2001 before the article was published.) Mayor Barry has been reelected to office after being set up by the FBI in a crack cocaine bust, completed his bid in prison, and come back to serve as perhaps America's most infamous public officeholder, and the only other acting mayor with a felony conviction since James Michael Curley was mayor of Boston in 1947.

While in France at the Cannes Film Festival in 1997 looking for backing for *MK-ULTRA*, Henri Kessler, Marc Levin, and I decide the time is right for us to pool our resources and strike out on our own to make a low-budget feature film. Given our unique access to the DC city jail and the thematic resonance of a story about mass incarceration set in the capital of the free world, we settle on a fictional story about a talented young spoken-word poet from the ghetto of Washington who gets busted for possession of a small amount of pot and is locked up in the brutally overcrowded city jail. The inspiration for the film is to show how the wholesale incarceration of young African American men on minor drug charges is not only corrupting the system but also creating a whole generation of alienated youth, often talented, ambitious young men who have very few options for avoiding the trajectory former Black Panther and prisoner activist Eddie Ellis identified as "from the plantations, to the projects, to the penitentiaries."

We take what is at the time an innovative approach in the making of what will become *Slam*; it is going to be a fictional film that will have the look and feel of a documentary. There is to be no script per se. Marc and I devise scenes, and I compose a written outline. Actors are given direction and suggested lines on how to get into the scene and how to get out. What they come up with during the actual filming of the scene will result in a kind of informed improvisation. There are no retakes. Most of the roles will be played not by actors but real prisoners, real prison guards, with spoken-word poets playing our male and female leads. The primary location is to be the DC jail and the streets of Washington DC's Anacostia neighborhood. We have just a week to shoot the DC scenes.

Slam is shot on Super 16 film by documentary-trained, handheld cameraman Mark Benjamin, who also shot the documentaries we made for HBO. The warden at the jail allows our crew just a few days to shoot the prison scenes. The climactic scene takes place in the prison yard, when prisoners from rival gangs face off to do battle and are then blown away by the Saul Williams character, Ray Joshua, who does a mesmerizing performance of a spoken-word poem about the journey of young black men that stymies the gang bangers and causes them to forget what they were ready to fight about. When doubts are voiced as to whether such a scene could work, we decide to try it out on the actual prisoners in the yard. After watching Saul perform his poem, the prisoners are stunned. No one speaks, and then they begin to chant, "South Side! South Side!" to claim Saul as one of their own.

While the crew prepares for a final courtroom scene, I get a call from Marc Levin on set who tells me that we have no one to play the judge. At the time, I am sitting in Mayor Marion Barry's office conducting the interview for *George* magazine. "Hold on a second," I say to Marc." And then, to the Mayor, "Mayor Barry, how would you like to perform a cameo role in our movie?"

"What's the movie about?" the mayor wants to know.

When I tell him, Mayor Barry signs on.

THE MAKING OF *Slam* combined fortuitous circumstances, raw talent, intrepid guerilla filmmaking, a timely subject matter, and high good energy, resulting in an independent film that would go on to win the Grand Jury Prize at the Sundance Film Festival in 1998, the Camera d'Or at Cannes, also in 1998, and several other awards around the world. *Slam* won Independent Spirit Awards for the male and female leads, talented spoken-word artists Saul Williams and Sonja Sohn. It sold to a distributor after its premiere screening at the Sundance Film Festival. Henri's investor made his money back and then some. For a brief period, we were besieged by eager agents at Hollywood agencies wanting to represent us and by producers and film company executives coming to us with scripts and deals for movies they wanted us to make. In a meeting at the William Morris Agency in Los Angeles, after a powwow with a room full of agents, I was approached by William Morris's head TV agent, Steve Glick, who took me aside and said, "You are going to make a TV series, and I want to represent you and help you get it set up."

Kim and I edited a book based on *Slam*. The book included a script written from the finished film and the poetry featured by the artists in the movie, as well as behind-the-scenes filmmakers' and actors' diaries telling the story of the making of *Slam* from several perspectives. Grove Atlantic published the book in 1998.

For me, a highlight of the *Slam* journey came when we were invited to screen the movie at the Latin American Film Festival in Havana. We flew down on the first commercial flight from the US allowed into Cuba since the embargo. They put us up in the Hotel Nacional, where I was visited by the ghosts of Charlie "Lucky" Luciano and Meyer Lansky.

La Flordita, Papa's favorite bar on Calle Obispo, evoked Hemingway's spirit for me. While I was in Cuba, Fidel Castro delivered a four-hour speech heard over loudspeakers outside my hotel room. As I walked the streets of Havana, I was reminded of the stories Joe Stassi told me of his time in Cuba, and I wondered whatever happened to the old man.

I would soon find out.

Chapter Eleven

WHITE BOYZ

THE WEEKS AND then months following the success of *Slam* recalls how some of my former smuggling partners and I carried on after bringing in a huge load of weed or hash. To say that the success of the film goes to our heads only partly describes what happens; it changes our lives. Hubris rears its ugly gorgon head. Henri in particular embarks on an empire building campaign. He leases and then builds out a vast production space in the Starrett-Lehigh Building on Twenty-Sixth Street and the West Side Highway. He christens the new company Offline Entertainment Group. He names Marc Levin head of production, I am named head of development, and he appoints himself chief executive officer. He begins a hiring spree to staff the office space with new employees. Executives Ezra Swerdlow and Alex Gibney, both established names in the business, come onboard with big-ticket salaries. Marc, Henri, and I have a meeting with Danny DeVito, Michael Shamberg, and Stacy Sher at the Jersey Films offices in LA. Danny gets down on his knees before us and tells how moved he was by *Slam*. He offers us a deal to make a film called *Knifehand*, written by former Black Panther Jamal Joseph, who I actually met years previously in the bullpen at the Metropolitan Correctional Center in Manhattan after the New York Panthers were arrested on the Panthers 21 case.

In my role at Offline as head of development, I read the *Knifehand* script and propose to my partners that we make the film. *Knifehand* is budgeted and already financed at $10 million, a big step up from our low-budget first film. And it feels like a good move for us to get into business with Jersey Films. Marc is not convinced; he's concerned that we will be seen as a one-trick pony because he feels the story is similar thematically with *Slam*. For his part, Henri says, "Who needs Jersey Films? We will be bigger than Jersey Films!" It is the beginning of dissension in the executive ranks at Offline Entertainment that will soon result in my leaving the company.

But before that, we make a second feature film, *White Boyz*, a comedy, sort of, based on a script by performance artist Danny Hoch and his writing partner, Garth Belcon. *White Boyz* tells the story of three young white kids from the cornfields of Iowa who listen to nothing but black gangster rap and aspire to become drug dealers and go to jail so they can get down with the black experience. The movie stars Danny Hoch and three new young actors, Mark Webber, Dash Mihok, and Piper Perabo as Danny's character Flip's crew. There are cameos and music by Snoop Dogg, Fat Joe, Dead Prez, Slick Rick, and Doug E. Fresh. Funded by Fox Searchlight, *White Boyz* is shot on location in Iowa and in the Cabrini Green projects in Chicago. The film opens in thirty-seven theaters the week of September 11, 1999, and has dismal gross box office returns of $22,451 during its entire theatrical run. It's a movie in search of a genre. It's a comedy with dramatic overtones as the would-be gangsters run into trouble on their foray into the drug business in Chicago. It's an extended rap video with a hilarious performance by Snoop Dogg as an imprisoned rapper who goes off on the staff in a prison mess hall. A failure at the box office, *White Boyz* has nevertheless become a cult favorite and has been broadcast many times on cable networks VH1, MTV, HBO, and the Fuse Network.

As for white boys Stratton, Levin, and Kessler, *White Boyz* heralds a divergence in creative and business aspirations that compels me to leave Offline Entertainment Group and venture out on my own. My experience working on *Oz* has convinced me that my future lies in scripted TV series. I pitch Chris Albrecht at HBO a dramatic series about undercover DEA agents working in Mexico and along the US border in and around El Paso, Texas. Albrecht likes the concept; he hires me and Kim to write a pilot script. The project is later shelved when Albrecht decides to devote all HBO's immediate development talent and resources to a new series they are producing called *The Sopranos*.

THE WHIRLWIND SUCCESS of *Slam* and my foray into the movie business is playing havoc with my marriage. I'm traveling a good deal and Kim is often left home alone with two, and then three, young children. At the New York party to celebrate winning the Caméra d'Or at Cannes, Kim, well in her cups, hauls off and smacks me across the face then storms out after a young woman I hardly know stops to greet me, recalling having met me in France. Kim increasingly appears to resent my success and suspect me of infidelity. With the money I'm making writing screenplays and producing movies, the disparity in our incomes has shifted. Her second novel, *Notes from the Country Club*, though a critical success, does not have the commercial value of *Rush*. We buy an apartment on Twenty-First Street in Manhattan and divide our time between a home upstate near Woodstock and the apartment in the city. When I make a unilateral decision to take a substantial chunk of our available funds and invest it in the making of a short film that I write and direct, Kim is irate, convinced of my financial irresponsibility, and the dissolution of our marriage appears imminent.

The gamble, however, pays off.

Chapter Twelve

STREET TIME

Soon after I leave Offline, I write a short script called *Street Time*, a drama set in the world of the Special Offenders Unit of a federal parole office. The inspiration had come to me while I sat in the Southern District of New York parole offices waiting to be called to report, and it never left. I kept thinking about the dramatic possibilities of pitting a conflicted, sympathetic parole officer with his own character flaws and issues against a conflicted, sympathetic parolee with a family, a rich criminal history, and the desire to make it in the world. I planned to play out their complicated relationship while following each character on his separate path. The parole office report room was a perfect setting for introducing new characters and new story lines while playing out the main characters' conflict. The fact of the periodic report, and placing the two main characters face to face in a small report room on a regular basis, struck me as rich with opportunities for dramatic tension and potential for a narrative structure to develop the characters and the themes of individual freedom and government control all to be played over several seasons.

Steve Glick, who I sign with as my agent at William Morris, sets up a pitch meeting for me with Jerry Offsay and Gary Levine at Showtime. In the meeting, Offsay wonders aloud if I can create a TV show with the same kind of documentary look and fresh narrative style as *Slam*. "Yes," I say, "given the right actors who are comfortable and talented working in roles where they become actively involved in creating their characters."

This is what all actors do to varying degrees, but in the *Slam* style the actor is given much more leeway, much more creative input in determining their character's essence and expressing who they are, even down to creating their dialogue. The words on the page of the script are just the starting point.

When I pitch my concept for a show set in the Special Offender's Unit of a New York federal parole office, Offsay says they don't do cop shows. I explain that this is nothing like a typical cop show; it's about a complicated relationship that develops between the parole officer, an authority figure, and the parolee, a person who is either trying to go straight and obey the rules of parole or who is set to revert to a life of crime and trying to get over on the authorities. The Showtime executives are interested but not convinced; they want to see a sample pilot script. I send them the short script I wrote and decide to do them one better and make the test pilot, a short version of what the series could be; direct it myself, shoot it *Slam* style using real parolees, former criminals, working parole officers, and set it in the actual federal parole offices in Brooklyn. I loot Kim's and my joint business bank account, hire Mark Benjamin as my director of photography, and set out to make the test pilot for what will become *Street Time*.

One of the parole officers I got to know from the Eastern District Office, Larry Goldman, signs on to help me gain access to the Eastern District Parole Office space over a weekend. Yes, we are actually shooting a movie in the space where I used to come to report to Ms. Lawless; it's a bizarre feeling, a curious metamorphosis from parolee to director of a pilot about parolees. I cast Larry Goldman as one of the parole officers. I cast Norman Mailer in the role of Saul "Two Canes" Cahan (Norman at this point is walking with the help of two canes), an aging Jewish mobster who has a boisterous confrontation with his parole officer, played by Norman's son, Stephen Mailer, a talented film and stage actor. The climax of the short film comes when Norman's character is taken into custody and dragged out of the parole offices by two US marshals for associating with other known organized crime figures. Cahan's parole officer has video proof—surveillance footage of the old gangster ambling along Mulberry Street in Little Italy and making contact with a known wiseguy, played by an alleged associate of the Gambino Crime Family, and the owner of a Mulberry Street café, a fiend known as Baby John, whom I met while locked up in the MCC. The finished *Street Time* test pilot is twenty-eight minutes long. VCR tapes are sent to out Offsay, Gary Levine, and a third Showtime executive, Pancho Mansfield. Offsay orders a pilot script.

Here begins a classic struggle in the world of scripted TV series. There is a much-revered species of TV writer/producer known as a showrunner who bears most of the responsibility for getting a TV show made. The showrunner is the key point person who answers directly to the executives at the network and production company. Once I deliver my pilot script, the executives at Showtime, and now Sony TV, who have come on board as the production company, go back on a verbal agreement they made with me and decide that they want to bring in another writer and showrunner with experience producing a TV series. What? I thought we agreed that if there was to be a showrunner, that person would be a producer and not a writer. I am supposed to be the writer and creator of the series. Yes, that's true; but, as I am about to learn, or not learn, over and over again, these agreements in the so-called legitimate world, unless they are in writing and unless you are willing to go to court, mean nothing. This is not the pot business where a man or woman is only as good as his or her word and hand-shake, where a deal is a deal or there are unfortunate consequences. In the legitimate business world, particularly in Hollywood, words mean nothing unless they are in a signed and executed contract and often not even then.

Over my objection, Showtime and Sony insist on hiring a TV writer named Steve Kronish, who was a writer and showrunner on a series called *The Commish*. I'm willing to give it a try, as I want to see the show get on the air, and I'm willing to learn to do whatever it takes. But it quickly becomes apparent that Kronish and I are from two different worlds and two opposing creative concepts as to what *Street Time* should be. Kronish comes out of the Stephen J. Cannell school of formulaic network TV series. In our first meeting, Kronish says to me, "I'm not in this to reinvent TV. I just want to get a paycheck, and hopefully get a show on the air."

Offsay may say he wants what we did with *Slam*, but Kronish assures that is not what Offsay really wants. "These executives don't know what they want until you show it to them," Kronish says. "And besides, that kind of improvisational, documentary-style filmmaking will never work in a TV series." He is hired by Showtime to do a pass on my pilot script. Kronish ends up doing a page-one rewrite, changing everything, even the names of all the characters, and recreating their back stories, changing the locations, the plot, virtually rewriting everything I had written so that, in accordance with the rules set down by the Writer's Guild, he is eligible for a co-creator credit, and will make more money. The executives at Showtime, however, reject Kronish's script and decide to go with my original version for the two-hour pilot.

Next, we must find a director. I meet with a couple of possible TV directors, but no one works out for different reasons. "What about Marc Levin?" I suggest. "You want the look and feel of *Slam*, Levin is the man for the job." But, the executives object, Marc has never directed a TV pilot. And herein lies one of the fundamental problems with TV executives at this early stage in what has now become a renaissance in the world of scripted television drama: if it hasn't been done before, and often done to death, executives who are interested primarily in keeping their jobs and wary of doing anything original are reluctant to, as Kronish put it, "reinvent TV." It is TV series lore that all the major networks and cable channels passed on David Chase's *Sopranos* pilot until it landed on Chris Albrecht's desk at HBO. Albrecht, with shows like *Oz*, *The Sopranos*, and *Six Feet Under*, is the visionary TV executive largely responsible for revolutionizing scripted TV drama and ushering in the era of exceptional quality shows we enjoy now.

I hold out and continue to lobby for Marc Levin to direct the *Street Time* pilot. I maintain that with Marc directing, at least I know we'll get the show we want. Steve Glick throws his considerable weight behind Levin as well, and Glick is soon given the job of packaging the series through the auspices of the William Morris Agency. Showtime wants to cast Rob Morrow in the lead role as Kevin Hunter, a former marijuana and hashish smuggler coming out of prison on parole in the Special Offenders Unit and doing his utmost to leave his life of crime behind. Rob had a hit with *Northern Exposure*. Levin and I are both sold on the choice of Scott Cohen from *The Gilmore Girls* series as the lead parole officer, James Liberti, who is assigned to supervise Kevin Hunter. Scott has a crease between his eyebrows that says to me the man can play conflicted. And I am utterly blown away by a young African American actress, Erika Alexander, whom we cast as the tougher-than-nails, outspoken, sexy parole officer Dee Mulheren. Naturally Marc and I want to shoot the pilot in New York, but at this time the tax credits available in Canada and the exchange rate of US to Canadian dollars favor producing the pilot, and the series if green-lit, in Toronto.

I have another issue with shooting in Canada: the possibility that I will be arrested on a number of dormant criminal drug smuggling charges once I step foot on Canadian soil, or, possibly, that I will not be allowed to enter the country in the first place. My former partner in the marijuana and hashish importation and distribution business is the so-called Hippie Godfather of Canada, Robert "Rosie" Rowbotham, at one time the major wholesaler of cannabis of all North America. Rosie did close to seventeen years in prison on a number of cannabis arrests, all connected to our efforts during the 1970s and 1980s to keep North America high by importing the best quality marijuana from Colombia, Mexico, Jamaica, and Thailand, and premium grade hashish from Lebanon and Afghanistan. I have been assured that the Canadian charges were dropped once I was sentenced to twenty-five years and six months in prison in the United States. But after my success in getting the US sentence reduced to ten years, there was some talk that the Canadians might still demand their pound of flesh. Ivan Fisher makes some inquiries and is informed that there are no outstanding charges in Canada and, with the proper paperwork, I will be allowed to enter our neighboring country to the north with no fear of being arrested.

After what I am told by Steve Glick and others in the industry is a remarkably short time from pitch to production, a little over six months, with our cast in place, Marc and I move into production offices in Toronto to prep, then shoot and edit, the two-hour pilot episode of *Street Time*. Steve Kronish, though still the nominal showrunner, stays in LA, where he will view dailies and coordinate production with the executives at Showtime and Sony.

We may not reinvent TV, but we do manage to bring a lot of the *Slam* style of documentary filmmaking to a scripted TV series. The actors are encouraged to cover what's on the page, and then to go off script, which infuriates Kronish back in LA. At one point, in answer to his complaints, Erika Alexander, as parole officer Dee Mulheren, turns to face the camera straight on and tells Kronish to back off with his objections and accept that what the actors are doing and viewers are reacting to favorably is working and is not going to cease no matter how much he resists it.

OVER THE NEXT two and a half years, we produce and Showtime airs a total of thirty-three hours of *Street Time*. Near the wrap of season one, Steve Kronish takes to his bed in LA, refuses to get up, and suffers what we are told is a nervous breakdown. There is a frantic search in Hollywood for a new showrunner while I take over as the acting showrunner on the set in Toronto. It's pretty much what I have been doing all along: sitting and talking with the actors to help them understand what their characters are going through and what they are feeling so that they can build on that and give it more commitment and integrity. The lead actors are not asked to recite lines that they either don't understand or don't believe given whom they have come to portray until they can talk it over with me. This results in lengthy meetings in my trailer with the lead actors to help them understand my vision for how their character is developing, allow them to give me their input, and make changes accordingly. It's an extremely collaborative process and most of the actors love it and embrace it. New directors come in with each episode. From the start, I make it clear that I will not tolerate directors abusing actors, and I resolve to fire anyone who screams or throws tantrums on set. The idea is to get everybody on board—from the crew, to the director of photography, to the actors—and have them all become invested in making the series, in fostering the kind of creative energy we found in making *Slam*, and, to some degree, in reinventing TV. It's working. The shows just keep getting better. Marc Levin not only directs the pilot; he comes on as an executive producer and directs nine more episodes.

At one point, after Kronish has left the production and the search for a replacement continues, Jeanie Bradley, an executive from Sony who has been a consistent supporter, tells me to just keep doing what we are doing, and that everyone in LA loves what they see in the dailies and the finished episodes. We will prevail, she assures me, and I should not worry about their attempts to replace me as showrunner. They'll get over it.

DURING THE SECOND season, we manage to do something that is almost unheard of in scripted TV: we move the writer's room from LA to a space in the former Offline Entertainment offices. The lease for the space is bequeathed to Marc Levin as part of his settlement with Henri Kessler and David Pipers when the company implodes. Marc and I also get the go-ahead to hire a new team of writers who come out of different writing disciplines: playwriting, independent feature film, and even a former parole officer. Larry Goldman, the federal parole officer from the Eastern District Office who helped me make the test pilot, comes on as our full-time technical consultant with an occasional cameo role.

Steve Glick gets a call from Ron Meyer, a founding partner at Creative Artists Agency and the current head of Universal Studios. Meyer tells Glick that both he and David Geffen are huge fans of *Street Time*. He asks Glick if they can receive advance videocassettes of each episode as it is finished so they don't have to wait for the show to air on TV. I receive a letter from David Geffen telling me how much he enjoys *Street Time*, and he invites me to his home for lunch on my next visit to LA.

DESPITE THE SUCCESS of the show, I earn a reputation in Hollywood for being headstrong and difficult to control. This comes to a head during the filming of the series finale, which I write and direct. Part of the problem is that we get sets of notes from the executives at Showtime that are often in conflict with the notes we get from Sony. The executives, though they may never admit it, have opposing views of where the show needs to go and what it needs to become based on their different business models. Showtime wants a soap opera with ongoing storylines arced out over a number of episodes in the series to attract repeat viewers who become invested in the characters and tune in to see what is going to happen to them. Sony, hoping to sell the show to foreign distributors, wants episodes that are complete in and of themselves with an A story, B story, and C story that are all wrapped up by the end of each episode. As the head writer and executive producer, my goal is to do both: tell a discreet story with a beginning, middle, and end in each episode but also develop storylines that will play out and develop along with the main character's arcs and plotlines over the entire series. It's the nineteenth-century novel on TV.

The notes we get on the script for what will become the season and series finale from Showtime and Sony not only contradict each other, but they make no sense when we consider how we intend to wrap up our main characters' storylines. I am aware that these people have a lot going on in their professional lives; *Street Time* is only part of a very busy schedule for executives at Sony and Showtime. But I sometimes wonder if they are watching the same show.

When Marc and I read the notes before commencing production on the final episode, we look at each other and shake our heads. The general rule of thumb on network or studio notes tends to be to incorporate those changes that make sense and may even improve the show and to ignore those that do neither. This can be tricky. In my experience, male executives in particular tend to be territorial; they want to claim the material or some part thereof as their own, and they are most offended and angered if their notes are ignored. I get the feeling that the notes have more to do with an executive wanting to piss on our show, mark it as his territory. (Jeanie Bradley at Sony is only one female executive working on *Street Time*, and she inevitably gives the best notes and seems to be most in sync with what we are trying to do with the show.) What to do? Our characters have come a long way. Parole officer James Liberti, Scott Cohen's character, is having an affair with his parolee, Kevin Hunter's wife, Rachel Goldstein, played by Michelle Nolden, a beautiful and talented Canadian actress. Liberti is a degenerate gambler in debt to his bookie, and he's fixated on locking up Kevin Hunter both for personal and professional reasons. Rob Morrow's character has a younger brother, Peter Hunter played by an outstanding Canadian actor named Chris Bolton. Bolton embraces the *Slam* style. He turns in a tour de force performance as the evil twin alter ego to Morrow's character. Over the course of the series, Bolton has made his character one of the most compelling to watch and wonder where he will go. While Rob's character was in prison, his brother took over the drug operation and blew all Kevin's stash of money by building an elaborate nightclub and endeavoring to become a freak crime boss. At one point during the filming of a particularly intense scene, Rob Morrow objects and says to me, "Why are you doing this to me? I feel like you're cutting my balls off." I tell him, "Yes, go for it. That's exactly how your character should feel being on parole and given what he is dealing with and what is happening to him."

A finale that will bring the series to a satisfying conclusion calls for a tragic, novelistic climax. I embrace my own advice and go for it. The episode, though uneven, has its moments, and it does complete the arcs of the main characters. By any measure, the series is a success. Ratings are consistently high, and critical acclaim is unanimous. The show has attracted a committed fan base and may well have gone on longer were it not for the all-too-frequent TV series and feature film spoiler known as the executive shuffle. Just before we are set to wrap season three, there is a changing of the guard in the executive offices at Showtime. Jerry Offsay steps down, and TV executive Robert Greenblatt, formerly of Fox and the Greenblatt Janolari Studio takes his place. *Street Time* is the only show Greenblatt carries over into his tenure; but, after a third season when Greenblatt has had time to develop new shows under his auspices, *Street Time*'s run is ended, and I am out of a steady job.

Chapter Thirteen

ORIGINAL GANGSTER: JOE STASSI REDUX

I HAD OFTEN wondered what happened to Joe Stassi after his parole was violated and they sent him back to the joint at age eighty-nine. I'd lamented never gaining access to what he described as a treasure trove of personal letters, family and criminal cohort photographs, FBI reports, government exhibits, and trial transcripts from his life that would have given me a detailed, unique look at the criminal career of a man whose history spanned the early days of the immigrant experience in New York City, Prohibition, the founding of Cosa Nostra, the expansion of Italian organized crime to include partnerships with powerful Jewish mobsters in what became known as the National Crime Syndicate, the mob's move to Cuba and their ouster once Castro took over, the building of Las Vegas, and the eventual crackdown on the mob that some speculate resulted in the Kennedy killings. Joe was there and experienced it all. What a missed opportunity!

And then one day in 2001 I am sitting in my office at the *Street Time* writer's room, formerly the Offline Entertainment office space, when I am introduced to a woman, a doctor from California who specializes in treating rare immune system disorders. She has come to New York to consult with Offline's financial backer, David Piepers, who has been diagnosed with Lyme disease. She mentions in passing that she was met at the airport and delivered to our offices by two men, whose names she mentions. I recognize them as organized crime figures, one of whom I met and became friendly with while we were both doing time at the federal prison in Petersburg, Virginia.

I'm intrigued. Her mentioning their names strikes me as odd. I can't resist asking why she would be met at the airport and chauffeured to our offices by men who are associated with the Mafia. Well, she says, she doesn't usually tell people this, it's not something she wants known to the general public, but, given my history, she feels comfortable telling me that she and her brother are the illegitimate children of Charles "Charlie Lucky" Luciano, as the founder of organized crime in America is referred to by his close friends.

Now I'm beginning to think this is all some kind of setup, though what kind I have no idea. Really, I say, you're Lucky Luciano's daughter. How did that happen? Yes, she says, her mother, who was also a doctor living in Westchester, a married woman when she met Luciano, had a long affair with him, and gave birth to a daughter and son fathered by the father of the mob in America. My initial response is to disbelieve her. Surely, she is trying to sell me some phony bill of goods. There is a vague resemblance to Luciano. She's got the dark Sicilian looks, the full lips, and sensuous mouth of Charlie Lucky but—really? Could she be telling the truth? It seems too farfetched and contrived.

"Then you must know my friend, Joe Stassi," I say as a test.

Joe and Luciano were very close, childhood pals who remained best friends all their lives. If this supposed daughter of Luciano has never heard of Joe, or if she doesn't really know Joe and of his relationship with Luciano, my guess is she's a fraud.

"Oh, yes," she says, "I know Joe. I spoke to him just the other day."

"Where is he?" I ask. "Last I heard they locked him back up."

"He's out. He's living with his son's wife in Miami."

Now I am beginning to believe her. I give her my cell phone number and ask her to please give it to Joe. The next day, as I am driving upstate for the weekend, my cell phone rings. It's Joe Stassi.

"Richie," Joe says, "I thought I was never gonna hear from you again."

He tells me that he lost my contact numbers when they locked him back up and seized his property. When I ask him about the lady doctor and her claim to be Luciano's daughter, Joe says, "She's the real deal, her and her brother. I know them both from when they were little kids."

Unbelievable. This is even more amazing than running into Joe on the subway. The illegitimate daughter of Charles Luciano—who knew? And that she would walk into our offices and not only know Joe but be in touch with him; it's a clear message that I must act upon. I make plans to fly down to Miami and visit Joe to rekindle our friendship, and hopefully pick up where we left off with our agreement for me to tell his story. When I tell Marc Levin, he is equally intrigued and suggests that, if Joe is willing, we should film the meeting and see if we can make a documentary based on Joe's life. I take a video camera along with me to Florida to shoot a sample interview.

When I arrive in Miami, however, and call for Joe at his daughter-in-law's home in North Miami—a single-story tract home that looks like the house where the Hyman Roth character based on Meyer Lansky was living in *The Godfather Part II*—she tells me that Joe had a fall, and though he was not badly injured, he had heart palpitations, and he was taken to the hospital and admitted. She gives me the name and address of the hospital. I find Joe laid up, held against his will in a double-occupancy room. When I take out the camera and start to shoot a bedside interview, Joe's not having it.

"Put that thing away!" he growls at me. "You gotta get me outta this place, Richie. These doctors are gonna kill me."

"Joe . . . How am I supposed to do that? Are they ready to release you?"

"Never mind! What the fuck's the matter with you? Since when do you need permission? Go get a wheelchair and get me outta here or we're finished."

There's one thing about these old mob bosses: when they give an order, it has such gravitas, such authority that I'm sure comes from years of having given serious orders to serious men in grave circumstances, that one does not wish to refuse such an order for too little. Might as well give it a try. I go nab a vacant wheelchair, wheel it to Joe's bedside, lift the old man out of his bed, and place him the chair. Operating under the tried-and-true method of the bold way is the best way, simply acting like I know what I'm doing and therefore I must have permission, I wheel Joe onto an elevator and take us down to the front entrance. When asked by a hospital staff member to see his release papers, Joe gestures to him to clear our way through the main lobby.

"Don't worry about my fuckin' release papers. Just get outta the way," the old man snarls. "I'm leavin'."

I go for the rental car, drive around to the entrance, and, lo and behold, Joe is still there sitting in the wheelchair, and he has even solicited the attendant's help in pulling off his escape. Once the attendant and I load Joe into the front passenger seat of the car, I ask him, "Where to, Joe?"

"I'm hungry," he says. "Take me to the House of Pancakes."

When we get there, I can't manage to get Joe out of the car and into the IHOP by myself.

"Never mind," Joe snaps. "Just go in, get the pancakes. We'll take 'em home."

WHEN I TELL the editor at *GQ* magazine about my rekindled relationship with Joe, he's sold. He gives me an assignment to write an article. "Oldest Living Mafioso Tells All" is published in the September 2001 issue. Marc Levin, Mark Benjamin, and I begin filming a series of interviews with Joe, first at his daughter-in-law's home in Miami, then in New York during a nostalgic trip to the Lower East Side neighborhood around Stanton Street where Joe was born and grew up, and later at some of the locations in New Jersey he frequented when he became a major bootlegger and powerful ambassador at large with the Genovese Crime Family.

Joe's wife of over sixty years, Frances Paxton, a Southern girl and former Miss America, died while Joe was back in prison on the parole violation. His son, Joe Junior, I learn, is a fugitive. And Joe's daughter wants nothing to do with him. Except for his daughter-in-law, Olga, the old man is alone in the world. Even while we were still locked up— when Joe first told me parts of his story and I read his file and learned of his background while I worked on his case, ultimately getting him released from prison—Joe denied any involvement in the narcotics business. He is so old school, so in denial about some aspects of his personal criminal history and about the mob in general that he'll admit to any number of murders, but narcotics? No, never; Joe will never cop to having dealt or imported heroin, and yet both his cases—his arrest and conviction in Texas and later when Joe was implicated in the French Connection investigation in New York City while he was in custody at the penitentiary in Atlanta, which resulted in his being tried and found guilty a second time—both convictions were for importation of narcotics. The parole violation that got him sent back to prison was also part of an investigation into organized crime heroin trafficking. Yet Joe remains steadfast in claiming that he was hounded by the Justice Department under Bobby Kennedy, pursued, arrested, and convicted because, as Joe says, Bobby Kennedy believed Joe had information about his brother Jack's killing (which, I'm certain, he does) and not because Joe was a major narcotics trafficker, professional killer, and a high-level member of the Genovese Crime Family.

At one point early in our renewed collaboration, while sitting in the rear garden at Olga's home in Miami, I ask Joe what he would like to do, and whom he would most like to see in these twilight years of his long and illustrious life of crime. Joe tells me, "I want to go back to New York and eat some decent food," and, he says, "I want you to bring me Arnold Stone."

Arnold Stone? I expected he would want to see his son or his daughter. But no, Joe wants to see Arnold Stone, the former Justice Department prosecutor under Robert Kennedy who, Joe claims, knows the truth of how and why Joe was targeted by the government, why he was hounded until his arrest in Boca Raton, Florida, and then prosecuted—not because of his stature in organized crime, no, but because he refused to cooperate with the government after he fled Cuba and was forced to give up his business interests there and return to the United States, having lost nearly everything. All this, Joe tells me, he can prove because it's all right there, in the files, in the documents, in the papers he has collected and saved all these years.

"Where are the papers now, Joe?" I ask him.

"Ah, this fuckin' bum," he says. "When I lost touch with you, Richie . . . when they locked me up, I lost all of my numbers. They took everything. I never would've found you, you never woulda found me if it hadn't been for that girl, Charlie Lucky's daughter. This other writer comes to me through a lawyer I know, and he says *he's* gonna write my story. Now . . . I give him all the boxes. He drives up from Florida in a truck and picks up all the boxes . . . with everything in 'em, all my papers."

"Okay, yeah, so . . . where are they now?"

"I don't know. He tells me he put 'em in some storage place or something. . . . You gotta ask him. I'll give you all the information. He never wrote a fuckin' word, this bum."

I MAKE ONE of my periodic trips to Hollywood to pitch the Stassi documentary in search of funding. Sheila Nevins at HBO passed on Joe's story; apparently, she has an aversion to old men. So far, Marc's company, Blowback, has been footing the bill. But as we plan to ramp up production, we need additional financing. Back while I was publishing *Prison Life* magazine, we did a cover story, "Hollywood Goes to Prison," featuring an interview with Oliver Stone around the time of the release of his film *Natural Born Killers*. Oliver and I became friends. We met again when we were both guests at the taping of a segment of Bill Maher's HBO show "Politically Incorrect," and I usually call Oliver and try to meet with him whenever I am in LA.

Oliver had been after me to introduce him to legendary ex-convict writer Eddie Bunker. Eddie had also been the subject of a *Prison Life* cover story and had become a close friend. We devoted one whole issue of the magazine to an excerpt from Eddie's classic prison novel, *Animal Factory*. When I call Oliver, he tells me he's hosting a dinner at a Chinese restaurant and asks me to bring Eddie Bunker. I pick Eddie up at his home in LA, and we drive to the restaurant where we are to meet Oliver. We arrive on time at eight o'clock. The hostess tells us we are the first to arrive and escorts us to a large private dining room. Soon other guests begin to wander in. A fellow who claims to be Oliver's psychiatrist joins us at the table set for at least twenty guests. Other characters arrive with stories of how they know Oliver, and then several beautiful Asian women join the gathering.

A good hour and a half after we arrive, Oliver is still nowhere in sight. Eddie is getting impatient. "Fuck this," he says, "I'm ordering food." Soon everyone follows suit, and dinner is served. I sit beside a gorgeous young Korean woman named Jayne Ku, who tells me she interviewed Oliver for Korean TV. When she asks me what I'm working on, I tell her about the Joe Stassi project, and she's fascinated. Koreans, Jayne tells me, love stories about American gangsters. She asks for my number in New York and says she'll be in touch. Finally, at around 10:30, after Eddie and I have eaten and Oliver still hasn't shown up, Eddie demands that I take him home. "Enough already," he says. "Let's go."

Later, past midnight, I am in bed back in my hotel room at the Chateau Marmont when the phone rings. It's Oliver. "Where are you guys?" he wants to know. "Where's Bunker? Why did you leave?"

Before I leave LA, Jayne Ku and I meet for lunch. She takes me home and introduces me to her parents. She says she is in talks with a wealthy Korean, a Mister Lee, whom Jayne thinks might be interested in funding the Joe Stassi documentary. Would I be interested in meeting Mr. Lee? Of course I would. Great, Jayne says, she will set it up.

The gods of film financing work in mysterious ways. You never know where the money might come from when looking for funding for a film project. You might meet a beautiful Korean woman who has a friend who loves gangster stories. My rule of thumb has become to chase every lead, pursue every possible source for money no matter how unlikely it may seem. When I tell Marc about Jayne Ku and her potential backer, Mr. Lee, Marc is all for following up. So when Jayne calls and asks us to meet her and Mr. Lee at Disney World in Orlando, Florida, we fly down and check in to a hotel. Our first night in Disney World, we have dinner with Jayne and Mr. Lee. He and Jayne would like to meet Joe. Of course, I will arrange it. Last I heard, Joe and his daughter-in-law were in the process of relocating to a new home in Kissimmee, not far from Disney World. Perhaps I can arrange for them to meet Joe while they are both here in Florida.

Mr. Lee speaks very little English. When Jayne translates, he takes out a packet of $1,000 traveler's checks, signs all of them, and hands them to Marc. There will be more money, he says, as needed. His one stipulation is that we agree to give Jayne a role as a producer. Yes, by all means, we are more than happy to bring Jayne on. Jayne says she's ready to relocate to New York to work on the film. But first, of course, Mr. Lee and Jayne want to meet Joe.

It's love at first sight. Joe is utterly smitten with the beautiful and gracious Jayne Ku. And she couldn't be more charming and solicitous. She holds and caresses Joe's wizened, liver-spotted hands. She gazes into his milky eyes and asks him how he feels.

"Are you all right, Joe?" she coos. "Can I get you anything?"

It's a done deal. Jayne will move to New York right away. Joe also will come to New York to eat some good food and revisit his old haunts while we film his journey back into his past. Mr. Lee will return to South Korea and arrange to have additional funds wired into an account set up for the production; Marc will have his lawyer draw up an agreement.

All proceeds according to plan until the *GQ* issue with my article "Oldest Living Mafioso Tells All" is published. Joe demands that I come to see him at Olga's in Kissimmee immediately. Marc Levin and Mark Benjamin come along to film the showdown. When we arrive at Olga's, Joe is apoplectic. If he weren't confined to a wheelchair, if he weren't nearly a hundred years old and could get to his feet and wrap his gnarled hands around my neck, if he had the strength, he would throttle me. If he had a gun, he would shoot me and bury me in Olga's backyard.

"Why, Joe, what did I do?"

"What did you do? You made me a rat!" Joe rants.

Made him a rat! Now I am the one who is angry. I made him a rat? I got the old gangster out of prison. I wrote the story he told me, and the story he wanted me to tell. What's he talking about?

There is only one way for me to deal with this. I know, at least I believe from past experience with wiseguys and in my previous dealings with Joe that I must not—no, I cannot just sit here and let him berate me. I cannot cower and allow myself to be intimidated by Joe or he will lose all respect for me. I have been called on the carpet. I have been summoned to report to a boss, and only a spirited and equally threatening defense will have any merit in Joe's eyes.

"What the fuck are you talking about, I made you a rat? You're the one who wanted me to tell your story. Not one word I wrote in that article came from anywhere but from you; every fucking word is what you told me, Joe! What you said you did! What you wanted me to tell as your story! How the fuck does that make you a rat?"

I'm on my feet, in Joe's face now, and ready to fuck him up no matter how old and infirm he may be. The man insulted me; he won't get away with it.

Joe is seated before a folding table on which there is a bowl of soup and a spoon. He's shaking the tray, rattling the bowl and spoon, barely able to contain his rage. I'm thinking any second he'd going to pick up the bowl and hit me over the head with it, make to gouge my eyes out with the spoon.

"What's this?" Joe says and stabs a page of the magazine with his finger. "How could you write this? Are you out of your goddamn mind?"

He points to photographs of Charlie "Lucky" Luciano and Meyer Lansky and to the caption under the pictures that identifies who the men are, and states, "men for whom Stassi worked, and murdered."

"How could you write this? Are you crazy? I didn't murder these men! I loved these men."

Oh, Jesus, now I get it. Joe may not have even read the entire article. I don't know if he can still read given his failing eyesight. But someone, maybe Olga, read him the caption under the photographs, and Joe completely misunderstood what it says.

"That's not what it says, Joe. Listen to me. It says that you *worked* for Meyer and Charlie Lucky, and that you *carried out hits* for them, under their orders, which is what you told me. The hit on Dutch Shultz. The guy you killed, your best friend, on orders from Meyer and Abe Zwillman. These are stories you told me that are in the article. It doesn't say you killed Lansky and Luciano; it says you killed *for* them."

We make up and embrace. I tell Joe I love him, and it's true, I do love the old killer, the multiple murderer, as insane as that may sound. We did time together. I lived in the next cell to Joe for three years, saw more of him day in and day out, and at closer quarters, than perhaps any other person I've ever known, including some ex-wives. I sat with him in his cell nearly every night and listened to his stories. When the arthritis in his hands became so painful he couldn't write legibly anymore, I used to go to his cell in the evening before lockdown and write letters he dictated to his family and friends. He always began with the salutation, "Dear so and so, how are you? As for me, I'm doing good." His cell was spotless, everything put away in its proper place. He would get down on his hands and knees and clean the floor. Joe did time like a captured enemy general. He never complained. He kept to himself. He rarely associated with the other organized crime prisoners in the joint, and they treated him with the respect due a don of his stature and history. He never mouthed off or bitched to the guards. His one comment to me about staff was, "They treat us better than we would treat them."

Much of my affection I feel for the old gangster comes from my own misguided youthful admiration of criminals. Growing up watching *The Untouchables* on TV and finding Al Capone much more compelling than uptight Eliot Ness. Then of course there are the Francis Ford Coppola *Godfather* films that further inculcated the myth of the honorable Mafioso. There was that adolescent urge to belong to something larger than myself—a gang, an army, a crime family, a band of brothers who took a vow and would be there beside you and have your back come what may. Joe Stassi was everything the government said he was, and that included being an organized crime member of unique status, trusted and respected by the legendary bosses of the underworld.

Once Joe understands what I wrote, and after I attack him verbally and threaten to walk out and abandon the project, he tells me to sit down and relax.

"Bring me Arnold Stone," he repeats.

It is a commandment with biblical overtones and one that I am determined to carry out.

AFTER SOME RESEARCH, I locate Arnold Stone, who is still alive and well and practicing law in Carteret County, North Carolina. When I reach him on the phone and say the name Joe Stassi, he takes a breath.

"That's a name I haven't heard in a long time," Arnold Stone says.

As well as being a lawyer and former Justice Department prosecutor under Bobby Kennedy, Arnold Stone is something of a literary man with some experience in the film business. He co-wrote a one-man play called *Secret Honor* about Richard Nixon that was performed in Los Angeles at the Actors Theater in 1983 and ran for three weeks

Off-Broadway. *Secret Honor* won Play of the Year and was produced as a film directed by Robert Altman in 1984.

Arnold Stone is surprised to learn that Joe Stassi is still alive. Would he be willing to come to Florida with me to visit with Joe and let us film the meeting?

"Why? What on earth for?" Stone asks. I tell him of the magazine article and of our production to make a documentary film about Joe's life.

But why, Arnold Stone repeats, why—first of all, why did Joe agree to be involved in such a project? And, secondly, why should he, Arnold Stone, agree to participate?

"Why?" I say, "Why, in the interests of history." Of course.

I go on to tell him that Joe has made certain claims about the government and about why the Justice Department was so interested in capturing him.

Arnold Stone says, "Well, how about the fact that Stassi was a major figure in organized crime. Joe Stassi was designated a 'Top Hoodlum' by the FBI and pursued by the Justice Department in an effort to identify and indict all the major organized crime figures of the era. Organized crime was and still is a threat to the economy and the integrity of our nation. Joe was suspected of firsthand involvement in several organized crime contract killings."

Yes, I say, but what about the whole Kennedy thing and Joe's close association with Carlos Marcello and Santo Trafficante and the long-whispered theories that those two and others were involved in the assassination of the president and senator? I tell Stone that I have long been good friends with Richard Goodwin, who worked under both Jack and Bobby Kennedy in the White House and who told me that Bobby was convinced the Mafia had a hand in killing his brother.

"Well," Stone says, "that's a whole different matter. Yes, we were certainly interested in anything Stassi might have had to say about that . . . and about a good many other things, crimes that remain unsolved to this day, and about which Mr. Stassi no doubt has significant information. We were definitely interested in having him come in after he fled Cuba and agree to be debriefed with regard to a number of . . . events we were aware that Mr. Stassi had firsthand information about."

So, I say to Arnold Stone, this is your chance to ask Stassi about some of those events—the last chance anyone may ever have. I appeal to him based on his literary accomplishments: "This will be like bringing Sherlock Holmes and Moriarty together at the end of their careers."

He chuckles. "That's pretty good," he says. "Holmes and Moriarty . . ."

I am to let him think it over and call me back.

Arnold Stone is a man with an adventurous streak and an interest in history. When he calls back, Stone asks if Joe will answer his questions. "Well," I say, "you know Joe. But he specifically asked for you. So let's give it a try, and see what the old Mafioso is willing to divulge after all these years of silence."

NOT MUCH, AS it turns out. In fact, very little. It's as though Joe simply wants to face the man whom he believes is responsible for his capture and long imprisonment, to be in the same room with him and gauge his substance, look into his eyes after so many years of dwelling upon him in his mind. Or maybe he just wants to prove that he endured all the government brought to bear and he survived. It's like putting two ex-heavyweight fighters together long after they have both left the ring, to let them come to peaceful terms, and see how each other has weathered the tests of time and chance. So if Joe is still who he became as a young man, still an old-school gangster, and he won't budge or give up his long-held secrets, he's stayed in character, and it makes for good drama to put these two arch enemies together opposite each other in the waning years of both their lives, and let them look into each other's eyes, gain the measure of the man in old age, and get the feel of the human being, the long-imagined foe gazing back at them.

Arnold Stone is no less in character. Typical prosecutor, his first question after the two men meet and greet one another is, "Mr. Stassi, were you a made member of organized crime?" Joe, equally intransigent, answers equivocally. "Yes, and no," he says. To which Stone rejoins, "Tell me about the yes, and tell me about the no."

In so many words, Joe answers that he was grandfathered in. They were kids running in the streets of New York, doing errands for what was known in those early years as the Black Hand. There was no formal swearing in or induction ceremony until later. He goes on to say that because of his childhood friendship with such men as Meyer Lansky and Ben "Bugsy" Siegel, and because he was Sicilian and had respect from the bosses of the Italian crime families, he developed a unique position as a kind of ambassador at large, someone who could go wherever he wanted, do whatever he wanted to do, work with different people from all the different ethnic criminal groups without answering to anyone in particular other than Meyer and Abe, who treated him as an equal.

Yes, it's true; Joe admits he had a falling out with Santo Trafficante in Cuba over the running of their club and casino the Sans Souci. And, yes, it's also true Joe had a meeting, as reported by the FBI, with Carlos Marcello and Santo Trafficante in New York City exactly one year before the Kennedy assassination.

"What did you talk about with Mr. Marcello and Mr. Trafficante?" Stone asks.

"Nothing," Joe deadpans. "We had breakfast."

"The Kennedys?"

"We may have talked about them, and how Bobby, that little son of a bitch, what he done to Carlos. But—" Joe is emphatic: "Santo didn't have the balls; Santo couldn't do anything . . . unless he had someone else to do it for him."

"Some patsy?" I ask. "Someone like Lee Harvey Oswald?"

Joe clams up. "I don't know," he says. "I never met Oswald."

"What about Jack Ruby?" I say.

"What about him?"

"Was he mobbed up?" Arnold Stone asks.

"Well," Joe says and shrugs, "you should know. You were the man in the Justice Department. Ruby . . . Yeah, Ruby was from Chicago. He had joints in Texas, nightclubs. So, you gotta figure, he knew people."

"People like Sam Giancana?" Stone keeps up the grilling.

"Sam was a good man," Joe asserts. "He never talked to nobody."

And that's about as much as we are going to get out of Joe, at least at this point. He's happy that we came through and brought him Arnold Stone. And for his part, Arnold Stone is equally impressed.

"He's like a sphinx," Stone says on the drive to the airport. "You look into those eyes, it's like looking into the eyes of some mythical creature who knows so much . . . has seen and done so much that he will never divulge. Did you ask him about the hit on Albert Anastasia?" Stone asks, referring to the famous barbershop murder of the so-called Lord High Executioner who had fallen out with the other bosses.

"Yes," I say. "And Joe did admit that he planned it."

"Well," Arnold Stone comments, "we had plenty of evidence that Joe came up from Cuba and put the assassination team together, that he made sure Anastasia showed up for his morning shave, and then stuck around to see the killing carried out before he went back to Havana. Maybe not enough evidence to charge and convict Stassi beyond a reasonable doubt, but we certainly had no doubt. It was Stassi, just one of many major killings Stassi planned and executed for the mob. When it came to that kind of thing Joe was in a class all by himself. You should ask his son, Joe Junior . . . if you can locate him. He's still wanted by the FBI."

THE FILMING CONTINUES with Joe's second request, that we bring him back to New York City so he can eat some good food, and even revisit some of his old stomping grounds from his earliest days as a bootlegger and killer in Newark, New Jersey. Jayne Ku comes along to accompany him. It's a trip down a grisly memory lane. Jayne flew to Florida, and then she and Joe fly to New York together. We put Joe up in a Manhattan hotel. Jayne has already moved into a midtown apartment paid for by Mr. Lee. Joe is confined to a wheelchair by this time. He's incontinent and so made to wear a diaper. Jayne has become his traveling companion. If nothing else, this project will have managed to warm some long dormant and hardened cockles in the old man's heart.

We take Joe to the West Orange, New Jersey, mansion where a man Joe considered his closest friend, the man he most admired, Abner "Longy" Zwillman, who Joe calls Abe, allegedly hanged himself in the basement when summoned to testify before the McClellen Committee Hearings on Organized Crime in 1959. There were rumors at the time that Zwillman had been murdered on orders from Luciano to prevent him from testifying. If Joe knows the truth, he's not willing to say. He'll admit only to being deeply saddened by Zwillman's death.

We spend a day in and around Newark, visiting the location of the original chophouse where Dutch Shultz was ambushed, and Joe recounts how he lured Shultz to a bogus business meeting at the restaurant, where he was met by a barrage of bullets from a hit team of practiced Jewish killers Joe recruited from the old Murder, Inc. mob. And we take him to one of his homes, a mansion he lived in while he worked with Zwillman running the gambling rackets in New Jersey. Joe was known as Hoboken Joe. The current owner of the home comes out and is thrilled to meet the actual Hoboken Joe, about whom she has heard so much, and she brings her young children out to meet the old gangster.

At a deli in the theater district, the owner is amazed to see that Joe is still alive. He recalls how Stassi was revered by all the top gangsters of the era. When we bring him to the hotel where Joe lived until he was forced to leave by Joe Kennedy Sr., who was having an affair with one of Joe's lady friends, he freaks out, starts protesting that he's been permanently banned from the premises. We have to remind him that was over fifty years ago.

MARC AND I travel to the Dominican Republic where we meet with Joe's son, Joe Stassi Junior, in a bar and brothel. Joe Junior tells us of his childhood, growing up in Havana as the son of one of the most influential American underworld figures of the era. His father wanted his son to go to a good prep school in the States, go to college, and become a legitimate businessman. But early on Joe Junior had a hankering for the Cuban ladies and for his father's glamorous gangster life. He soon quit school and went to work for his father in the casino at the Sans Souci. His dad, Joe Junior tells us, was highly regarded by all the bosses of the different families, not only those in New York but also the Tampa, New Orleans, and Chicago families, for his acumen and skill at resolving critical disputes. When there was an issue, some disagreement or problem that involved high-level members from different families, Joe was often consulted, asked to mediate and to deliver a ruling. He would listen patiently to both sides, hear any other evidence from outside sources, and then he would retire to his home and spend however long it took him in seclusion as he deliberated and reached his decision. He would then call the parties to meet and deliver his verdict. Men from all over the world of organized crime would come to Havana specifically to ask Joe for advice on how to settle disputes.

Perhaps the most debated revelation Joe proclaimed, which still has so-called experts on organized crime disputing his version of events, involves the murder of Joe's childhood friend, Ben "Bugsy" Siegel. As recounted in the *GQ* article, Joe claimed that it was not the mob who shot and killed Siegel, supposedly on orders from Lansky and Luciano, but it was actually the brother of Siegel's girlfriend, Virginia Hill. Joe told me he was sent to Los Angeles by Luciano and Lansky soon after Siegel's murder to determine who was responsible. Hill's brother was an ex-Marine, a sharpshooter who Joe determined shot Siegel from across the street with a high-powered rifle. He was even able to locate the owner of the gas station where Virginia Hill's brother kept the weapon he used to kill Siegel. When Joe reported his findings to Luciano and

Lansky, the decision was made not to retaliate since Siegel's killing had been over a personal matter and not business.

"Listen to me," Joe says, "if we are gonna kill a guy like Ben Siegel, we wouldn't do it with a rifle from across the street. We would have some friend, someone Ben trusted, shoot him in the head and make sure he was dead, and then leave the gun."

The original story of Siegel's killing, as recounted in *The Last Testament of Lucky Luciano* by Martin A. Gosch, and then accepted as mob lore, that Siegel was killed on orders from Luciano and Lansky at a sit-down in Havana because of the runaway costs of building the Flamingo Casino in Las Vegas is, according to Joe, all nonsense. "Meyer loved Ben. Charlie Lucky, all the bosses who invested money in Vegas knew it was gonna be a gold mine. Ben was an honorable man. Nobody was worried about getting their money back. It was Virginia Hill's brother who killed Ben because Ben beat her up. And that's the truth, that's the real story."

MARC AND I complete a short version of the documentary, a teaser, and screen it at the Tribeca Film Center to a full house, a good 20 percent of which is made up of former gangsters and actors who play gangsters. I also screen the teaser at the Hudson River Film Festival and sit for a Q and A after the screening. One fellow in the audience, who I suspect is an FBI agent, wants to know where and under what conditions we met with Joe Stassi Junior. I am left to ponder the impact of Stassi Senior's life of crime on his family. From what I'm able to gather, Joe Stassi Junior is wanted by the government as much for what he supposedly knows about his father's life as for what he personally may have done.

Joe Senior's wife, who as a young beauty queen was forced to forfeit her title when it was learned she had been married and divorced, lived without her husband most of the years of their marriage. Joe's daughter, once she realized who her father was and what he had done, would have nothing more to do with him. Joe Junior, at the top of his class in prep school, refused to return to school after his Christmas vacation as a teenager in Havana, seduced by his father's life and the sexy Cuban women.

Mr. Lee, ah, yes, let us not forget Mr. Lee. What was his hidden agenda? No great mystery there. How many men of means foray into the movie business in hopes of getting laid? A good many, we may presume. Harvey Weinstein is not alone. And how many film projects have foundered on the unrequited lusts of horny financiers? Mr. Lee may join the legions, as he underestimated the resolve of good Jayne Ku. She was not giving it up, at least not for married Mr. Lee. No, this was a business transaction, not an assignation, no agreement to become a kept woman. Jayne is a woman of real aspirations. When it became clear to Mr. Lee that he wasn't getting any, he shut off the cash flow and disappeared. Jayne was forced to give up her Manhattan apartment and return to LA. Marc and I were left with hours of unedited film, archival footage that would need to be licensed to be used, and a main character, original gangster Joe Stassi, who was increasingly shuttered in his own dark memories and paranoid fears, tormented by his murderous rage and his guilt-ridden memories, still rummaging in his wallet looking for the numbers of long-dead hitmen to put a contract out on me for telling his story, for enabling him to violate his oath of omertà—the man who liberated him from prison so he could curse the world at large.

Joe died in 2009 at age ninety-five, alone, sequestered in a nursing home. And what of his papers, that collection of documents and photographs and letters that would enable me to tell the real story, Joe's story, what he saw and what he did, the true story of the founding years and personalities of organized crime in America? The papers supposedly moldered in a storage unit somewhere in Florida. They were soaked with rain from a leaky roof, Joe told me, and never recovered. Like Joe's misspent life, the records of his time on earth, saturated and spoiled, turned to waste.

Chapter Fourteen

THE INFORMER: WHITEY BULGER AND THE FBI

*We loathed informers. It wasn't a conspiratorial thing—
our folklore bled with the names of informers who had
sold out their brethren to hangmen and worse in the lands
of our ancestors.*

—William "Billy" Bulger, *While the Music Lasts*

I AM INVITED to meet Sonny Grosso, a former New York City narcotics detective who is now a successful producer of film and TV. After a long and celebrated career as a detective—Sonny was one of the detectives who made the famous French Connection case—he has gone on to achieve an even more auspicious success as the producer of *The French Connection*, the classic, multiple-Academy-Award-winning crime film directed by William Friedkin and starring Gene Hackman and Roy Scheider. Sonny was one of the creators of the long-running reality show *Cops*, and he and his LA-based partner have made a number of TV films, series, and documentaries.

When Sonny and I meet in the spring of 2002, he's intrigued to learn that I met and had dealings with infamous Boston crime boss James "Whitey" Bulger. Sonny, who says he is a fan of *Street Time*, wants me to meet former special agent John Connolly, Whitey Bulger's beleaguered FBI handler. Connolly is out on bail awaiting trial in federal court in Boston on numerous charges related to his long, complex, and now allegedly criminal relationship with Bulger and Bulger's right-hand man, Stevie "the Rifleman" Flemmi. Both were what are known as Top Echelon (TE) Criminal Informers, who worked closely with the FBI while also running a lucrative and murderous criminal enterprise. Top Echelon informers are allowed to continue to commit crimes and promised they will never be revealed as informants, never be arrested for their crimes, and never have to face trial and imprisonment so long as they continue to provide valuable information to their FBI agent handlers.

John Connolly's relationship with Bulger was the subject of a book, *Black Mass*, by two Boston newspaper reporters, Dick Lehr and Gerard O'Neil, which is to be the basis of a movie. Like nearly all of the reporting done on the case, *Black Mass* portrays Connolly as a corrupt federal agent acting on his own to become a co-conspirator with Bulger and Flemmi in their long reign as major players associated with a multiethnic criminal group known as the Winter Hill Gang. It's a superficial understanding of the TE/FBI relationship at best.

Sonny Grosso, John Connolly, and I meet for dinner at a restaurant a few blocks from Sonny's offices on Third Avenue. Both Sonny and Connolly are relieved to learn that I'm already familiar with the long-held secrets of what is known as the FBI's Top Echelon Informant Program. I had received a tip and written a magazine article entitled "The Grim Reaper's Girlfriend," published in the August 1996 issue of *Penthouse*, about another murderous wiseguy, Colombo Family capo Greg Scarpa, who had personally killed a number of enemy combatants during the bloody Colombo Family internecine wars, while a member of the elite FBI/TE club.

So, I get it; I know how the FBI/TE relationship works, and I'm not shocked or scandalized to hear that the FBI had long-standing deals with high-level mobsters of the likes of Jimmy Bulger, Stevie Flemmi, and Greg Scarpa. The program works. Major government prosecutions, including the case that made Rudy Giuliani's career as a prosecutor, the Commission Case in New York—in which the bosses of all five Mafia families were convicted and sentenced to hundreds of years in prison—were based largely on information the FBI got from Scarpa and other TE informers. And in Boston, the New England Patriarca Crime Family was decimated through information the bureau got from Flemmi and Bulger, provided by Special Agent John Connolly.

Law enforcement depends on information gathered from informers. In order to arrest and convict the bosses of sophisticated, secret criminal groups, agents need access to intelligence from the highest levels of organized crime. That kind of information can only come from members or trusted associates who are accepted, respected, and often feared in criminal circles, men who are killers themselves and therefore never suspected of working for the FBI and yet are willing to work in the informer's dangerous netherworld.

The TE program worked for John Connolly and his supervisors in the bureau for many years. The FBI was even able to record an actual Mafia induction ceremony based on tips from Bulger and Flemmi, and the recording was used as evidence in organized crime cases all over the country to prove the existence of the various crime families. But then, a decade after Connolly retired, having been feted and decorated, extolled as a hero, a new federal prosecutor arrived in Boston. Around this time, the Scarpa case involving FBI handler Linley DeVecchio broke in New York. The Justice Department and FBI circled the wagons and went into cover-up mode. The new prosecutor in Boston reviewed the Bulger and Flemmi file and decided to renege on the deal, to go after Bulger and Flemmi and deny there ever was a "special relationship" between the two gangsters and the FBI. Even though he was retired, Connolly was called in and told he would have to go along with the change of policy, admit everything he knew about the crimes of Whitey and Flemmi, and disclaim their covert relationship with the FBI—indeed, maintain that no such relationship ever existed—and disclose everything he knew about other Boston-based

FBI agents who may have been involved in working with TE criminal informants. More importantly, Connolly was ordered to divulge everything he knew about Whitey's younger brother, William Bulger, the former president of the Massachusetts State Senate, and current president of the University of Massachusetts—specifically what Billy Bulger may have known about his brother's criminal activity and his current whereabouts as a fugitive. Connolly refused.

When he refused to go along with the cover-up, Connolly was charged with accepting cash gifts from Whitey and with obstruction of justice for allegedly tipping Whitey off that he was about to be indicted and arrested in Boston, thus supposedly enabling Whitey to flee. When Connolly and I meet, Whitey is still the subject of one of the largest international manhunts ever mounted. He is second only to Osama Bin Laden on the FBI's Ten Most Wanted list and will assume first place after Bin Laden is captured and killed.

Like many others, I was surprised to learn that Whitey had been an FBI informer. Still, it made perfect sense. When one considered how an Irish crime boss from South Boston associated with the ragtag, infiltrated, and much-indicted Winter Hill Gang had managed to survive and even thrive during the bloody Boston gang wars, there had to be more to the story. And when one saw how Whitey remained unscathed on the sidelines and then rose to power as the Patriarca Crime Family was wiped out with dozens of arrests and convictions based on multiple informers, wiretaps, and surveillance videos, including the recording of a Mafia induction ceremony, the pieces of the puzzle came together when it was revealed that Whitey had been protected by the FBI, and much of the success of the FBI's war on organized crime in New England and New York could be attributed to Whitey, Flemmi, and other TE informers.

Of course. That's how it works. It's the art of war, right out of Sun Tzu. Whitey was a student of military warfare tactics. He would have seen the advantages of working both sides to his benefit.

Connolly is relieved to know that not only is there no need for him to try to explain the TE program and the handler/informer relationship and process to me, but that I'm sympathetic, even respectful of his decision not to double-cross Whitey and Flemmi. That is the agreement he made, and it is not a deal one reneges on for too little. Certainly, I respect Connolly's resolve not to rat on his fellow agents or give evidence on his close friend, Billy Bulger, whether or not Billy actually had any substantive information on the whereabouts of his fugitive older brother. I'm willing to believe Connolly is not corrupt, that in fact he was just doing his job and doing it well, as directed by his superiors in the bureau, and with approval from the highest levels within the Department of Justice, going all the way up to the attorney general's office. The government had declared war on organized crime, specifically on Cosa Nostra, and in such a war it is often necessary to make deals with enemy combatants and turn them into spies.

How then to account for the fact that there were now federal and local prosecutors eager to make Connolly and fellow FBI agent and TE handler Lin DeVecchio scapegoats or fall guys for the controversial program? The simple answer is careerism. Prosecutors in Boston and New York are willing to hang Connolly and DeVecchio out to dry, make them take the heat for the inevitable scandal once the TE program is revealed, in order to enhance their own careers while protecting higher-ups in the Justice Department and federal government who had signed off on the TE program. The TE program itself was to be covered up and denied, with the Bulger and Scarpa cases made out to be aberrations rather than part of bureau policy.

I like Connolly. Despite my long career as an outlaw, or perhaps because of it, I understand what it takes to survive in that world both as a criminal and as a cop. You are only as good as your word, and you are only successful if you are working with reliable information and dependable, loyal partners. No matter that Whitey and Flemmi are vicious criminals; that was understood. They had valuable inside intelligence on high-ranking members of the Patriarca Family. They had access to the bosses' inner sanctums, the backrooms where the conspiracies were conceived. Of course, it gets dicey working with gangsters and killers like Flemmi, Scarpa, and master manipulator and murderer James Whitey Bulger. Innocent civilians suffer and die. That was never part of the deal, but such is war. Look at how many innocent women and children perished in Vietnam or in Afghanistan and Iraq.

In New York, the bureau rallies around Lin DeVecchio, and he beats the case brought against him by prosecutors in Brooklyn. It's another story for John Connolly in federal court in Boston. There are other factors at work. Connolly is caught up in a local power struggle that goes back decades and involves class and ethnic warfare. Whitey is still at large, and Billy Bulger still has powerful enemies who would like nothing better than to see him disgraced and jailed along with his brother.

At trial in federal court in Boston in 2002, Connolly's FBI supervisor, John Morris, an admitted corrupt alcoholic who accepted cases of wine, airplane tickets, and money from Whitey and Flemmi, had made a deal with the government to avoid prosecution and testified against Connolly. Morris told of a phone call he got from a "Mr. White" after Bulger fled Boston. Morris was so terrified when he picked up the phone and heard Whitey tell him that, if he went down Morris was coming with him, that Morris suffered a massive heart attack and had to be rushed to the hospital. Such was the infamy of Whitey Bulger in the criminal underworld: a phone call from Whitey could give a man cardiac arrest.

A few weeks after we meet, Connolly is acquitted in Boston on the corruption charges of accepting money and gifts from Whitey, but he is convicted of obstruction of justice for supposedly tipping Bulger and Flemmi off about the pending indictments. This count in the Connolly indictment strikes me as being fabricated and ridiculous, but it's typical of how the feds work. When they have a weak case, prosecutors will pile up a number of charges on the assumption that if the jury decides against some or most of them, they will assume the defendant must have done something wrong for the government to have charged them with so many crimes, and they will often vote to convict on those charges that are the most difficult to prove and to defend against.

Connolly had already retired; he was working for Con Edison, and he was no longer privy to investigative details in the Bulger and Flemmi case. Whitey was on the lam and had been gone from Boston on an extended road trip with one of his girlfriends for months by the time the indictments came down and Flemmi was arrested. Connolly didn't have to tip Whitey off about anything; Whitey was always the one with access to information. He was savvy enough to understand that once Connolly retired and the new federal law enforcement regime came to power in Boston, the deal he and Flemmi had with the FBI would be scrutinized by ambitious Justice Department prosecutors. Whitey had amassed a fortune in cash, and he knew that once word got out that he had been a longtime rat for the feds, not only was he going down but so were his allies in the bureau, and he was as good as a dead man in the Boston and New England underworld. He picked up one girlfriend first and then dropped her off when she said she wasn't up to a life on the run, then he picked up another longtime lover, Catherine Greig, and they took off. It's not until sixteen years later, with Connolly still in prison, that Whitey would finally be captured hiding in plain sight in an apartment complex near the beach in Santa Monica, California. The elusive crime boss was located based on a tip from an actress living in Iceland who recognized Catherine Greig in a TV report on the fugitive couple.

When I meet John Connolly a second time in 2009, he had been convicted after the 2002 trial, sentenced to ten years on the obstruction of justice charge in the Boston federal case, and served close to seven years of his sentence. Then, just weeks before his release, Connolly is indicted again, charged with conspiracy to commit murder in a 1982 Miami case. The body of a shady Boston businessman, John Callahan, had been found in the trunk of his Cadillac in long-term parking at Miami International Airport. Prolific Boston hitman John Martorano is convicted of murdering Callahan on orders from Whitey, who, Martorano claims, had been tipped off by Connolly while he was still with the FBI, and told that Callahan was about to cooperate with federal investigators. At trial in Miami in 2008, Connolly is acquitted on the conspiracy to commit murder count, but he is convicted of a lesser-included offense, "second degree homicide with a firearm," that the prosecutors had added to the indictment in case they couldn't prove the conspiracy. Although Connolly was fifteen hundred miles away, at his home in Massachusetts in 1982 when the murder of Callahan took place in Miami, and although the firearm Martorano used to kill Callahan was never in Connolly's possession, Connolly is convicted on the theory that he was in possession of a firearm—his government-issued FBI service weapon—at the time Martorano killed Callahan. Connolly is sentenced to sixty years in Florida state prison. Numerous appeals all fail. At the time of this writing, Connolly is still locked up, the only person in the whole bloody Bulger, Flemmi, FBI/TE informer scandal to remain in prison nineteen years after the case first went to trial in Boston.

It doesn't seem possible. When I tell people the circumstances that led to Connolly's conviction in Miami and his long imprisonment, they find it hard to believe. Things like this don't happen in America, particularly not to decorated ex-FBI agents. Oh, but they do. If you piss off the right people, and if you refuse to knuckle under and go along with the program, woe is you. Connolly's Miami prosecution and imprisonment begs credulity until one looks into the hidden facts of the case and understands all the high-level machinations at work to cover up Department of Justice malfeasance and protect the careers of men still in office and currently in the news. It takes years of first-hand experience with the US criminal justice system to understand how powerful, vindictive, and duplicitous the men working for the government can be when their agenda is to bring you to your knees and have you beg to do their bidding, including lie for them, to enhance and protect their careers. Even Whitey got his comeuppance, however indirectly, when he was left to be beaten to death by convicts in a West Virginia prison.

AFTER OUR FIRST meeting with Connolly, Sonny Grosso hired me to write a screenplay on the Whitey Bulger and John Connolly story. I am fascinated, and I want to focus the story on the complicated, intimate, and parlous relationship between the FBI handler Connolly and his TE informer Whitey. It's like a marriage made in hell. Vows are taken: I will not leave or forsake you till death do us part; our lives must and will depend on our faith in one another. Inevitably in such a relationship, one member of the couple will become dominant. Connolly's success in the bureau depended on the high-level intelligence he got from Whitey and Flemmi. That in turn gave the gangsters a certain amount of control over Connolly as well as his boss, John Morris. The same is true of Greg Scarpa's relationship with his FBI handler. Their lives become inextricably entangled in a secret relationship fraught with risk—and with the promise of abundant reward. Street-smart criminals, unscrupulous men like Bulger and Scarpa are adept at manipulating people and controlling relationships. Often the TE informer ends up handling the handler.

The French Connection director William Friedkin signs on to direct the film based on a screenplay I write. While working on the script for Sonny Grosso with Friedkin, I write two articles on the Bulger and Connolly story, both published in *Playboy*. "Super Rat" appears in the January 2009 issue while Whitey is still in the wind, the subject of alleged sightings at remote locations all over the world—Ireland, supposedly protected by the IRA, South America, and Europe. "The Secret Life of Whitey Bulger" is published in December 2012 after Whitey's capture in California in June 2011. When Friedkin reads my finished draft of the screenplay, he pronounces it too condensed. He tells me that he and Sonny have come to believe that the story is too big and cannot be told adequately in a two-hour film. They decide to take it to

Kevin Reilly at NBC and pitch it as a four-hour miniseries. I'm paid for writing the feature screenplay and then hired to expand it for NBC. Now, with an enlarged canvas, I am free to look deeper into the character of superrat James Whitey Bulger and even to see him, his brother Billy, and John Connolly as archetypes of the American immigrant experience: the cop, the politician, and the gangster bound together in an emblematic covenant.

These men grew up in the same South Boston housing projects at a time when there were signs in shop windows in Boston that read HELP WANTED. NO IRISH NEED APPLY. I want to know more about the Bulger household, to try to understand and show how conditions that produced one brother who grew up to be a vicious, powerful gangster and informer for the FBI in a relationship with an agent he had known since childhood also nurtured his younger brother to become what is known as a "Triple Eagle": graduate of Boston College High School, a classics scholar at Boston College, and awarded a law degree from Boston College School of Law. Billy Bulger went into local politics and became a fierce defender of his tight-knit Southie neighborhood, no more so than during the violent street wars over the forced busing of schoolchildren, which both Bulger brothers actively resisted: Whitey with threats of violence, and Billy with his political clout. Billy spent seventeen years as a member of the Massachusetts State Senate, and he was that body's president for over a decade. During his long, controversial tenure, Billy made his share of powerful enemies from among the Yankee Protestant bluebloods of Beacon Hill and wealthy Boston suburbs, who perceived him as a presumptuous, despotic, shillelagh-wielding mick usurper from the wrong side of town.

Renowned for his iron-fisted rule, Billy Bulger displayed stubbornness, loyalty to family and neighborhood, an incisive intelligence, and a charming Irish wit that endeared him to his constituents often at the expense of his political rivals. Upon his retirement from the state senate in 1995, Billy was named president of the University of Massachusetts. Long hounded by allegations of corruption and plagued by innuendo about his relationship with his notorious older brother, Billy Bulger was ultimately driven from public life by then Massachusetts governor Mitt Romney. He was threatened with obstruction of justice when he refused to testify before a grand jury investigating his infamous brother's disappearance. Billy told his interrogators, "The Fifth Amendment's basic function is to protect innocent men who might be ensnared by ambiguous circumstances. I find myself in such circumstances." He refused to testify.

I was born in Boston, that city on a hill known as "the Athens of America," also arguably the most ethnically divided city in the country. And though I grew up in the WASP bastion of Wellesley, Massachusetts, while in the marijuana underworld, I met Whitey. He interceded on my behalf and backed down a Boston wiseguy with connections to the family in Providence when he tried to shake me down and muscle in on a hashish importing operation run through an air freight catch at Boston's Logan Airport.

Who better to tell the Bulger brothers/John Connolly story? And how I want to tell it, and really get into developing it over several hours on TV. I also want to explore Whitey's relationship with his father. Bulger senior was injured in a work-related accident and lost one arm. He was unable to work, became bitter sitting around the cramped tenement apartment watching the Red Sox on TV, and the family fell on hard times. Young Jimmy, as the oldest boy, a smart, tough, and ambitious kid, went out on the streets at an early age and began to hustle, embarking on a life of crime as a bank robber in part to augment the family income as well as to show up his disabled father. Like many ruthless gangsters, Whitey was devoted to his mother. A vicious, good-looking kid with platinum blond hair, as a teenager Jimmy Bulger was the idol of the younger boys, like John Connolly, growing up in the Old Colony housing projects in South Boston. At sixteen, Whitey was driving a red convertible and dating a red-headed stripper from the Old Howard Theater in Boston's Scollay Square.

No doubt I am the man to write the saga of Whitey Bulger, Billy

Bulger, and John Connolly, and to show the inner workings of FBI's Top Echelon Informant Program. But, alas, it is not to be—at least not yet, not in this configuration. Just as we are getting ready to go into production at NBC, Kevin Reilly leaves the network.

Once again, the executive shuffle results in a derailed opportunity. The project is abandoned.

Chapter Fifteen

THE BRAND

I GET A call from a woman named Lisa Fielding, a producer who lives in LA. Lisa tells me she has formed a new partnership with a producer who optioned an article from *The New Yorker* magazine. They would like to talk to me about possibly adapting *The New Yorker* piece as a screenplay.

"You are the perfect person for this project, Richard," Lisa tells me.

"Sure," I say. "What's the article?"

Lisa says, "It's called 'The Brand.'"

"Forget it," I tell Lisa. "I read it. It's a great story, but no one is ever going to make that movie."

"Please, meet this guy, my partner. His name is Anthony Mastromauro. He'll come to New York to meet you. Just hear what he has to say."

I am working out of offices at *High Times* magazine on Park Avenue South. Along with Norman's son, John Buffalo Mailer, and Annie Nocenti, a talented writer and former editor at *Prison Life*, I have been brought in to try to rebrand the now forty-year-old publication and to take it from the essentially cannabis cultivation magazine it has evolved into and reposition it more in keeping with founder Tom Forcade's original vision for the publication as a magazine about the impact of cannabis on the larger culture in America. It's a thankless task. We are up against a trend of dwindling sales of print magazines and magazine ad space. The staff at the magazine, and the trustees of the family trust that took control of the company after Tom's death, are resistant to change. They claim to want to see *High Times* increase its subscription base and newsstand sales, but no one appears willing to go along with what I believe is necessary to keep the magazine profitable while repositioning it in the marketplace: fire three-quarters of the staff, move from the expensive Park Avenue office space, cut the overhead way down, and bring in new writing and editing talent as well as a new ad sales team while we beef up the magazine's online and multimedia presence.

Anthony Mastromauro comes to New York and meets me at my *High Times* office. What do I think of his project to make a film based on the article in *The New Yorker*? I repeat what I told his partner, Lisa. Yes, I read the piece; it's an amazing story. I know the material well. I did time with some of these guys while in prison in California. But the movie will never get made. Why do I believe that? Because the subject matter is too provocative and way too dark. I tell Anthony he'll never find backers willing to put up the money to make the film.

But, Mastromauro counters, "What if I have Sean Penn on board to direct the movie?"

"Well, that's different. With someone like Sean Penn attached, you've got a shot."

Mastromauro says he's headed back to Los Angeles, and, if he can set it up, would I be willing to come out to LA or San Francisco to meet with Sean?

"Sure," I tell him. "Of course. I have tremendous respect for Sean Penn."

The *New Yorker* article, "The Brand," written by David Grann, tells of a huge racketeering case brought by a federal prosecutor in Southern California. The feds have indicted the entire ruling council of the imprisoned faction of the Aryan Brotherhood (AB), some forty defendants known as the Brand. They are accused in a RICO (Racketeer Influenced and Corrupt Organizations) indictment with committing more than thirty murders while running a far-reaching, powerful criminal organization from inside some of America's most secure federal penitentiaries. These guys are all doing life without possibility of parole; many of them are locked down in solitary confinement twenty-three-plus hours a day, never allowed out of their cells unless they are cuffed behind their backs and escorted by at least one prison guard. Most have been convicted of killings while in custody, both of rival gang members and, in some instances, of prison guards, as well as arranging hits on the street carried out by AB members. Some of these men are legendary convicts in the prison system; most have been locked up for nearly their entire adult lives. Men like T. D. Bingham, known as the Hulk, whose chilling short story of revenge won a *Prison Life* magazine first prize for fiction and was published in the magazine, and Barry Mills, known as the Baron, who, along with Tommy Silverstein, a talented visual artist who has been locked up continuously since his early twenties, was convicted of four separate prison homicides, including the murder of corrections officer Merle Clutts at the maximum-security penitentiary at Marion, Illinois.

David Grann's *New Yorker* article details how the Aryan Brotherhood prison gang bosses are able to communicate and dispatch orders to other AB members through an elaborate prison messaging system, sending what are known as "kites," coded notes from gang leaders in solitary confinement at supermax prisons to their lieutenants and underlings in penitentiaries all across the country. Grann lays out the byzantine inner workings of the AB's ruling council, the characters themselves with their intricate body art tattoos and secret rituals of blood in and blood out, and the breadth, reach, and diversity of their criminal enterprise throughout the federal and state prison system. And certainly the story of how these convicts have adapted and learned to control their environment while in the strictest confines of the American gulag not only has the makings of a great prison drama, but the story says much about our deeply flawed American penal system and the kinds of supercriminals who are being shaped and educated by life in our prisons.

But my reservations persist: Who is going to put up the money to get such a film made, even if Sean is on board to direct and will possibly star? I have my doubts even as I board the plane and fly out to San Francisco to meet with Anthony Mastromauro and Sean Penn.

Meanwhile, I have been in touch with my friend, the ex-con novelist Eddie Bunker, who knows several of the men who comprise the Brand. Eddie did time with T. D. Bingham and Tommy Silverstein and several other members of the Brand while in the California prison system at San Quentin where the AB was founded. Eddie was on a trajectory not unlike that of T. D. Bingham and Tommy Silverstein, destined to die in isolation in a maximum-security prison until he was saved through becoming a writer. He assures me that he can help me get some inside perspective on the story of these men's lives, and how they have come to rule a criminal organization from within America's toughest prisons.

AT THE AIRPORT in San Francisco, Mastromauro meets me along with another man, Paul Herman, an actor originally from New York who is now the celebrity meeter and greeter at Robert DeNiro's restaurant, Ago, in Beverly Hills. Paul is a close friend of Sean's and the one who has made the connection for Mastromauro. We rent a car and drive up to Sean's home near Sausalito. Sean is pumped after just having finished a workout. He says he's definitely interested in the story, and he wants to hear more about my take on the material. That night we load in a car and head into San Francisco, where we meet with a writer friend of Sean's. I immediately like Sean. He's smart, engaged, not at all full of himself, and eager to put his energy behind telling relevant, important stories. He spent some time in jail and understands the need to expose the truth about a prison system that is an intense microcosm of a distorted larger culture. By the time I'm ready to leave the next day after a morning meeting with Sean, he and I agree to work on the project together. We make plans to meet in LA and visit the prosecutor who is behind the RICO case against the Brand. Sean says he knows someone who might be willing to put up the money to get the screen-play written.

Sean does have an investor, Bill Pohlad, the son of billionaire financier Carl Pohlad, owner of the Minnesota Twins baseball team. Before the agreement can be made, Paul Herman is ready to strangle Mastromauro when he attempts to cut Paul out of the deal. Finally, I am contracted to write the script. Sean is committed to direct the movie, until he's not. He and Pohlad go off to make another film Sean is directing, *Into the Wild*. It comes as no surprise when Pohlad drops "The Brand" from his production company's slate after reading my first draft of the screenplay and pronouncing the subject matter "too violent."

Well, one is inclined to say, I told you so.

Sean and I remain friends. He agrees to do a cover story for *Details* magazine when asked by the editor and requests to have me write the article. I spend a few days with Sean in New Orleans while he is work-ing on *All the King's Men*, directed by screenwriter Steven Zaillian. And I join Sean in Toronto for a few days during the Toronto Film Festival. The story is published in the *Details* December 2004 issue.

THE TRAVELING, THE long and frequent separations, and finally Kim's drinking have made our marriage untenable. We separate soon after *Street Time* wraps and are soon in the process of divorce. I've left our home in the Hudson River Valley and have moved into the city full time. In one bitter exchange, Kim tells me, "You'll leave this marriage the way you came into it—with nothing." Ah, yes, but when I came into the marriage there was one child on the way, Maxwell; and now there are three children, Max's younger brother, Dash, and their sister, Sarah Alexandra, called Sasha. They are the ones who will suffer.

But, it seems clear that, had we stayed together, things would only have gotten worse.

I have begun seeing the woman I met in Sonny Grosso's office, the lovely Antoinette Harrington. She is with me after some months go by, possibly even a year, when Sonny calls again. He's pissed off, accuses me of stealing Antoinette away from him. The real reason for his call, however, is to invite Antoinette and me to join him for dinner with Kevin Reilly, who is in town for the TV industry Up-Fronts, where the major television networks preview their upcoming fall and midseason shows for advertisers, the press, and other networks.

Sonny's health has deteriorated significantly. He needs help just getting around. Antoinette and I arrive before Sonny and Chris, his longtime companion, show up. We sit at a table with Kevin Reilly and Sonny's development executive. Reilly is eager to talk about Whitey Bulger now that there has been a new and seemingly final chapter in the saga with Whitey's arrest in Santa Monica on June 22, 2011, his conviction at trial in Boston two years later in June 2013, and his two consecutive life sentences imposed on November 14, 2013. I expound on what interests me in this story: the ethnic tribal warfare in Boston, the long simmering conflict between the Yankee WASP blue bloods and the Irish who came to control local and even national politics with the Kennedys and to dominate the police force and the Boston headquarters of the Federal Bureau of Investigation. All of that came to a head when Billy Bulger stood firm in his defiance of the federal court order to integrate Boston public schools, when the Brahmins of Beacon Hill and Wellesley forced busloads of black kids from Jamaica Plain and Roxbury to attend school in Southie's militantly white Irish neighborhood. This resonated for me as rich background to the story of Whitey, Billy, and Connolly—three Irish kids from Southie who grew up to be the archetypes of the immigrant experience.

Then I launch into a discussion of the scapegoating of John Connolly, which brings a whole new dimension to the story. I explain how and why my take on Connolly's relationship with Whitey differs from pretty much all the writing and public discourse on the subject. Reilly is even more intrigued in the story now, given the saga of John

Connolly from decorated FBI agent to convict. He turns to me and says, "I want to do eight, ten hours on this story, possibly even an open-ended series. I want big actors, top directors, for a major event series. And I want you to write it."

Sonny comes in midmeal. "What's going on?"

We are going to do a series on the Connolly/Bulger story. Sonny is to be an executive producer. Reilly asks if I have an agent. Yes, Steve Glick. Reilly says great, he knows Glick well, and he tells me to have Glick contact his office tomorrow and make the deal.

Glick is excited: another Whitey Bulger deal! This is the story that keeps resurfacing and paying the bills. But will it ever get made? *Black Mass* does get made, with Johnny Depp as Whitey. But it's as superficial and misguided as the book and performs poorly in the box office.

Months go by. I write a bible for the series and a pilot episode and get paid once more. Sonny drags his feet, insisting on running the production through his New York company, which becomes a nonstarter for Fox. A new company is brought in to oversee production. Sonny is irate. He accuses me of negotiating behind his back. Antoinette and I go to dinner with Sonny at one of his favorite restaurants in Long Island City. He again chastises me for stealing Antoinette away from him. Midmeal, Sonny gags on a rigatoni and nearly chokes to death. Antoinette leaps up and saves him with a Heimlich maneuver.

"You should have let him croak," I say on the way home.

Of course I don't mean it; I'm fond of Sonny, and he's been good to me. I lived for over a year on the various writing fees from the Bulger/Connolly project. We had many joyous evenings with Sonny and his entourage dining at his table at Rao's, the celebrity wannabe restaurant in East Harlem. I have stayed in touch with John Connolly and done what I could to try to see him get released from prison—I got paid, and I did get the girl. Had it not been for Sonny and the Whitey Bulger/John Connolly project, I would never have met Antoinette. But by the time Sonny finally gives up on his demands to run the show and signs his deal, it's too late. Reilly is already on his way out the door at Fox.

Once again, the Whitey Bulger/John Connolly project perishes in Development Hell.

Chapter Sixteen

DOG EAT DOG, CRUDE, AND MORE FALSE STARTS

AFTER WE PUBLISHED the *Prison Life* cover story on Eddie Bunker, "America's Greatest Living Convict Writer," in the September 1995 issue, Eddie sent me the manuscript of a novel he had written called *Dog Eat Dog.* The book had been rejected by several New York publishers Eddie's agent submitted it to; they all found it too violent and the characters unsympathetic. I read the manuscript in one sitting and was impressed. I felt it was the best work that I had read of Eddie's since *Little Boy Blue,* his autobiographical novel based on his childhood as a runaway in Los Angeles, and his induction into the criminal underworld while locked up in various juvenile detention centers on his way to San Quentin at seventeen—the youngest man ever condemned to the California animal factory.

Dog Eat Dog is the story of three boys brought up state-raised in the California criminal justice system who go on to the penitentiary as finishing school, get out after years spent in hardcore joints like San Quentin and Folsom, and want nothing more than to wreak havoc on society and use whatever skills they have learned and perfected while locked up to become master criminals.

I send Eddie's manuscript to an editor I know at St. Martin's Press, James Fitzgerald. Fitzgerald loves the book and ends up not only publishing *Dog Eat Dog*, but St. Martin's makes a deal with Eddie to reissue his earlier novels: *No Beast So Fierce*, which was made into a film called *Straight Time*, starring Dustin Hoffman; *Animal Factory*; and *Little Boy Blue*; and his 2001 memoir, *Education of a Felon*. I tell Eddie I want to adapt *Dog Eat Dog* and direct the film. He gives me his word that the job is mine.

Eddie is in New York in the late fall of 2002 to meet with documentary filmmaker Joe Berlinger, who has optioned *Education of a Felon* and wants to develop it as a feature. Eddie suggests Joe meet with me to discuss adapting *Education of a Felon*, and I drive in from Upstate to join Joe and Eddie for dinner at an Upper West Side restaurant and to discuss the possibility of adapting Eddie's book.

The *Education of a Felon* project never really gets off the ground. While we are looking for backing, Berlinger asks me to collaborate with him to pitch and develop a series about a criminal defense attorney. He has been offered a development deal at FX. After meeting with executives in LA, I am hired to write a pilot for a series I call *Solomon's Law*, about a high-profile criminal defense attorney straddling the ever-nebulous line between criminal and attorney—not unlike my former employer Ivan Fisher, and based on the careers of various trial lawyers I have come to know over the years, in particular Gerry Shargel, who represented John Gotti until he and Bruce Cutler were disqualified from the defense team by Judge I. Leo Glasser, who ruled that the two attorneys had become "house counsel" for the Gambino Crime Family.

Berlinger also hires me to adapt another book he has optioned, *Facing the Wind*, a harrowing, beautifully told true story of madness and familial murder. My script adheres closely to the book. The author, Julie Salamon, thanks me for being respectful of her work. *Facing the Wind* appears ready to go into production, literally on the verge of casting, when one of the investors insists that Berlinger hire his girlfriend as an actress. Berlinger refuses, and the project dies.

Around this time, a close friend, actor, and activist, Robert Galinsky, brings another attorney in to meet with me at the former Offline

Entertainment offices and one-time *Street Time* writer's room, now Marc Levin's Blowback Productions headquarters. Galinsky's friend is a man named Steven Donziger. They have a concept for a reality TV crime show they would like to develop with me. Steven edited a book I read and thoroughly admire called *The Real War on Crime*, published in 1996, which discredits much of the political pap being force-fed to the public to justify the massive build-up of the criminal-industrial complex. He's a young Harvard Law School graduate, a former public defender who worked in the DC system and experienced the war on crime at the street level.

When Donziger and I meet, he is the lead American attorney involved in a huge civil suit against oil company giant Chevron. Donziger represents the indigenous peoples of the Oriente region in Ecuador, comprising the eastern slopes of the Ecuadorian Andes and the lowland areas of tropical rainforest in the Amazon basin. Their class action suit charges Texaco, now wholly owned by Chevron, with massive oil-related contamination of the local inhabitants' lands making up an area the size of the state of Connecticut.

We soon abandon the reality crime TV show while the Ecuador litigation takes up all of Donziger's time. The more I hear about the case, the more interested I become in the possibility of making a documentary about this epic struggle of a Third World people against a powerful multinational corporation. Steven invites me to travel with him to the rain forest region to see the contamination for myself and to meet the local residents. I decide to bring along my thirteen-year-old son, Max, an aspiring filmmaker. Max brings his video camera and films the plague of pollution Texaco and Chevron left in their wake after sucking out the oil and dumping the toxic waste in dozens of open, unlined pits that allowed heavy metals and other carcinogenic contaminants to seep into rivers and streams and pollute the water supply, infecting and poisoning the local wildlife and inhabitants who depend on the unfiltered water from rivers and streams. The pollution left behind by the oil company has precipitated an outbreak of cancers and skin diseases hitherto unknown to the local people.

The visual images are cinematic—stark and horrifying: pristine rain forest jungle marred with open pits of black sludge; rivers and streams covered with oily film; fish and other wildlife with obvious tumors; young women in treatment for ovarian cancers. By any standards, the contamination of the Amazonian rain forest in Ecuador is one of the worst oil-related environmental disasters on the planet, dwarfing the Exxon Valdez oil spill, and on a par with the Chernobyl nuclear meltdown.

In the United States and other developed countries where oil is extracted, the by-products from drilling are re-injected deep below the ground surface to keep them from contaminating the water supply. In Ecuador, because the oil company executives knew they could get away with it, they simply dumped it in open pits throughout the remote, rain forest jungle instead of spending the extra money to dispose of the toxic waste. And yet Chevron refuses to take responsibility and to pay to clean up the malignant mess left behind by Texaco. Donziger's case has resulted in a major human rights campaign.

The trip is an unforgettable bonding experience for father and son. Max and I are both deeply moved by the plight of the indigenous tribes, whose water supply and food chain have been polluted. We sleep in tents in tribal villages reached by canoe and days away from the nearest vestiges of twentieth-century civilization and technology. Max observes as I partake in a ritual ayahuasca ceremony around a campfire at midnight with tribal elders and medicine men. One morning I wake up and step on a scorpion that has taken up residence in my boot. I hobble around with a swollen foot for the next couple of days.

Max makes a short film he calls *Oro Negro* (Black Gold) that Antoinette arranges to have screened at the Queens Film Festival. When Berlinger sees Max's short, he asks if I would be willing to introduce him to Steven Donziger and possibly work with him on a feature-length documentary entitled *Crude* about the Ecuador case. I introduce Berlinger to Donziger. We get independent funding for the film and shoot in Ecuador over several months as the case comes to a head. Donziger eventually wins a $9.5 billion judgment on behalf of the local residents against the oil company to pay to clean up the contamination. Chevron appeals but loses all the way up through Ecuador's highest court.

Originally, I signed on to co-direct the documentary with Berlinger. Early in the production phase, it becomes apparent that Berlinger is doing his utmost to exclude me from the process and take over the production. I acquiesce; my goal is to get the film made, and if Berlinger needs "A Film by Joe Berlinger" credit to assuage his ego, so be it. My role is redefined as a producer, but even as producer I am marginalized, as Berlinger makes it clear he wants no input, no collaboration; this is to be his film. When I see the finished film, I'm disappointed. It is obvious that Berlinger has issues with Donziger, issues that have nothing to do with the case, and he goes out of his way to curry favor with Chevron while disparaging Donziger. *Crude* wins several awards, including the prestigious Berlin Peace Prize, but does little to help the cause. Chevron continues to refuse to pay for the cleanup in Ecuador. The oil company executives instead retaliate by bringing a civil racketeering case against Donziger and his clients, the indigenous people of the Amazon, filed in the Southern District of New York. The beleaguered lawyer is charged with having obtained the judgment in Ecuador through bribery and fraud.

As of this writing, litigation in the Chevron Ecuador contamination case has been going on for more than twenty-five years. After Donziger's work in the public defender's office in Washington, DC, his life work as an attorney became trying to get Chevron to clean up the environmental disaster in Ecuador. Donziger and his clients refuse to give up. He's like a general commanding a ramshackle army of local tribesmen and human rights attorneys against a superpower. The civil suit against Chevron was originally filed in federal court in the Southern District of New York. Upon motions brought by the oil company, the court in New York ruled that the proper venue for the litigation was Ecuador. But after losing in Ecuador's courts, Chevron changed tactics and filed the New York civil racketeering case against Donziger with demands against the attorney for $60 billion in monetary damages. Donziger asked for a jury trial. The oil company eventually dropped its demand for monetary damages, which would have necessitated a jury trial. The case was assigned to a decidedly probusiness, pro-Chevron senior judge, Lewis A. Kaplan. Donziger was found guilty of supposedly bribing officials in Ecuador to win the judgment. Chevron, with more than sixty lawyers and tens of millions of dollars expended on legal fees, still manages to avoid paying to clean up the contamination left behind in the Amazon rain forest.

During the lead-up to the civil racketeering case in New York, Judge Kaplan orders Berlinger to turn over all the outtakes from the filming of *Crude*. Berliner at first makes a show of asserting his privilege as a journalist to protect his sources and his work product. He initiates a campaign to raise money for his defense. But, to the dismay of documentarians and journalists around the world, Berlinger caves when he begins to contemplate the remote possibly that he will actually be jailed if he continues to refuse to give up the outtakes. No doubt, the prospect of having to go to jail can be daunting and inspire fear. But it's doubtful that, even had Kaplan found Berlinger in contempt and ordered him to jail, the judge's order would have withstood appeal, and Joe would have been seen as a hero.

Steven Donziger continues to fight the case. He and his clients take Chevron to court in Canada where the oil company has significant assets. Again, he wins judgments up through Canada's highest courts. Chevron still refuses to pay to clean up the mess they left behind, and they choose instead to continue to attack Donziger, aided by their ally, Judge Kaplan. The bar association in New York suspends Donziger's license to practice law based on Kaplan's specious finding of fraud. Numerous celebrities rally behind the people of the Amazon. Sting and his wife, Trudie Styler, make a trip to Ecuador and donate money to provide a system for the locals to gather rainwater so they won't have to depend on the polluted waters of their rivers and streams. Roger

Waters of Pink Floyd and *The Wall* takes up the cause; he travels with Donziger to the rain forest and brings attention to the plight of the local inhabitants with a video he posts on social media.

THROUGH ALL OF this—the successes and failures, the hits and near misses, the paychecks and paybacks—at least I have realized my abiding ambition of becoming a professional writer. I manage to make a living from what I love doing: putting in the long and demanding hours at my desk; working at the solitary, sedentary craft of the writer. It never gets any easier, even when I pull together a collection of my magazine journalism, *Altered States of America: Outlaws and Icons, Hitmakers and Hitmen*, published by Nation Books in 2005. The successes I achieve in the film and TV business with *Slam* and *Street Time* continue to bring new opportunities, as well as new frustrations.

But through it all my marriage to Kim continues to suffer. The relationship deteriorates and ultimately ends in divorce. My dream of having a family and of becoming a father is never nearer, never further away.

PART THREE
FATHERHOOD:
THE BEGINNING OF A GREAT ADVENTURE

Chapter Seventeen

GODFATHER AND SON

*I know my father loved me, but I got to wonder how much,
to put me with all these wolves. This is the world you put
your son in: so much treachery. My father couldn't have
loved me to push me into this life.*

—John Gotti Jr. in a taped conversation
with a government informant

MY EDITOR AT *Playboy*, A. J. Baime, calls to ask if I would be interested in writing a feature story on the trials of John Gotti Junior; and, if given the assignment, do I think that I could get John Junior to agree to do an interview. Good question.

John Gotti Senior, known in the media as the "Dapper Don" for his sartorial flair, or "Teflon Don" for his apparent invincibility to government prosecution, is the most notorious Mafia godfather since Al Capone. After several courtroom victories, Gotti Senior was finally convicted in 1990 of racketeering and ordering a number of murders in furtherance of a racketeering enterprise. He was sentenced to life in prison with no possibility of parole. As the heir apparent to the leadership of the Gambino Crime Family, Gotti's first-born son and namesake, John A. Gotti, known as Junior, has the dubious distinction of having endured three previous trials in 2005, 2006, and 2007 in New York federal courts. All three trials ended in mistrials when jurors were unable to reach a unanimous verdict as to guilt or innocence. It appears some of Gotti Senior's Teflon rubbed off on his son.

But the federal government does not give up easily, particularly when your last name is Gotti. John Junior is to be tried again in yet another, a fourth racketeering case set to go to before a jury in the Southern District of New York. This time the government claims that they have damning new evidence.

I tell my editor that I can certainly cover the trial and write about it, but it is going to be difficult, perhaps even impossible, to get an interview with Gotti Junior while he is in custody. The feds are notorious for keeping their prisoners from meeting with the press, particularly someone as high profile as he. And in any case, there is a story here with or without an interview. Three mistrials in federal courts in New York City: that is unheard of; it must constitute some sort of record. The feds don't often lose or fail to get a conviction at trial, and certainly not in New York City's two federal district courts—the Southern District in Manhattan and the Eastern District in Brooklyn. They have a 95 percent conviction rate, with 98 percent of those who choose to go to trial ending with a guilty verdict. Mistrials due to hung juries are also rare in federal criminal cases, and even more so in the Southern or Eastern Districts of New York, where many of the major criminal cases brought by the government are tried. Judges will ordinarily order jurors to continue deliberating until they reach a verdict.

In 2009, when John Gotti Junior stands trial a fourth time in federal court in Manhattan, charged with being the boss of the Gambino Crime Family, the specter of his dead father haunts the courtroom. Gotti Senior died a lonely, inglorious death in 2002, wasting away of throat and neck cancer at the federal prison medical facility in Springfield, Missouri, while serving the tenth year of a life sentence. Now his son faces a similar fate. If convicted of the racketeering, cocaine trafficking, murder, and murder conspiracy charges brought by the government, John Gotti Junior will be sentenced to a mandatory term of life in prison with no possibility of parole, like his father.

But what kind of a life was it? I wonder going into the trial in the magisterial new Daniel Patrick Moynihan United States Courthouse just a twenty-minute walk from my home. Is Gotti Junior like his father—as the government seeks to prove—a merciless killer, a mob boss who made tens of millions of dollars moving a mountain of cocaine through the streets of Queens, New York, and Tampa, Florida? Is he a street thug who matured into a made Mafia member and took up the mantle of his imprisoned father to become boss of the largest and richest crime family in America?

Or, as Gotti's lawyers contend, did John Junior come to see the horror and treachery of his father's and his own criminal life, recoil from it, and quit the mob over a decade ago after having admitted his guilt in 1999, been sentenced to seventy-seven months in prison, served his time, and come out to dedicate his life to his wife and children? The government, the Gotti defense maintains, is going after John Junior yet again and seeking to lock him up for the rest of his life not based on anything he may have done, for which he has already been punished, but because of who his father was, and because they can't stand losing in court—particularly to someone named John Gotti. The Gotti name alone, many in law enforcement seem to believe, is a crime in and of itself.

"GOOD MORNING, I am John Gotti," John Junior introduces himself to the jury pool on the first day of voir dire, the process by which a jury is selected. "Here I am again," he says, to remind potential jurors that this is the fourth time the government has attempted to convict him and lock him up for the rest of his natural life.

He was arrested early on the morning of August 5, 2008, when a dozen FBI agents, some arriving in helicopters, swooped in on Gotti's Oyster Bay, Long Island home, where he lived with his wife and five children, and took him into custody on charges that originated out of a Tampa, Florida, indictment. Gotti was held without bail, transported to the Pinellas County jail in Clearwater, Florida, where he was brought before a federal judge who ruled that the government had to take him back to New York to stand trial. In a pretrial victory for the defense, the judge wrote a nineteen-page ruling that held there was no basis for moving the case to Florida and that the Tampa indictment gave the "disquieting impression of forum shopping" by federal prosecutors who had been unable to convict Gotti in New York courts.

Junior, as he is known on the street, appears smaller, diminished by the year plus he has been locked up in solitary confinement while awaiting trial. A burly man, a weight lifter and reputed tough guy when climbing the ranks of the mob on the streets of Queens, Gotti has shrunk and gone gray—not just his hair, his flesh too has taken on the dull ashen patina of jail cell walls. His perennially tanned dad had swaggered into spectator-packed courtrooms in his three-thousand-dollar suits, looking like a movie star with his silver-gray hair impeccably coiffed, flanked by his flamboyant, A-list attorneys, Bruce Cutler and Gerald Shargel. Junior shambles into a near empty courtroom, squinting from behind a pair of tinted, oval-shaped glasses, dressed in what appears to be prison-issue-clothes, and escorted by deputy US marshals. He takes his seat at the defense table with lead counsel Charles Carnesi, a balding, jovial sparkplug of a man with shoulders nearly as wide as he is tall, and a corrosive voice that could melt the grease off an engine block. Carnesi is second-chaired by co-counsel John Meringolo, an affable regular in New York mob trials.

The prosecution has assembled an equally disparate team. The young, hyper Manhattan assistant United States attorney Elie Honig reminds me of Ben Stiller in *Along Came Polly* as he scurries around the courtroom trying to clean up the government's mess. He seems somehow chagrined by the awesome responsibility of trying to accomplish what more experienced prosecutors failed to do in the past. Next to Honig is James Trezevant out of the Tampa, Florida, US attorney's office. Trezevant is confined to an electrically powered Rolls Royce of a wheelchair. He drives in and out of the courtroom like Ironside accompanied by his Playboy Playmate–worthy paralegal, Ms. Rodriguez. To Honig's left sits assistant US attorney Chi T. Steve Kwok, a buttoned-down rookie apparently drafted from the government's farm team. Rounding out the prosecution's squad is FBI case agent Ted Otto, who looks like a slightly shorter version of Lyle Lovett, with a pile of curly light-brown hair on his long, angular head.

Word around the federal courthouse in downtown Manhattan, where superswindler Bernie Madoff recently pled guilty to a $50 billion Ponzi scheme, is that the seasoned, top-tier government prosecutors and criminal defense attorneys don't want to try these organized crime cases anymore. There is no glory in it, not since then United States Attorney Rudy Giuliani took down the bosses of all five New York Mafia families in the Commission Case, and not since John Gotti Senior's final, precipitous fall from grace and disappearance from the front pages of New York City's newspapers. Lawyers and prosecutors prefer the high-profile, white-collar securities and fraud cases where defendants are charged with stealing millions and even billions with a pen and a briefcase instead of a machine gun. Then, the prosecutors reason, they can leave government service and take jobs that start at $200,000 a year at New York's top corporate law firms.

Prosecutor Elie Honig, stopping by the press section, laments, "What, *The New York Times* doesn't even send one of its people to cover the trial?"

The Mafia is so eighties.

As the trial progresses, however, the room gradually fills with courthouse buffs, lawyers and detectives, FBI special agents, internal affairs cops seeking to gather intelligence about corrupt officers who may have worked for the Gotti clan, members of the press, and Gotti groupies. Even Jerry Capeci, who bills himself as "the nation's foremost EXPERT on the American Mafia" on his Gang Land News website, shows up. Federal Judge Kevin Castel, an avuncular, solicitous jurist with seemingly inexhaustible patience, moves the trial to a larger courtroom to accommodate the growing crowd of spectators. Victoria Gotti, the defendant's sister and a celebrity Mafia princess in her own right, the former star of the reality TV series *Growing Up Gotti* and an author with a new book to promote, makes periodic appearances. With her mane of waist-length bleach-blond hair and model slim figure, Victoria will scowl and sit beside the other Gotti women, dressed in somber dark clothing, looking like a flock of grieving Sicilian widows at a funeral as they cluck and hiss at the government's witnesses.

John Junior's life, as depicted by Charles Carnesi in his opening statement to the jury, is a sadly foregone outcome of his father's doomed existence. John Gotti Senior was, in Carnesi's words, "a gangster through and through. You could cut John Gotti in half and all you would find is gangster."

"Cosa Nostra forever," that was Senior's mantra. Never plead guilty, never appear before a grand jury, never admit anything: that is the code John Gotti Senior lived by—and died by. Not so John Junior, Carnesi avers. By the early 1980s, when Gotti Junior began hanging around the social club with his father, Gotti Senior had risen to the position of capo or skipper with a powerful crew of made Mafia members and associates operating out of the Bergin Hunt and Fish Club on 101st Avenue in Ozone Park, Queens. Soon John Junior began to assemble his own crew, headquartered at the Our Friends social club just blocks away from the Bergin. In every way except his choice of wardrobe, the younger Gotti emulated his father. Junior preferred expensive warm-up suits and sneakers to his dad's elegant DeLisi and Armani suits and Bruno Magli shoes.

If the government rats are to be believed, John Junior imitated his father in another aspect as well: he made a fortune through the sale of illegal drugs. It has long been a popular myth that the Mafia does not deal in narcotics. The reality is, as the government's star witness, John Alite testifies, three-quarters of the wiseguys have got a hand in the dope business, and half of them are using drugs. Alite puts it this way: "As far as the world was concerned, we didn't deal cocaine. We're not in the drug business. We are in the drug business, but we're not in the drug business." In other words, "Don't get caught." As Sonny Corleone opined in *The Godfather* when the Don demurred over getting into the junk business, "There's money in that white powder." And the mob is all about one thing over all else: money—just like corporate America, the biggest drug dealers of them all. Respect, honor, omertà: all have a price tag.

John Gotti Senior ran afoul of the Gambino Family leadership in the mid-1980s when it became known in mob and FBI circles that the Gotti crew, through Senior's trusted lieutenant and boyhood pal, Angelo Ruggiero, known as "Quack Quack" for his relentless chatter, in partnership with Gotti's brother, Gene, were generating millions for the family in the heroin business. The FBI had tapes of Ruggiero discussing countless junk deals over the phone from his Long Island home. After a series of high-profile busts of Gotti lieutenants on narcotics charges, the "charade," as Junior's main accuser John Alite describes the mob's prohibition of drug dealing, was debunked. Paul Castellano, Carlo Gambino's brother-in-law, who had assumed leadership of the crime family (and who also received millions in drug profits from a crew of Sicilian junk dealers paying tribute to the boss) demanded to see transcripts of the Ruggiero tapes. To be implicated in heroin transactions would have meant a death sentence for Ruggiero, and probably for John Gotti as well. Castellano would be pleased to find any excuse to have Gotti killed. The powerful upstart capo already represented a threat to Castellano's leadership. Then, in December of 1985 in a preemptive strike, Castellano and his bodyguard, Thomas Bilotti, were shot and killed outside Sparks Steak House in Manhattan. The daring, classic mob hit in broad daylight during the Christmas season was brilliantly planned and coordinated by Gotti and Sammy "the Bull" Gravano. Gotti Senior became the new Gambino godfather and Boss of Bosses.

Growing up, Junior Gotti idolized his father. In her book, *This Family of Mine*, Victoria says Gotti Senior was a tough but adored dad who was often either in prison or in the headlines. When a gang of local kids attacked Junior with baseball bats, John Senior beat three of them to a pulp, and forced the others to beg for their lives. He then ordered his son to fight each of his attackers one-on-one to regain his honor.

"My father on the street made you want to be part of it, because he was that kind of guy," Victoria Gotti writes. Gotti Junior said, in a conversation recorded in a prison visiting room, "You had to be part of it. You wanted to be as close as possible to him. The only way was by being that. You wanted to be in it."

"Mob fathers almost never want to involve their sons," Sonny Grosso (no relation to murder victim George Grosso) tells me over dinner at Rao's, the famous mob restaurant and hangout in East Harlem. "But it's almost impossible to keep them out. Sons look for their fathers' approval."

BY ALL ACCOUNTS, John Gotti Senior was different. He gloried in "the life," as those who live in it refer to the Mafia milieu. He broke with Mafia custom and upset mob traditionalists like Vincent "the Chin" Gigante, boss of the powerful Genovese Crime Family, by publicly flaunting his wealth and criminal status, and by shepherding his son into the secret society. While John Gotti Senior angered his peers and put a target on his back for law enforcement agents, he became a folk hero to a gangster-adoring public. He was cheered and feted at block parties in Queens and Brooklyn neighborhoods to celebrate his acquittals on state and federal charges. Movie stars and sports celebrities sought Gotti's company when he held court at Manhattan's best restaurants. Anthony Quinn and Mickey Rourke made guest appearances at his trials. His face graced the cover of *Time* magazine in a portrait by Andy Warhol. Surrounded by his entourage of eight bodyguards, drivers, and button men, gleaming for the paparazzi, a cocky Gotti Senior reveled in his role as Mafia godfather. John Junior, standing on the sidelines, could not help but be impressed.

There was another side of Gotti Senior that few but his closest intimates, criminal underlings, and FBI agents got to see. "He was a sucker," a mob bookmaker tells me. "A degenerate gambler. And a tyrant. He squeezed everybody around him for money, then blew millions on stupid bets." On FBI tapes, Gotti Senior was revealed as a foul-mouthed dictator with an explosive temper and scatological sense of humor. He ordered the killing of Gambino soldier Louis DiBono for the crime of not coming in to report. "You know why he's dying?" Gotti Senior asked his underboss, Sammy Gravano, in a conversation secretly recorded by the FBI. "He's going to die because he refused to come in when I called. He didn't do nothing else wrong." According to John Alite, Gotti Senior gave responsibility for carrying out the hit on DiBono to his son, John Junior.

Senior was a tyrant at home as well. On the witness stand John Alite tells of Senior Gotti raving at his son about how he should treat his friends. "Fuck your friends!" the father yelled. "Use them and abuse them!" Gotti Senior had not noticed Alite camped out on the living room sofa. "Oh," he said when he saw him, "I didn't know you were here."

Caught on tape complaining about FBI wiretaps after the feds bugged Angelo Ruggiero's house, Gotti Senior joked, "You know how they invade your privacy. You hear a baby crying, your wife crying. You say, 'It could be my house, my baby, my wife.' Where the fuck are we going? Maybe you wanna throw a fart in the bathroom, you hear it in open court. They hear you farting. Like that poor fuckin' 'Frank the Wop.' His phone was in the bathroom. He's takin' a shit, and he's talking. That's a fuckin' shame. . . . Then he goes, Phphphhh! *Bing!* He said, 'I feel better now. I couldn't move.'" Gravano cracked up. Gotti too was laughing, clapping his hands. "In open fuckin' courtroom. Madonna!" he went on. "You gotta get a heart attack."

The boss might have had a heart attack if he had known the feds were listening in and busting a gut laughing.

Gotti Senior was a notorious womanizer who spent long hours

at Manhattan nightspots like Regine's sipping Rémy Martins with his various high-profile mistresses. He fathered a child with girlfriend Sandy Grillo, the common-law wife of a wiseguy, thus disdaining Cosa Nostra's strict prohibition against consorting with another made member's woman.

In time, John Gotti Senior became enamored of his own myth and began to see himself as invulnerable to the onslaught of criminal investigations swirling around him. He seemed to set himself up for his own fall, allowing himself to be captured on an FBI bug in an apartment above his headquarters at the Ravenite Social Club as he discussed a mounting body count and bad-mouthed his vicious underboss, Sammy Gravano.

In 1991, both Gravano and Gotti Senior were in custody, locked up in the maximum-security unit on the ninth floor of the Metropolitan Correctional Center in downtown Manhattan—the same federal lockup where John Junior resided during his trial. The two most feared and powerful gangsters in the world were awaiting court dates on a massive racketeering case that detailed thirteen counts of murder, including the brazen hit on Paul Castellano. Gravano soon flipped on his boss after FBI agents showed him transcripts of the Ravenite tapes. Gotti was caught on the wire calling Gravano a "mad dog killer," criticizing him for being too greedy and creating a "family within a family." Convinced Gotti's defense strategy was to heap blame for the killings on him while Gotti portrayed himself as a peace-loving boss, and because he couldn't stand doing time in jail, Gravano made a deal with prosecutors. He pled guilty to a single count of racketeering, admitted responsibility for nineteen murders, and took the stand to betray his oath and summon the Gotti curse. Both the father's and the son's most trusted brothers in blood would stab them in the back. For his testimony against Gotti, Gravano's admitted nineteen homicides were forgiven. He was sentenced to five years, and back out on the street in less than two years.

TWO YEARS AFTER John Junior became a made member of the Gambino Crime Family in 1990, he was elevated to the level of captain. In 1992, soon after his father was locked up for good, Junior was promoted again. His father anointed him acting boss. It was an all-too-swift rise to the top of the underworld. Mafiosi both inside and outside the Gambino Family questioned the wisdom of naming Junior, only twenty-eight at the time, boss of what was then the most powerful Mafia family in the country. Even Junior would later claim he was unprepared to lead the crime family. An old Mafia saying has it that "the Family is only as strong as its boss." The elder John Gotti, cognoscenti maintained, had demoralized the Gambino crews by imposing his son as a surrogate boss.

Sometime after taking over the family, John Gotti Junior began to change his image. He started wearing expensive business suits in place of the warm-up suits. He donned a pair of wire-rimmed glasses. He would come to appear more as a distinguished, thoughtful, and businesslike version of his father. In 1990, Gotti married Kim Albanese in the most lavish Mafia wedding of all time. Wiseguys, mob associates, and their wives and families from around the country were in attendance. At the reception held in the Helmsley Palace in Manhattan, each of the five New York families and the New Jersey branch had their own tables. The newlyweds moved into a six-bedroom Colonial mansion on three acres of rolling hills in Mill Neck, an exclusive community on the North Shore of Long Island and began to grow their young family. In 1997, during a search of one of Junior Gotti's properties, FBI agents found over $300,000 in cash and a typed list of the made Mafia members who had attended Junior's wedding with the dollar amounts of their gifts. News of the discovery enraged imprisoned Gotti Senior and earned Junior the moniker "Dumbfella" in New York tabloids.

But Carnesi tells the jury that the Mafia life is over and done with for John Junior, and it has been over for many years. He tells the jury that in 1998 John visited his father in prison to seek his permission to plead guilty to federal racketeering charges of bribery, extortion, gambling, and fraud. According to Carnesi, Gotti Senior reluctantly gave his son permission to take the plea and withdraw from the family, even while maintaining that it was something he himself would never do. Gotti Junior was sentenced to serve seventy-seven months in prison. His father died while John Junior was still locked up.

Then, just days before Gotti Junior was to be released in 2005, the government hit him with a new indictment. This is a favorite government tactic, exactly what they did to FBI agent John Connolly. If they can't break you the first time around, they wait until you are about to be released, and then bring a whole new set of charges in hopes of getting you to surrender. Again, Junior was charged with a pattern of racketeering, and the prosecutors added a new count to the indictment to allege that Gotti had ordered the 1992 kidnapping and beating of Guardian Angels founder Curtis Sliwa. A popular radio talk show host, Sliwa had infuriated the Gottis by calling John Senior "Public Enemy Number One" and repeatedly denigrating the powerful crime boss on his morning radio show.

Jeffrey Lichtman, then a rising star of the Manhattan criminal defense bar and most recently appearing as Mexican drug lord El Chapo's lawyer, represented John Junior at his first trial in 2004. Lichtman eviscerated Sliwa on the witness stand with a vicious cross-examination. Sliwa admitted he concocted multiple stories of having been attacked in the past and fed them to the press to gain sympathy for himself and the Guardian Angels. Sliwa also confessed to being "addicted to publicity." Lichtman so discredited Sliwa's testimony that by the time of Junior's trial in 2009, the government thought better of recalling him to the stand.

Lichtman secured the first in the series of mistrials by presenting the novel defense that Junior Gotti had formally withdrawn from organized crime. Gotti's withdrawal defense, what is known as an "affirmative defense," contends that, yes, the defendant, John Gotti Junior, was a made member of the Gambino Crime Family, indeed he became acting boss of the family after his father was sent to prison. But he pled guilty to those charges; he went to prison, where he renounced his position as boss, and severed all his connections to organized crime while serving his six-and-a-half-year sentence. He quit the mob and became, in his words, "a civilian."

The government counters with the argument that the withdrawal defense is no more than convenient fiction concocted by Gotti and fronted by his lawyers. The prosecutors and government agents maintain that it is not possible for Gotti Junior to have quit the Mafia, as he contends. Nor can a made member withdraw and become a civilian because it is not allowed under penalty of death. Haven't you seen *The Godfather*? Of course, we all know after having seen Coppola's masterpiece that once you are sworn into Cosa Nostra that's it; it's a blood oath, you are a made man and a member for life. The only way out is death. Or you become a government rat, you join Team America, debrief, and testify against other organized crime figures for the government, like Sammy Gravano—and then spend the rest of your unhappy life in the Witness Protection Program. Furthermore, the prosecution maintains, with regard to the present indictment, Gotti's withdrawal defense is null and void since there is no statute of limitations for murder or conspiracy to murder.

But wait a minute: First of all, who says you can't quit the Mafia besides novelists, filmmakers, snitches, and government agents? That may be true in the movies or on TV, but in real life we've seen it done before. Sonny Franzese's son Michael quit, as did Joe Bonanno's son, and neither of them were killed as a result. Bonanno Senior, like Gotti Senior, was a boss when his son decided to quit. Still, it is difficult to imagine that the son of John Gotti, first-born son of the charismatic don of the most powerful crime family in the country—the man who famously proclaimed, "Cosa Nostra forever!"—would be allowed to leave the life his father embodied even if he wanted to.

The Boss of Bosses, Gotti Senior died a slow and agonizing death, locked up in solitary confinement for over ten years to pay for his sins. Gotti Senior never wavered from his position as a staunch and resolute defender of, and a believer in, "the life" of organized crime. It was what defined him as a man. He accepted his punishment and never complained of the unduly harsh treatment he received. Whatever else he may or may not have been, Gotti Senior was no hypocrite, and he was no rat. To imagine that John Senior would ever consent to allowing his son to renounce his position as his father's stand-in, to break his vow of omertà, and to give up his claim to rule the Gambino Crime Family through his son—no, that is unthinkable. Although I have taken the assignment to cover the trial, I am far from convinced of John Junior's defense—until I hear all the evidence.

"THIS IS A case about fathers and sons," defense attorney Jeffrey Lichtman told the jury in his opening statement at the 2005 John Gotti Junior racketeering trial. "One son, my client, John Gotti, wants to reverse and forever rewrite his father's legacy, and another set of sons, the government's cooperating witnesses who are following in the bloody footsteps of their Mafia father, the most famous turncoat in history, Sammy 'the Bull' Gravano.

"The relationship between fathers and sons is something that has been examined for as long as there have been fathers and sons on this earth," Lichtman continued. "Anyone who has ever been a son can tell you they want to please their fathers, earn their approval. Sometimes a son will do anything just to be around his father, to be accepted by him. When your father is John Gotti, the flamboyant Mafia boss that everyone wants to be around, the oversized personality everyone wants to touch, it is even harder to get a minute with him let alone have any father-son moments that kids want.

"You will learn when John had these moments, they weren't at the Yankee games, they were not in the park on a Sunday afternoon, they weren't spent on a boat fishing on a lake. Instead, they were in social clubs surrounded by wiseguys where Mafia talk and criminal activity was all around. You will learn most of the time John's father wasn't even around to take him to any place or spend any of these quality moments with him. He was taken around by his uncles because his father was in prison most of the time. None of you could possibly know that. When you hear the name Gotti, you just shut off. It is normal. When you hear the name Trump, you think of money. When you hear the name Gotti, you think of crime."

As argued by Jeff Lichtman, the withdrawal defense worked well enough to cause Gotti three mistrials after juries became hopelessly deadlocked. For the fourth trial, the government has brought new charges, including murders that were not charged previously and are not protected by the statute of limitations, and they have a new star witness, John Alite, who they unearthed from a Brazilian jail. The prosecutors also managed to get the case transferred to a male judge after Gotti's previous trial judge, United States District Court Judge Shira Scheindlin was believed to have been too accommodating to the defense.

"The defendant has killed with his own hands," Assistant United States Attorney Honig declares in his opening statement to the jury. Honig tells us that government witnesses will testify that Junior Gotti stabbed to death a kid named Danny Silva, nicknamed Elf, in a senseless barroom brawl at a Queens pub called the Silver Fox. The killing took place in 1983 when Gotti was just nineteen. Honig says that the jury will hear from government witnesses that after the Danny Silva murder, Gotti Junior bragged how now that he had killed, he had proven himself "capable," and "a tough guy," mob vernacular for being a killer, like his father.

As I observe the trial, I soon come to understand why the government is having so much trouble getting a conviction, why previous juries were unable to reach a unanimous decision: the government's case is full of holes and based entirely on dubious cooperating witness testimony, and there is ample evidence that John did indeed quit the mob. When considered in light of the indisputable facts, the case doesn't hold up. The rats trotted out by the prosecution are tried and true, but it's all old history. John already pled guilty and served time for most of what the rats allege; they have no new relevant evidence that falls within the statute of limitations.

The prosecution's co-star witness, Michael "Mikey Scars" DiLeonardo, a turncoat Gambino captain from the Bensonhurst section of Brooklyn and now a government rat, is right out of central casting. He looks like he just stepped off the set of *The Sopranos*. Mikey Scars walked the walk and talked the talk, and he has been flipping on his former goombata like flapjacks at the International House of Pancakes ever since. DiLeonardo was born into the mob and became a made member in the same induction ceremony as Gotti Junior. DiLeonardo's grandfather was a wiseguy; he has Cosa Nostra bloodlines going back eighty years to when the Mafia was known as the Black Hand. A practiced stool pigeon who testified at John Junior's three previous trials, Mikey Scars regales the jury with his machine-gun mouth, retelling first-person, insider stories in mob vernacular, of hits and "hospital beatings; a beating bad enough to put the guy in the hospital but not kill him," such as DiLeonardo claims Junior ordered for Guardian Angel and radio talk show host Curtis Sliwa.

"He deserved a beating," DiLeonardo says with a shrug when prosecutor Honig asks why Sliwa was attacked. "We were infuriated with Curtis Sliwa spouting off. Junior sent some of his kids to give him a baseball bat beating." Junior's kids, DiLeonardo goes on to explain, comprised the young crew of wannabe mobsters who had come up with Junior from the streets of Queens. They kidnapped Sliwa from in front of his home in a taxi. Instead of adhering to the plan to beat Sliwa with baseball bats, a Gotti kid hiding on the floor in the front seat of the cab jumped up and immediately opened fire on the stunned Guardian Angel, shooting him several times in his abdomen.

"How did John Gotti Junior react when he heard that Sliwa had been shot?" Honig asks.

"Junior was upset," DiLeonardo tells the jury. "He said, 'This is a cluster-fuck.' We could get destroyed for that. We don't kill press."

Sliwa, however, survived. He jumped out the window of the cab and ran off.

DiLeonardo describes how the Gambino Family and other "borgatas," as the Mafia clans are known, extort legitimate businesses like construction, garbage collection, and in the garment industry; how they control labor unions; run "pump and dump" stock fraud scams; shake down strip joints and night clubs; and launder the hundreds of millions of dollars generated by crime.

Several times during Mikey Scars' testimony, Judge Castel has to tell the witness to slow down and translate what he means by, for example, "a piece of work for the Family" (murder); "he was on the move" (he was part of the killing crew); "get a line on someone" (follow them around, learn their habits so as to prepare to kill them); and "sneak hits" (murders not put on record with the Family's higher-ups). "We can't kill on our own," DiLeonardo explains. "We're not supposed to."

"Were you close to John Gotti Junior?" Honig inquires.

"Very close," DiLeonardo claims. "I baptized his son. Junior was learning about the life from his father. But his father got arrested too soon, just when Junior was learning the ropes."

Finally, DiLeonado tells of Junior Gotti's attempt to rewrite the rules of Mafia membership, which he describes as "complete hypocrisy."

"*Omertà* means silence," DiLeonardo explains. "Meanwhile everybody's talking. You got Junior Persico, boss of the Colombo Family, admitting there is a Mafia in the Commission trial. John Senior called Persico a rat for saying there is a Mafia. Meanwhile Persico is doing a hundred years. There's an edict, you would be murdered if you're dealing drugs. I look around the table, there's ten captains there and they're all dealing drugs. We're not supposed to take part in stock fraud."

"How often was that rule broken?" Honig asks.

"Every day," says DiLeonardo.

DiLeonardo goes on to debunk Junior's withdrawal defense. "You can't admit there is a mob or that you are a made member of the Mafia. Junior wants to change that. As his defense, he wants to say okay, we admit there is a Mafia. Everybody knows there is a mob. But we deny the crimes. John Senior would have a great issue with that."

"Was that a lie?" Honig asks the witness.

"Of course. That's my job as a Costa Nostra member. To lie."

But this is all ancient history, testimony as to events that took place prior to John Junior's previous guilty plea, his time in prison, and his alleged withdrawal from the Mafia. There is evidence in tapes of visits and telephone calls between Gotti Junior and other members of the Gambino family that supports John's claim to have made up his mind to leave the crime family, to take his blood family, move out of New York, and "go fishing."

The jury has heard of no new crimes, no allegations of homicide or conspiracy to commit murder to overcome the statute of limitations, until the prosecutors introduce their star witness, John Alite.

"He was capable," DiLeonardo says when Honig asks him if he knows fellow rat Alite.

"Capable meaning what?" Honig asked.

"Oh, he was a murderer," DiLeonardo replied.

One can feel the tension in the courtroom ramp up as Alite saunters in and takes his place on the witness stand. Alite had fled the United States to dodge a number of serious criminal charges, including home invasions and homicide. He had reached out to the FBI with what he claimed was evidence of Gotti Junior's participation in those same murders and murder conspiracies. Alite was willing to give up his evidence in hopes of being returned to the US from Brazil and ultimately set free by testifying against Gotti—always a reliable get-out-of-jail-free card.

John Alite is John Gotti Junior's Sammy Gravano. If we are to believe Alite, he was Junior's confidante, his muscle, his best friend, and his "mad dog killer" on call twenty-four hours a day, seven days a week until Gotti, according to Alite, turned on him. Now Alite is getting even. Because he is of Albanian descent, Alite could not become a made member of the Mafia, and that rankled, left him feeling used but not accepted. He was told to leave the room when secret Mafia business was discussed. Junior had been best man at Alite's wedding. The jury is shown photographs of a beaming John Junior holding Alite's infant son. Gotti invited Alite into his home. On an FBI surveillance tape, John Junior is shown greeting several burly men in overcoats outside the Ravanite Social Club with John Alite at his side. Alite claims he killed and beat people senseless on orders from Gotti, "baseball batting them" he calls the beatings.

"I was around John Gotti Junior," Alite explains to the jury, meaning he became an associate of the Gambino Family under John Gotti Junior who reported directly to his father. "He, John Gotti Junior, would direct me as to what crimes we would commit each day."

When he testified at a previous trial against Mafia hitman Charles Carneglia, Alite claimed to have had an affair with John's sister, Victoria Gotti, who was married at the time to Gambino soldier Carmine Agnello. At John Junior's trial, under direct examination, Alite stops short of saying he and Victoria were intimate.

"We started having feelings for each other," he tells the jury. "I had feelings for her, she had feelings for me. We talked to each other. I wasn't just fooling around with her. It wasn't that."

Alite says Victoria came to him for comfort after being beaten by her husband. She had a swollen lip and a shiner, but she was afraid to tell her brother or her father for fear they would kill Agnello.

Outside the courtroom during a break in the trial, the striking blond erupts in outrage. "The only feelings I had for John Alite were that I despised him. Feelings?" Victoria Gotti sneers. "He flatters himself."

According to Victoria, Alite's revised testimony proves he lied about the affair, and proves he is lying now about his relationship with John Junior. As for being beaten by Agnello, "Do you think my brother would have allowed that?" Victoria asks. "Is he a criminal, a thug? Or a big softy who would have allowed someone to mishandle his sister?"

When his testimony resumes, Alite says that John Gotti Junior ordered him to murder a Gotti-protected drug dealer named George

Grosso for using the Gotti name as sanction for his coke-dealing enterprise. Though Grosso paid Gotti Junior tribute for being able to deal drugs under the Gambino umbrella of protection, he was warned not to mention the Gotti name. When he defied the warning and kept running his mouth about being "with" the Gottis, Junior, according to Alite's testimony, ordered him killed. "He pushed the issue," Alite says on the witness stand. "John Gotti Jr. kept saying, 'You didn't kill this kid yet,' trying to say I didn't have enough balls to do it."

Alite and another witness, a retired corrupt New York City cop named Phillip Baroni, describe how Grosso was taken for a one-way ride. Alite sat in the rear of the car behind Grosso with Baroni beside him. Alite shot Grosso in the head, spit on him and called him a "motherfucker." After the killing, Alite says he reported to Junior, who was having his nails done at a salon next door to Gotti Senior's Bergin Hunt and Fish Club. Junior told Alite to leave Grosso's body where it would be discovered. "Don't bury him, don't hide him. Put him out on the street so people know what you did. Send a message: Don't use our names." Alite claims Gotti wanted to visit the scene to "verify that the guy was dead. I watch a lot of movies, where the killer always gets caught going back to the scene of the crime. I didn't want to go back."

But he did because, as Alite repeats ad nauseam in his testimony, John Gotti Junior was his boss and what the boss ordered, Alite did. "Otherwise, I go, if I don't execute his orders." When they drove past where the body had been dumped beside Grand Central Parkway, the scene was swarming with cops and staff from the medical examiner's office. "He doesn't look that good," Gotti Junior joked after seeing Grosso's corpse. Four days after the Grosso hit, on Christmas Eve, 1988, at the tender age of twenty-four, Junior Gotti followed in his father's footsteps and became a made member of the Gambino Crime Family.

In her book *This Family of Mine*, Victoria Gotti describes the night her brother was inducted in a secret mob ceremony that Junior likened to joining King Arthur and the Knights of the Round Table. "This was one of the most important days of his life," Victoria writes, describing how proud Junior was to become a made member of Cosa Nostra. The ceremony was held in an apartment belonging to Joe Butch Corrao on Mulberry Street in the Little Italy section of Manhattan just doors away from the Ravenite Social Club, where Gotti Senior took command after usurping control of the Gambino Crime Family. Junior was given a picture of a saint stained with a drop of Gotti Senior's blood. As the saint's picture burned, Junior recited the ancient oath.

"If you should betray *La Cosa Nostra*, your soul will burn like this saint," Junior was warned. The other men in the room began to chant. "Now you are born over. You are a new man."

After the ceremony, Gotti joined his father at the Ravenite. "He was the happiest man alive," Victoria writes. John Senior had not attended the induction to avoid the appearance of nepotism, already a persistent, though whispered, complaint in mob circles. It is also legend that a father's presence at his son's induction could bring bad luck to the Family. Present, however, was underboss Sammy Gravano. Another budding wiseguy who got straightened out (became a made member of the family) that night with Junior was Michael "Mikey Scars" DiLeonardo, who would later testify against him.

In his gravelly voice, with his head cocked back on his thick, tattooed neck, dressed in a baggy gray sweatsuit, Alite rarely passes up an opportunity to belittle his former boss. He characterizes John Junior as a petty, greedy loudmouth who hid behind the Gotti name but was afraid to stand up to his despotic father. Alite says Gotti Senior ordered Alite to get a beating when Junior and his crew were called to a sitdown over the wounding of a Genovese captain's nephew in a Queens nightclub shootout. "We wanted to hear him say, 'Dad, I shot him,'" Alite testifies. "But, as usual, he said nothing."

On another occasion, according to Alite, Junior got pissed at one of his crewmembers when he called the gun Gotti was carrying, a .25 caliber automatic, a "baby gun." Gotti grabbed a shotgun and growled, "This big enough?" then shot the guy in the hip.

Both Alite and another government witness, Michael Finnerty, a big, ruddy Irish leg-breaker for the Gotti crew, recount how when Finnerty bested John Junior in a drinking contest, Junior ran off to the men's room to puke, then returned with a steak knife and stabbed Finnerty in the shoulder twice. "John hated to lose," Alite says.

Alite goes on to tell of making tens of millions of dollars with Gotti Junior running his cocaine distribution business through dealers operating out of "forty or fifty bars that we had, moving four to eight kilos per month," under protection of "the Gambino umbrella." Alite claims they robbed and extorted other drug dealers, shook down bouncers and bar owners, ran book-making and loan-sharking operations, and beat and murdered anyone who did not bow to the Gotti rule. "I would do anything for this man," Alite says.

They traveled around the world, blew tens of thousands of dollars over a weekend gambling in Vegas. They bought lavish homes, condominiums, and businesses: a trucking company, a glass business, nightclubs and after-hours joints, a junkyard, and an auto parts outlet. "I spent money like a wild man," Alite admits. "I was a nut."

Like Gotti Senior's entourage, Junior, Alite, and the crew were ushered into the best restaurants and clubs without ever having to wait in line. They mimicked the high-profile gangster lifestyle they watched Gotti Senior take to a whole new level of public exposure. "The mob is a secret society. His [Gotti Junior's] family changed all that. They were in the news all the time," Alite reminds the jury. He embellishes his testimony with irrelevant details, telling the jurors he kept a derringer in his jockstrap, for whatever reason he does not say. "I was elated. I was happy. I was with the Gotti regime. . . . Yes, I was a gangster," Alite proclaims. "I liked the attention, I liked the money. I liked everything about *the life*."

Then, in the early 1990s, it all turned ugly, "treacherous" Alite says, over his beef with Victoria Gotti's husband, Carmine Agnello. Alite claims he wanted to "hurt" Agnello for abusing Victoria. Junior, however, according to Alite, sided with Agnello. "I believed John cared for me," Alite said. "Then I learned I was just another guy he used to hurt people. The friendship deep in my heart changed. I was not blood."

Agnello, however, was blood through his marriage to Victoria and also as a made member of the Gambino Crime Family. Agnello and several of his henchmen paid a visit to Alite and threatened him. Alite retaliated by shooting one of Agnello's men, Stevie Newell, without "going on record" or getting permission from his boss, Junior Gotti. After that, according to Alite, he became a marked man. Though their business relationship continued through intermediaries, Alite separated himself from John Junior and his immediate circle. He moved to Cherry Hill, New Jersey, and reported to Gotti, who was now acting boss of the crime family, through Ronnie "One Arm" Truccio and Charles Carnesi, John Junior's lawyer. At a meeting with Junior in a public setting at Aqueduct Raceway, Alite claims Gotti tried to lure him back into the fold so he could kill him. "He invited me to go Upstate hunting," Alite tells the jury. "I said 'Sure, I'll put on a pair of Bugs Bunny ears and you can all shoot at me.'"

On the seventh day of Alite's testimony, as Gotti's lawyers wrap up their cross-examination with questions about the strangling death of a young woman in a Queens motel room, spectators in the courtroom get to see a dramatic demonstration of the famous Gotti wrath. The jury has been removed for the lunch break. Deputies from the US Marshals WITSEC unit are escorting Alite from the room. Alite will claim later that Gotti mouthed the words, "I'll kill you!" during Alite's testimony that it was Gotti's uncle, Vinnie Gotti, who murdered the woman for disrespecting him. "They were getting high," Alite had said from the witness stand. "They had a bit of an argument, and he put her in the bathtub and strangled her.

"That's not the first time with that family, killing girls and raping them," Alite added before prosecutors cut him off.

Now, as he leaves the courtroom, Alite stops walking, he faces his former boss and demands, "You got something you want to say to me?"

Gotti goes ballistic. "You're a dog!" Junior shouts at Alite, insulting man's best friend. "Did I kill little girls, you fag? You're a punk! You're a dog all your life—you always were. Do I strangle little girls in motels?"

All considered, I believe Alite's testimony does little to bolster the government's case against John Junior. During the cross-examination by Gotti's amiable and adroit attorney, Charlie Carnesi, I watch as the jurors turn stony and even appear exasperated, with a few shaking their heads in disbelief as Alite admits to one heinous crime after another—home invasions, murders, beatings, drug rip-offs—but claims he never acted on his own volition, that he committed these crimes always with the qualifier that "John Gotti Junior told me to do it." Alite would have the jurors believe he never had an original idea, never made a move without Gotti to tell him what to do. By the time Alite slinks out of the courtroom after Carnesi's bruising cross-examination and an ineffectual redirect by the government that does little to affirm the witness's testimony, and despite John Junior's name and his admitted position in the crime family, Gotti's withdrawal defense is beginning to seem plausible. It is at least credible enough to cause real doubt in the jury room.

To those who are close to John Junior, there is another, private side of the man that is in stark contrast to the street thug described in witness testimony and that bears little resemblance to his father's public reputation as a brutal killer. Defense attorney Jeff Lichtman was a longtime member of the Gotti inner circle until he quit the defense team, which Junior saw as a betrayal. Lichtman tells me that when he first met Gotti Junior in the law offices of Michael Kennedy, John struck him as, "intimidating, sullen, a wild animal." But when they met again six years later, after Lichtman had gone to work for alleged Gambino house counsel Gerry Shargel, who represented Gotti Senior, Lichtman found he and Junior had a shared interest in and sympathy for the plight of Native Americans. In particular, they were both fascinated by the life of Sitting Bull and the Battle of Little Big Horn.

Junior, according to Lichtman, has a sensitivity he found likable. "We hit it off. Gotti would plop down in a chair, and we would talk for hours. We talked about boxing. Sports—and family. I found him intelligent, caring; he would ask a lot of questions. He was introspective. Human. Sensitive . . . even warm, especially when he talked about his family. We bonded over a love for our kids. John did not want to take a plea [to the 1997 racketeering case]. He was practically crying, talking about how much he loved his kids, and how he wanted to be there for them when they were young."

Lichtman says he and John Junior had similar relationships with their fathers, who were not around when they were boys growing up. They both wanted to stay close to their children and experience the joys and trials of fatherhood while hopefully setting a good example. "He changed his kids' diapers," Lichtman tells me. "All he cared about was his kids. He would insist on calling in to parent/teacher conferences from prison. I loved the guy."

The tragic inevitability in John Gotti Junior's life is that he was destined to become who he is and end up on trial for his life. How does a young man grow up in the shadow of this ubergangster—named for him, following him around as a young boy, and watching adoring fans and sycophants fall all over themselves to be around him—and not want to follow in his father's footsteps and become a gangster like his dad? You either renounce your father and his life—a virtual impossibility—or you embrace it.

"You've got to understand what it's like to live in these neighborhoods," the wife of a friend who comes from a mob-infested Brooklyn neighborhood tells me. "You don't think about the police or politicians when it comes to who is running things. You don't even know who they are. What you know is the local Mafia guys. Everyone knows who they are, and everyone accepts it."

Fathers and sons. Two boys brought up by the same dad, and one may become a crook, the other a man of God, as in the family of Genovese boss Vincent "Chin" Gigante, whose brother is a priest. Or as in the Bulger family, where one son becomes the president of the Massachusetts State Senate and the other a killer and FBI informant. John Junior has a younger brother, Peter Gotti, who is not involved in organized crime. Peter bonded with his father watching professional sports on TV. "Who do you like in the Giants game?" Senior would ask the boy. Then he would place his son's bets along with his own. Peter became a compulsive gambler like his father.

There was another Gotti son, known as Frankie Boy, who was run over by a car and killed while out riding on a friend's minibike. Frankie was just twelve years old when he died. He was the favorite son: a good student, an athlete, and he had an outgoing and engaging personality. Gotti was devastated by the death of his middle son, and Victoria never got over it. John Junior changed as well after Frankie was killed. According to his brother, Peter, John Junior became hardened and distant.

John Favara, the neighbor who ran over Frankie, did not attempt to show any remorse. He didn't bother to have his car repaired but kept it as a visual reminder of the accident. He had outdoor parties in his yard adjoining the Gotti's backyard within days of the boy's death. Victoria had to be heavily sedated for weeks. One night she was found trying to break down the door of the funeral home where her boy was lying in his coffin. She said Frankie Boy was cold and she had brought him a blanket. She showed up at Favara's door with a baseball bat and gave the neighbor a hospital beating. After he was released from the hospital, Favara put his home up for sale. But a few days before he was to sell his home and move, he disappeared. Witnesses would later claim Favara was whacked over the head with a two-by-four and thrown into the rear of a van, never to be seen again. Gotti Senior had an alibi: he was vacationing with his wife in Florida at the time Favara vanished. FBI informants said Gotti ordered his men to keep Favara alive until he returned so he could personally cut him to pieces with a chainsaw.

But vengeance would not bring the Gottis peace. Each year on the anniversary of Frankie's death, an announcement runs in the *Daily News*: *Frank: The pain of losing you never leaves our heart. Loving you, missing you always, and always hurting.* Years after his son was killed, as John Senior was followed by FBI agents on what became a weekend ritual outing to the graveyard where Frankie was buried, they watched as Gotti placed a bouquet of red roses at Frankie's headstone. Gotti sat staring at his son's grave for half an hour, quietly talking to himself . . . or to his dead boy's spirit.

Once the reign of Gotti Senior ended, and when the father died and John Junior went on trial, the Gotti regime had changed the face not only of the Gambino Crime family but also of the modern American Mafia in New York City. Between them, Gotti Senior and Gotti Junior broke all the long-held rules of the secret society. They tore the mask off the hidden visage of the Men of Honor. Senior was a celebrity gangster who basked in the limelight and who thrust his son into the life. Junior, caught in the harsh glare of his father's infamy, tried to take a bow and leave the stage. Rats lined up on deck ready to leap from the sinking Gotti ship into the welcoming arms of the FBI. Their testimony would forever blaspheme the criminal brotherhood. John Junior balked. Whether he was afraid or incompetent, whether he was brave and determined, he made it clear that he did not want to be his father, he did not want to be the Godfather. He wanted to be a father to his children.

Whatever John Gotti Senior might have thought of his namesake for violating his Cosa Nostra blood oath—first by admitting there was such an organization, and that he was a member, and, finally, by the traitorous blasphemy, as far as the elder Gotti was concerned, of renouncing his Mafia membership—whether he loved or hated his son for what he had done, the old don may twist and turn in his grave for eternity with one guilty certainty: John Junior was the better man. He may have followed his father's example, but only up to a point. He would come to defy him. He would renounce the treacherous criminal life his father embraced. He would become his own man, a father to children, uncle to his nephews and nieces—the engaged, loving father that he never had.

FURTHERMORE, THE GOTTI defense will claim, there is evidence to prove John Junior's withdrawal defense. Yes, Charlie Carnesi says, there is actual, physical proof of John's claim that he quit the Mafia and stepped down from his role as Gambino acting boss. And the evidence will prove that he did it with his father's approval.

Throughout the trial, when the jury is not present, and after the prosecution witnesses have testified, I keep hearing statements and argument from both the prosecutors and the defense lawyers concerning a videotape that recorded a final visit between father and son while John Senior was at the Federal Medical Center in Springfield, Missouri, being treated for the cancer that would ultimately kill him. Both sides request the court's permission to enter specific portions of the videotape, along with transcripts, as evidence to prove their opposing positions.

The tape was made in 1998 while John Junior, who was also in custody, was awaiting trial in New York. A federal judge granted John a special visit with his father to seek Senior's permission to plead guilty to the outstanding racketeering charges for an agreed-upon sentence of ten years rather than risk going to trial and receiving a certain life sentence if convicted. This, according to the government's theory, is proof that John Junior was the acting boss of the Gambino Crime Family— it's clear in the interplay between father and son—and that in his position as acting boss, John takes his orders directly from his father.

Yes, the defense agrees: the tape establishes John Junior's leadership position in the crime family, which Gotti Junior does not dispute. But the defense maintains that the tape also proves Gotti's contention that he went to his father specifically to ask for his permission not only to plead guilty to the indictment but also to ask his father to release him from his vow, to give him leave to quit the crime family, to withdraw from his role as the acting boss and, in John Junior's words heard on the tape, to get "closure" and to "move on with my life," which the defense argues is John Junior specifically asking for his father's permission to quit the crime family.

The judge must decide whether or not to admit the tape and, if so, which parts will be played for the jury.

Really? There is a tape of this singular meeting between a father and son—but not just any father, the godfather, John Gotti, and his first-born son, his successor to the position of boss of the Gambino Crime Family? Where is it? Who has this tape? How can I see it?

When I ask the defense attorneys, they say no, they do not have the tape. They assume that the government must have it since they keep bringing it up. The actual physical existence of the tape seems to be of less importance to the litigants than the arguments concerning its content and admissibility.

In keeping with my documentary filmmaker's maxim to always go for the videotape, to at least try to get ahold of whatever actual footage that might exist in any given story I am working on, on a whim, I go down to the clerk's office on the ground floor of the courthouse, and I ask one of the staff for the Gotti tape.

"Who are you?" the young man inquires. I say something to the effect that I am "with the lawyers," which is partially true as I have only just left them upstairs in the lawyer's conference room, and I mention that I am, "covering the trial."

I must appear believable because once again the gods of documentary filmmaking smile upon me. The man goes and gets the videocassette tape; he hands it to me without so much as asking for my name, asking me to show identification, or asking me to sign a release to record who I am and that I have received what turns out to be the only copy of the tape in existence.

This has become an uncanny boon: first there was the Mike Tyson Junior Olympics footage; then the Troy Kell prison murder surveillance tape; and now this, Gotti father and son. Part of me is inclined to flee from the courthouse before the clerk realizes what he has done. Instead, I go back upstairs to the lawyer's conference room where Gotti's attorneys are still meeting. John Junior has been returned to his cell in the MCC.

"I have the tape," I tell them.

"What tape?" they ask.

"What tape? The tape you guys have been arguing about with the government for the past several days."

"You have it?"

"Yes," I say and show them the videocassette.

Then, before anyone can inquire how I got it and what I intend to do with it, and perhaps even demand I hand it over, I put the tape back in my bag, turn, and leave the courthouse.

What can I say? These things happen. My motto is "Go for the tape." You never know; sometimes you get lucky.

THIS TIME, AS with the Troy Kell prison murder tape, as soon as I watch the video, I know that I have something unique, something journalists, magazine editors, and TV executives covet, and something readers and viewers would otherwise never have an opportunity to see or to learn about. This is the goods, the real stuff of insider storytelling. It is a look into a room in a prison where an intimate, private father-son meeting takes place, and it allows viewers to eavesdrop on an emotional conversation between a proud, dying Mafia godfather and his heir-apparent son. To me, watching the tape, it is like something out of Shakespeare. John Junior is Hamlet—to be or not to be a gangster. He meets Julius Caesar, his proud, doomed emperor warrior father, who has been betrayed by his Brutus, Sammy Gravano, and who knows that his empire is in peril, entrusted to his reluctant heir, and besieged by enemy forces. It is a ninety-minute visit duly recorded by the Bureau of Prisons, and it is the last time these two men will ever see each other. The bureau recorded all of Gotti Senior's visits with his family and friends, even visits with his attorneys, although to do this is specifically forbidden by law as a violation of attorney/client privilege. You can only get away with doing it when the defendant's name is Gotti.

The Gotti father-son tape, an hour and a half of extraordinary, intense, and emotional conversation between a dying father and his deeply conflicted, emotionally devastated son, is not only proof to me of John Junior's innocence and corroboration of his claim to have quit the Mafia; it is also striking evidence of the courage I know it must have taken for John to go to his father and ask his permission to essentially disclaim and repudiate everything his father stood for and believed in. It is true-life Mafia drama at the highest levels in a universal, intimate relationship any father or son can relate to and hope to understand. And the jury will never see it—at least not during the trial.

A frail, sick, but still proud and ramrod erect Gotti Senior shuffles on camera draped in chains, shackled, handcuffed, and surrounded by prison guards. He meets his son, John Junior, who wears a sports coat and looks like a supplicant bowed under the heavy weight of his request. The men approach the prison captain, who is accompanied by two FBI agents. The agents say they have been sent to observe the meeting. Really? "Well," Gotti Senior looks at his son and says, "I love you, John, and as glad as I am to see you, it's not going to happen." To the guards he says, "Take me back to my cell." Gotti refuses to sit in the room with FBI agents present. The captain intercedes. He says that the visit was ordered by a federal judge, he has the court order, and nowhere in the order does it say that the FBI is to be present during the visit. He tells the agents they must leave, and he orders the visit to proceed.

Father and son take seats across from each other at a long table in the prison conference room. A prison official is present to operate the single video camera on a tripod offering a stationary two-shot and affording poor quality audio that it will take several viewings to fully transcribe. John Junior is a bodybuilder, but despite his obvious physical size he appears diminished in the presence of his father. He slumps in his seat, looks up to and up at his father. Gotti Senior is a wraith of his former self. He's not so much lean as he is physically wasted, clearly ravaged by the disease eating away at his once handsome face. And yet he appears unbowed, sitting up straight, leaning into his son, and in full command, ever the boss, ever in control. He has a sheaf of court papers he brought into the room with him, as well as some paper napkins he uses to blow and wipe his nose of the drainage from his disease.

John Junior winces when he sees how the cancer has disfigured his father; he wipes away the tears from his eyes. Senior jokes about it. He says that the doctors removed a chunk of his chest and attached the flesh to his face and neck where they had removed the cancerous tissue.

"You mean they took the skin?" Junior asks.

"They took the meat," Senior tells him.

He turns to the camera operator and says, "I just wanna show him the scar."

Senior rips open his jumpsuit to show his boy where the doctors removed a slab of his pectoral flesh and stuck it to his face.

Senior jokes, "Yeah, I told your mother, I don't even have tits, and they gave me a mastectomy."

Now I see why the defense attorneys sought to have the entire tape played for the jury. It is no help to the government's case, not at all. Indeed, it supports John Junior's claim that he quit the crime family with his father's blessing. Watching the meeting between these two men and listening to the conversation, however difficult to understand at times, it is clear that John Junior did ask for his father's permission to plead guilty so that he could, in his words, "have closure . . . and give the government their pound of flesh," do some time and live to make it out of prison in time to once again become an active, free man and personally involved father to his own kids and his father's many grandchildren. At first, Senior demands of his son, "Where's your dignity, John? Where's your manhood?" He says, "Closure? That's a word for overeducated and underintelligent motherfuckers." But then, about three-quarters of the way through the meeting, there is an amazing moment, a kind of transformation as the godfather changes and becomes a father. Gotti Senior looks at John Junior and sees his son for who he is: a man who has found his dignity and his manhood not in being a crime boss but in being a husband to his wife and a father to his children. Senior tells him, "There's nothing in the world, no one in the world I love more than you, John."

John Junior replies, "I'm not one tenth the man that you are."

Senior says, "No, John, when it comes to being a father and a husband, you're ten times the man I am." He appears to have given up.

But Gotti Senior did not rise to become the boss of the Gambino Crime Family and Boss of All Bosses by chance or simply by force, nor even by acquiescing to the will of others. The man is a master manipulator, and a brilliant negotiator. He has a physical presence that cannot be denied, even as he is a disfigured ghost of his former self. He killed and connived his way to the top of the mob. He broke all the rules, including the ultimatum that a boss is beyond reproach, and certainly must never be murdered by his own men. And Gotti's ability to control other men, not excluding his own son, comes through over the course of the meeting in such a way that by the time he has given John Junior his permission to plead guilty to the government's charges against him, even to move on with his life, Senior manages through sheer egoism, by relating everything that happens in the world to him and to his view of how things must and should be done, to turn it all around. By giving in, by giving John Junior what he asks for, what he thinks he wants, he causes his son to question his motives, question the very idea of who he is, and finally to change his mind.

"You know how I am, John," Senior says. "When it comes to the government, I raise the black flag. Do you know what that means?"

"The whole world knows what it means, dad," Junior answers.

"No," Senior says, "it means you give no quarter. I kill you, or you kill me. That's the end of the fucking story. They could accuse me of robbing a church, I could have the steeple stickin' out of my ass, and I'm gonna deny it."

"I'd follow you off a cliff," John Junior says. He's in tears now.

"No, that's not right," his father tells him. "You're your own man, John."

The boy is so in awe of his father, so in love with the man, that even to get from him what he came for in the first place undercuts his resolve. He doesn't want to win at his father's expense. All Junior ever wanted was to be loved and respected by this man. Senior says, do it, John, if that's what you want to do. But he tells him that the government will never leave him alone. They will never accept it, never allow it—unless he beats them at trial. He is a Gotti. He is John Gotti Junior. And the fifteen hundred–plus extended family members, all those cousins and brothers-in-law and friends of friends and associates—subtle reference to the Gambino Crime Family members—and their families, their wives and children who depend on the family, what are they to do? What are they to think? Have you considered that, John? How, Senior asks in so many words—as indeed both men talk not so much in coded language, as the government would claim, but with words that have more than one meaning—how do you plan to deal with all of that, John? All of those extended family members out there to whom we have an obligation as men, men who have chosen a path and, as Senior believes and lives by and will die holding on to that belief, which is all he has left: the conviction that once a man chooses a path, once he decides on a way of life, he must see it through to the end no matter that he comes to understand the error of his ways, no matter that the path he has chosen leads to prison or to death. A man finishes the journey he sets out on, or he is not a man.

John Junior says he disagrees. It may well be the one and only time in his life that John has ever questioned or disputed his father's faith in Cosa Nostra and his concept of what it means to be a man of honor. No, John Junior says to his father; as a father himself, he believes that his first obligation is to his wife and children, to his blood nieces and nephews, to Senior's grandchildren. "It's about the kids," he says. Who is going to be there to take care of the kids if he ends up like his father, doing the rest of his life in prison? Or dying in the street?

Senior sits back in his seat, he rustles the court papers, he blows his nose on the napkins, he rants on about President Clinton getting a blowjob in the White House and denying it, how they are all a bunch of lying scumbags and he hates them all, how he could have been president himself if he had been born in different circumstances: "I didn't choose this life," he says, which hardly seems believable. "It was forced on me." He's losing ground, or so it seems, and, appearing to acquiesce, he gives his son his permission. He tells him, okay, do it, John, do whatever you decide; it's your life. But make sure you get what you want out of the deal. Make sure you have your deal with the government set in stone because they will come for you again and again. You are a Gotti, and Gottis are not subject to the rules of fair play.

It is mesmerizing to see the old mobster in action. No wonder he evoked such blind loyalty even when it was plain he was on a path that would lead to the destruction of the entire crime family. The guy is who he is, the force of his personality will not be denied, and it must be reckoned with. John Junior may have gone into the meeting with a plan, but in acquiescing to the plan, and releasing him from his position in the crime family, with a masterful stroke of what appears to be compromise, his father manages to cause John Junior to doubt his plan, and to question and reconsider everything he stands for. The kid is really in a quandary: To be or not to be a gangster, whether it is nobler to stay true to his doomed father's way of life or to become his own man and a father to his children?

John leaves the meeting with his father determined to go to trial. Then, sometime later, John tells me in one of our first interviews, he was in the backyard at his home in Mill Neck watching his kids play soccer. One of his young daughters sat on his lap and asked him about plans for her upcoming birthday party. "Will Pop Pop come to my party?" she asked her father, using the nickname the kids have for John Senior.

"No," John told her, "Pop Pop won't be able to come."

"Why?" the girl asked. "Because he's in that place?"

"Yes," John says. "Pop Pop loves you and he wants to come to your party . . . but he can't."

The girl looked at her father and said, "Are you going to go to that place, too, Daddy? And then you won't be able to come to my birthday parties?"

That is when John Junior changed his plans yet again. He pled guilty. He went to prison, he served his time, seven years, and he was about to be released when he was indicted, went to trial three times, and now finds himself back in this courtroom facing his fourth verdict and a possible life sentence.

THE DEFENSE RESTS. The lawyers give their closing arguments. Although the tape is never played for the jury, after they are sent out to deliberate, I leave the courtroom convinced there is enough dubious testimony from sleazy prosecution witnesses, along with enough evidence from the defense in taped visits and recorded telephone calls with Junior while he was in prison where he states emphatically his resolve to "move on with my life" and refuses to accept the role of Gambino boss upon his release from prison, to give credence to his claim of withdrawal, so that it looks likely that trial number four could result in an acquittal or another hung jury. No matter that Judge Castel excused one of the jurors and ordered the jury to go back to deliberate with an eleven-member panel over objections from the defense. (In an ironic note, the government cites my own case, *United States v. Stratton* et al. as precedent to allow for a verdict from eleven jurors when one of the jurors is excused for reasons having nothing to do with the case.)

The jury comes back in and claims that they are unable to reach a verdict after more than two weeks and after several charges by the judge, known as Allen charges, ordering them to go back into the jury room and continue to deliberate. The Thanksgiving holiday looms. Finally, the jury foreman stands firm and declares that they are hopelessly deadlocked. The judge has no alternative but to declare yet another mistrial. The government prosecutor makes a startling admission that the government is unwilling to try Gotti again. He even places his hand on John's shoulder and wishes him luck.

John Junior leaves the courtroom and walks out from the courthouse and into the midst of a media blitz on the courthouse steps as a free man after ten years of trials, seven years of imprisonment, having forfeited millions of dollars in cash and property to the government, forsaking everything his father lived and died for, walking out now into the world to try to rebuild his life with a name that has become synonymous with organized crime.

"How does it feel to be free?" one of the reporters asks Gotti.

"I'm just looking forward to getting home to see my wife and kids," John says.

Over the several weeks of the trial, I met and became friendly with members of John's family: his mother, Victoria, who clearly was every bit a loving mother devoted to her children and a force to be reckoned with as a fierce wife to a husband she fought bitterly over his decision to bring John Junior into the crime family. When I asked Victoria about how she reacted when she learned John had brought her son into the life, she told me she was enraged, she refused to speak to him on the phone or go visit him in prison for over two years. She told him she hoped he would rot in hell.

"He told me he did it to protect him," Victoria told me. "That—if they couldn't get to him, they would go after John. But if he was . . . one of them," Victoria shrugged and gave me a look, "it wouldn't be so easy."

She didn't appear any more convinced by this Mafia reasoning than I was. We both knew that Senior broke his word to his wife and brought his son into the crime family because it meant more to him than anything else. That was the vow he took, to put his loyalty to the crime family before everything else, even his wife and kids.

I met John's sisters Angel and Victoria and his brother, Peter. We often ate lunch together in the courthouse cafeteria. They are a close-knit clan, and they adore Gotti Senior. Whatever else one might wish to say about John Gotti, he undoubtedly evoked powerful family ties. I met Senior briefly when we were both locked up in the Metropolitan Correctional Center. He was the only man I ever saw who looked good in a blaze-orange prison jumpsuit. Gotti was not only handsome, he not only had charisma, but he had something more—gangster élan. John had a personal style and easy sense of himself that came down somewhere between being the scariest, toughest guy you ever met and the most charming, the most fun to be around. He exuded confidence and a love of life. Most of the mob bosses I met and got to know over my years in MCC and other federal prisons were more like Joe Stassi: haunted, festering with contained rage and bitterness over their fate. Or they were sullen, trapped in the inescapable reality of where their lives of crime had brought them. John Gotti seemed to love being who he was; even prison could not dampen his enjoyment of being John Gotti, mob star.

Once I learned about John Senior's childhood from his wife and children, I began to understand how and why he became the man who would be a celebrity crime boss, the dapper don glorying in his extravagant wardrobe, and in love with his role as a Mafia prince who would become king.

"Do you know why my husband had so many pairs of shoes?" John's wife, Victoria, asked me one day. "Because when he was a boy growing up he sometimes had to go to school with two shoes from different pairs and both with holes in them. The kids would tease him and call him poor white trash."

John Senior was one of thirteen kids, eleven of whom survived, born to a loving mother and an abusive father who often disappeared for weeks at a time and gambled away most of the money he made at menial jobs or blew it on booze and other women. When John Senior, in talking to John Junior about his father—who was also named John Gotti (so, in fact, John Senior is a junior, and John Junior is a third)— Gotti called his father "a bum." He regularly beat the kids when he returned home from one of his absences simply to let them know he was back: "a preemptive beating," John Junior called it, just in case they were considering doing something wrong. He mellowed as he got older—or perhaps his tough son, who was a leader even as a boy, called

"Crazy Horse" by his friends for his indomitable spirit, had intimidated his father into becoming less abusive. The children all said Gotti Senior's father would have been locked up now for the way he abused John and his brothers and sisters.

John Senior was on the street from his early teens in the tough Brownsville, East New York, neighborhood. The family moved from the tenements to church welfare housing while the father was off on one of his gambling and boozing binges. At one point John Senior was sleeping in a pool hall. Later, an African American family took him in. Soon he was a member of a street gang, the Fulton Rockaway Boys, and hanging out at the local social club running errands for the neighborhood boss, a Gambino lieutenant named Carmine Fatico. With his intelligence, his nerve, his ambition, his ferocious temper, and his charm, Gotti quickly distinguished himself. He killed a man, an Irish thug named McBratney who made the mistake of kidnapping the nephew of Gambino boss Carlo Gambino. Gambino paid the ransom, but instead of returning the nephew, McBratney and his cohorts killed him. Gotti, with his lifetime right-hand man, Angelo Ruggiero, and another Gambino associate located McBratney in a Staten Island barroom. They posed as police detectives and tried to get McBratney to leave the bar with them. McBratney refused to go, there was a struggle, and when things began to get out of hand, Gotti took out a gun and shot McBratney. Carlo Gambino hired Trump mentor and criminal defense attorney Roy Cohn to represent Gotti. Cohn managed to get Gotti a deal to plead to a lesser charge of manslaughter instead of homicide. John went to prison and did his time. When he got out, with Gambino's blessing, Gotti was inducted as a made member of the family. He rose to the position where he was able to effect a coup within the Gambino Family by plotting and carrying out the audacious, dramatic hit on his predecessor, Paul Castellano.

THE DAY AFTER the end of John Junior's fourth and last trial, I am doing my morning workout routine when my cell phone rings.

"Is this Richie Stratton?"

"Yes."

"This is John Gotti."

I congratulate John on yet another hung jury and what appears to be a final victory. John thanks me and asks if I have the videocassette tape of his meeting with his father. I admit that I do. John says he would like to have it, as it was to be the last time he would see his father alive. I agree to give him the tape, which I have already had digitized, and ask if John will agree to let me interview him for my *Playboy* article. We meet, along with John's lawyer, Charlie Carnesi, at a pizzeria on Long Island. The article, "Godfather and Son," is published in the April 2010 issue of *Playboy*. It wins the 2011 New York Press Club Award for Crime Reporting.

In a meeting in 2012 with executives Molly Thompson and Brad Abramson at A&E network, I pitch them a multipart documentary series based on the Gotti father-and-son story as told in the *Playboy* article.

"Can you get John Junior to agree to go on camera?" they ask. I say I believe I can. John wants to tell his story. While Senior was still alive, it is doubtful John Junior would have gone on camera. But, after sitting mute in courtrooms for the past several years and listening to cooperating witnesses and FBI agents tell their versions of the Gotti story, John has much he wants to say that never came out in any of his trials. He has written and self-published a book, *Shadow of My Father*, and he wants to profess publically his decision to quit the Mafia and become a civilian in the hopes that even the FBI might come to believe him.

What about the FBI? the executives ask. Will they cooperate? Well, let's find out. My producing partner, Doug Biro, and I shoot a sample interview with John at his office in Oyster Bay, Long Island. Gotti strikes everyone who sees the interview as being not only articulate and intelligent but also empathetic and an engaging storyteller. If I can get the FBI to agree to come on board, A&E will greenlight the project.

The docuseries for A&E is derailed once the *Playboy* article makes the rounds and John Junior sells his life rights to a producer who intends to make a feature film. I get a call from Sylvester Stallone, who says he read the *Playboy* article, and he wants me to write the screenplay. He's going to direct the film and play the part of Gotti Senior. John Junior goes out to Hollywood and meets with Stallone. The producer, who has never made a feature film before, is able to raise millions of dollars based on having secured the rights to Gotti's story.

It quickly becomes evident, however, that the neophyte producer has no idea what he's doing. He blows millions of dollars of the financier's money on rich pay-or-play deals with actors before there is even a script. Stallone bows out, as do I when it becomes clear that the producer is in way over his head and is too arrogant and full of himself to listen to people who at least have some idea what they are doing. The project appears doomed. With the feature film in development limbo, John Junior comes back on board to be interviewed, and the documentary series is back on track at A&E.

At first, the FBI agents I contact want nothing to do with the documentary when they learn that John Junior has agreed to be interviewed. It takes a call from Joe Pistone, a.k.a. undercover FBI Special Agent Donny Brasco, whom I met and became friends with while working on the Connolly/Bulger story, to get me access to FBI agents who were involved in both John Senior's and John Junior's investigations. After speaking with Pistone, the agents are willing to talk to me. When I assure them that I am seeking to tell a balanced story and give both sides an opportunity to present their case, a number of agents who were active members of the FBI's Gambino Squad and were responsible for the arrest and conviction of John Senior as well as agents involved in the investigation and prosecution of John Junior, along with Judge Shira Scheindlin, who presided over three of John Junior's trials, and a former federal organized crime task force prosecutor all agree to go on camera. When I track down Gotti Senior's infamous, flamboyant criminal defense attorney, Bruce Cutler, now practicing in Chicago, and he agrees to be interviewed, I know we have a compelling cast of characters.

WHEN I INTERVIEW Judge Scheindlin, she says she believes that the government made a mistake when they entered clips from the Gotti father-son tape into evidence in the trials she presided over—which is probably why it was alluded to but kept out of the last trial. Judge Scheindlin says she felt the tape hurt the government's case and worked to support the withdrawal defense and evoke sympathy for John Junior from jurors.

The FBI agents and federal prosecutors who were determined to convict Gotti and lock him up for the rest of his life or flip him and turn him into a cooperating witness have an entirely different view. They are apparently still smarting over their inability to get a conviction after four tries. They are unwilling to accept that John quit the life of organized crime to become a civilian; some even hint that after all these years he may still be in the life and under active investigation. In my interview with FBI Special Agent Lou DiGregorio, he takes the party line and insists John Junior would never have been allowed to leave the mob. He holds to the belief that a made member can leave Cosa Nostra only by coming to the government, renouncing his vow of omertà, and agreeing to become a witness against other organized crime figures. A casket is the only other way out, according to DiGregorio. But, I ask, what about the visit at Springfield where John goes to his father and asks his permission to plead guilty and become a civilian? DiGregorio insists that it never happened. But there is a tape, I say, a videotape of John Junior in a visit with his father asking for, and receiving, Senior's blessing to leave the life. At first DiGregorio says the tape does not exist, because the visit never happened. But when I assure him that I have the tape and have watched it, he maintains that, in the first place, it makes no difference to the FBI if in fact Senior did release his son; that is not the same as coming to law enforcement and declaring that you want out. Besides, the FBI agent insists, the entire meeting between John and his father at the Springfield Medical facility was an act, it was a sham devised and rehearsed by the two men to make it appear John Junior had stepped down and quit the Gambino Crime Family when in fact it was all a ruse the gangsters staged to win over a gullible jury.

How, I ask, were John and his father able to compose the lines and rehearse their parts so that the staged meeting plays so convincingly, with Junior in tears and emotional turmoil when at the time Senior was dying in isolation in Missouri and Junior was held in solitary with no phone privileges except to speak with his lawyer in New York? If indeed they were acting, they were compelling performances. The Gottis missed their calling when they became criminals. They should have gone to Hollywood instead. But DiGregorio, like most of the FBI agents we spoke to, remains as steadfast in his view of the gangsters as the gangsters are in their opinion of the agents. Once a gangster, always a gangster—unless you become a rat. DiGregorio will later assent, off camera, that perhaps John Junior did withdraw; or, in mob terms, he was "put on the shelf," forced by the ruling body of the family to go into retirement, given that he does not appear to have been involved in criminal activity for the past several years. The agent maintains, however, that if they (the Mafia) were to come to John and order him to act on their behalf, Gotti would have to do whatever they ordered him to do, or he would be killed.

While we are in production on the four-hour documentary series based on the *Playboy* article, and with extensive interviews with John Junior, the feature film is revived, this time with John Travolta playing Gotti Senior. Kevin Connolly, an actor on the HBO series *Entourage*, directs. We visit the set at Sparks Steak House and do an interview with Travolta in character as Gotti.

It takes a little over two years from the time the deal is signed to complete the A&E documentary. The four-part series, *Gotti: Godfather and Son*, airs on A&E over two nights to record-breaking audiences in June 2018. It is later picked up and aired by Amazon Prime and other video streaming services.

Chapter Eighteen

FATHERS AND SONS

He died hating that kid, you know that.
—Mob rat Lewis Kasman, Gotti Senior's so-called
"adopted son," speaking of Senior's feelings for
his son in a taped conversation with Gambino
consigliere Joseph "JoJo" Corozzo

DURING THE Q&A after the premiere screening of the first two hours of the A&E documentary at the IFC Theater in Manhattan, when questioned about what drew me to the story, I remark that had it not been for John Junior's decision to quit the mob and his resolve to go to his dying father in prison and ask his permission to do what went against everything his father lived for and would die defending, I never would have wanted to make the docuseries in the first place. Without John Junior's decision to quit the mob, and without the videotape of his visit with his father to ask his permission, it would have been just another show about gangsters. What impressed me was John Junior's courage. He could have waited until his father died to plead guilty and become a civilian. But he had the integrity and the fortitude to face his father with what he knew was going to be an affront to everything Senior stood for.

It is the universal father-son story that attracted me. The unique dynamic between these two men as bosses of a powerful crime family and as men like other men when it came to their relationship—a boy and his dad. And finally, the decision John Junior made to quit the life and his brave commitment to confront his dying father moved, intrigued, and inspired and challenged me to want to tell this story. I knew there was a story worth telling as soon as I got a view into their relationship through the tape of John's final sit-down with his father. But how to give context and emotional depth to that meeting? How to bring in voices that could fill in all the necessary background and make these characters' stories resonate in a way that would move viewers to feel the same empathy I felt watching John with his father in that prison conference room?

John Junior's unique talent as a storyteller and the FBI agents' counterpoint is what made it all work. What impresses me, and I believe will move the audience, is John Junior's devotion to his wife and kids. He made the choice to be an engaged father to his children. He decided not only to leave the mob but to step down from a position of tremendous power, to walk away from a vast and immensely profitable criminal empire to become a traitor in the eyes of Mafia legions, a target for both government agents and wannabe tough guys who would view him as a rat who betrayed his vow of omertà by even talking about his life in Cosa Nostra—a violation that calls for a decree of death. That will always be something Gotti has to live with.

"Where's your dignity, John? Where's your manhood?" Those words of John Senior can be asked of any man. But they are especially relevant and poignant when one is faced with the possibility of being shot to death in the street at any time or spending the rest of one's life in prison. I have to wonder if, given the same set of circumstances, I would have been able to make and carry out the choices John Junior made to find my dignity, to define my manhood.

I had no family when I was arrested; I was separated from my wife and had no children. What if I had had a family, young children at home waiting for me when I stood trial in federal court in New York faced with a possible life sentence? Would I still have had the will and courage to resist the government pressure to join Team America and rat out my friends? It's a tough decision, maybe the toughest decision a man or woman will ever face. Even Senior in that final meeting with his son had to admit that John Junior was the better man when it came to being a father and a husband.

Isn't that the real test of a man?

I recall once seeing Victoria Gotti, John's wife, when she was stopped by reporters in the street and asked what her husband did for a living. She replied, "He provides." A telling reply. She didn't say, "Never mind what he does for a living. He's a great dad." That requirement of a man—to provide for his wife and kids—must also be factored in to anyone's assessment of a father. John Junior had a much easier time coming up in the world than his father. Everything was provided for Junior except what he wanted most: undivided love and time with his dad. Senior had had to fight for every morsel of food; he had to go to school in his brother's worn-out, hand-me-down shoes. He was on the street in early childhood, and he was in prison for most of John Junior's childhood.

It is clear by the end of the father-son tape that both Gotti men are as perplexed and challenged as are fathers and sons everywhere with their given roles that often seem to be at cross purposes. How to be a man in the world and a devoted father? To constantly measure and test oneself against the will or financial resources or even the physical force of other men, men who are not necessarily there to help you face the challenges to be a breadwinner while also a loving, dutiful father and husband who endears and engenders love and respect? It strikes me how much simpler this question of manhood and fatherhood is when one is in prison. It all comes down to basic survival, staying alive one day to the next without the challenges of fatherhood or the demands of earning a living and supporting a family. There is little to nothing you can do to be a father when you are locked up. Your manhood is all about respect and your personal survival. It's such a self-centered existence, it does not prepare you for the conflicting challenges of fatherhood.

My oldest boy, Max, is in the front row of the audience with his girlfriend at the IFC Theater. Discussing John's relationship with his father during the Q&A after the screening, I admit to my own lingering feelings of inadequacy, of having failed as a father, and how that feeling of not measuring up to my own concept of what it means to be a good father had also drawn me to the subject. To be a father and have a family was the one thing I believed I wanted most to succeed at upon leaving prison, and yet it had eluded me. I remember sitting in prison visiting rooms seeing fathers with their kids and feeling their pain when they were separated at the end of the visit. I remember the days and long, lonely nights in prison when I wondered if I would ever make it out alive and have enough life left in me to share with a wife and children. And I remember Kim's adamant demand that I give up criminal activity before she would agree to marry me and have a family; yet what was I to do? From my late teenage years, all I knew was the outlaw life. I needed to reinvent myself in my midforties. I remember the joy I felt when we learned Kim was pregnant, and the joy we felt as each of our three children was born. I lost all that through my own failure as a father.

"No," Max tells me later at the reception after the screening. "You were a good father, a loving dad." Perhaps, when Max, his younger brother Dash, and their sister, Sasha, were kids and I was there for them, I had been a good dad. But once the marriage fell apart, and when I left to pursue my career . . . no, it was inevitable, or at least so I believe, that my role as father to my boys and to my daughter suffered. I simply wasn't there when they needed me. I was off trying to make a living. It is the undeniable tragedy of divorce; the kids suffer. I still feel the pain of losing my family every day these many years later. I failed at that which I wanted most of all to achieve: to be a good dad, to be a present and loving father—to be the father I never had.

For the truth is, I had no training at fatherhood, no example of hands-on paternal love and guidance to follow. My own father, Emery Paine Stratton (my mother used to call him Emery "Pain in the Neck"

Stratton) was typical of his background and generation yet even more so. A quiet, reserved, handsome, old-school Yankee WASP, he was wrapped up in his own world as certainly I have proven to be wrapped up in my career. I don't recall ever sitting on my father's lap as a boy, of being hugged by him, definitely never kissed. We didn't go out in the yard and throw a baseball, though I did play in a couple of father-son golf tournaments with him, and a few times he took me fishing. About the only sure way I knew to get my father's attention was to get in trouble with the police, something I started doing and would prove good at from an early age.

Coming out of prison at forty-five, even as I pursued a family and fatherhood with Kim and our children, I was also fixated on my career. I felt I had a lot of catching up to do—indeed, I had to remake myself in the world. In time, I would come to learn that you can never catch up with something that is lost and gone forever. For an ex-con and lifetime criminal to remake oneself as a citizen with a career is an ongoing, day-to-day process and challenge.

When the boys were young, I used to wrestle with them on the big king-size bed. They loved it; I loved it. And while we lived in Manhattan, I walked them to school each day at PS 11. The day my daughter Sasha was born, I took the boys on a long walk on the land we owned upstate and showed them a new adjoining seven-acre parcel we had purchased. There was a spring on the new land that we named after Sasha.

WHILE I WAS working on the *Street Time* series after 9/11, Kim and the kids moved to Toronto to join me in a big home we rented. The production van would pick me up for work each day, and Max and Dash would come to the set with me. Those were happy times. As the second season was nearing completion of the final few episodes, we had a long break over the Labor Day weekend. I took Kim and the kids to a camp on a lake in Ontario. It was one of the happiest times in our marriage.

But there was a fissure in the relationship between Kim and me that would continue to widen and solidify as I spent more time traveling and Kim was left at home with the kids.

I take at least half the blame for being unable or unwilling to do the work needed to mend the marriage. When Kim told me on our first date that she didn't drink, I didn't understand that what she was saying is that she couldn't drink. Years later, when it was obvious that alcohol was a major contributing factor in the unraveling of the marriage, I was not willing to do what it appeared needed to be done and quit drinking to help Kim stay sober.

Who knows if it ever could have worked? Yes, we stayed together for thirteen years, and though Kim accused me of being unfaithful, I never was. A serial monogamist, I take my vows seriously. I was devoted to her and to our children, but two self-absorbed writers in the same household is a challenge no matter who they are. And in my case, though I make no excuses, I will say that a long stint in prison takes years to get over and does not leave one prepared for fatherhood. The cauterizing of emotion one needs to survive a long-term imprisonment may be permanent, and one's emotional self may never be fully resensitized. Even now, nearly thirty years after my release, the prison experience is as indelible as a convict's tattoos. I avoided the tattoos, but the emotional scar tissue is still there.

If there is one piece of advice I would give to any young, or even not so young, couple considering marriage, it would be to make certain they both want to live in the same geographical location, be it city or country, New York or the Hudson River Valley. Don't let your careers and your desire to put down roots pull you in different directions. When Kim and I met, we were both living in New York City. I have never wanted to live anywhere else.

I first saw New York City as a twelve-year-old boy when my father uprooted us from our home in Wellesley, Massachusetts, and moved the family to Puerto Rico, where he had taken a job as assistant pro with Chi-Chi Rodriguez at the Dorado Beach Hotel and Golf Club.

We spent a night in transit in New York before boarding the plane to San Juan the next day. I was fascinated by what my mother told me was the greatest city in the world, and where, if you could make it there, you could make it anywhere. When I was a young teenager, a close friend's father brought us to New York for a weekend, and again I was captivated by the energy and diversity of the place. During my years in the marijuana underground, though we worked all over the country and all over the world, smuggling marijuana and hashish from South America, Asia, the Middle East, the island of Jamaica in the Caribbean, it was always to New York that we came to distribute the product in the world's biggest illegal marketplace and to celebrate with the proceeds. Even after I was locked up, it was while at the MCC in Manhattan that I met the celebrity criminals who would become characters in my writing and where I would have my richest experiences in the criminal justice system that became the subject matter of my journalism and my books.

Kim had come to New York from Texas, and I assumed she was equally committed to living in the city. But she was convinced that New York City was no place to bring up children. Now, having lived here full time since the divorce and brought up another son here, I'm convinced that kids who grow up in New York City have a lot of advantages over their rural or suburban contemporaries. The move to the Hudson River Valley, with my work in the city and frequent travel taking me away from home, precipitated the beginning of the end of our marriage.

THE DAY MY father died, I was at work at the Fortune Society editing *Fortune News*. Max was still a toddler and had been sick when I left for work. I was already worried about him when I got a message at the office to come home immediately. All the way across town in the taxi I prayed that Max was okay. When I walked into the apartment, Kim was on the floor in the living room playing with Max. When I asked her what was wrong, if he was okay, she said, "No, he's dead." I thought she had lost her mind. What was she talking about?

"What do you mean, he's dead?"

"No," she said, "not Max. He's fine. It's your father. He was killed this morning."

Emery had been out for a walk, taking his morning constitutional. Nearing eighty, he was still in good shape. He stepped into the street to go around a parked car blocking the sidewalk. He was hit by a van and killed instantly. I went from thinking I might have lost my son to realizing that it was my father who was gone, who I would never see again. We set out to drive from New York to Massachusetts for my father's memorial service, but we were stranded in Connecticut in one of the worst blizzards of the season. Emery was gone from my life in much the way he had lived: beyond his son's ken, ever out of my reach. A man I never really knew.

I was closer to Norman Mailer than I was to my own father. Mailer was my intellectual progenitor. And I spent more undivided time in close quarters with Mafia don Joe Stassi than with anyone I've ever known. Stassi was my gangster guru. Mailer and Stassi were the mentors of my twin personae: the artist and the criminal. Mailer was dying at Mount Sinai hospital on the Upper East Side of Manhattan in October 2007. When I went to visit him, he couldn't speak. He had had a tracheotomy and could only mouth or write words. His illegible scrawling reminded me of Joe Stassi's handwritten notes that I used to decipher and transcribe in letters to his family and friends. To see Mailer at pains to communicate, this man who had so distinguished himself by his monumental talent with words, was as poignant as seeing Joe Stassi in his diaper in a wheelchair raging against the Kennedy brothers. Mailer would regain his ability to speak before he died. His biographer, J. Michael Lennon, told me that Norman awoke once from a dream or some near-death altered state and exclaimed: "I have met God!"

Mailer died peacefully surrounded by loved ones. His work will endure for as long as there are books and people to read them. Gotti

Senior choked to death on his own blood while in solitary confinement in a prison hospital cell. John Gotti Junior is still a free man and a devoted father. Joe Stassi died alone in assisted living still believing that I had betrayed him by telling his story. His son remains at large. That should give me some indication going forward which path to follow, which division in my conflicted psyche to fortify and honor.

And it has. I rest my case. Let the troops lay down their arms. The artist won. And let the truce endure.

Afterword

A PLACE YOU NEVER WANT TO BE

IT HAS NOW been just more than thirty years since I was released from prison. Yes, *thirty* years. It hardly seems possible. The experience is still as much a part of who I am today as it was on the day I walked out of the front gate at the federal prison in Ashland, Kentucky. I may not think about it as much. I may not have the nightmares of being locked up in some abstract prison anymore. But I am still conditioned by the experience. It informs my sensibility. I am not easily intimidated. Nor do I bitch and complain about minor inconveniences. I still measure everything I am forced to endure, as well as everything I hear or read or see on TV or on the news or in the movies about crime, criminals, and prison life in America against my own experience of having lived in that world and having been locked up for eight years in the vast American federal prison system. I am still, and always will be, an ex-convict with all of the depth of experience, stigma, and advantages and limitations that entails.

When I read that James "Whitey" Bulger had been shipped from the Federal Transfer Center in Oklahoma City to the United States Penitentiary in Hazelton, West Virginia, and that, within hours of his arrival, as he sat alone in his diaper in a wheelchair in a temporary holding cell awaiting formal classification and cell assignment, a couple of prisoners entered the unlocked cell and proceeded to beat Bulger to death with the old lock-in-the-sock prison sap, and cut his tongue out, and gouged his eyes out, I thought: *Okay, good riddance. The guy had it coming. It is business as usual—that is what happens to high-level rats in the Federal Bureau of Prisons.*

Civilians less familiar with the way things work in the BOP might ask, "How could something like that happen?" How does a well-known rat like Whitey Bulger, easily the most infamous FBI informer in federal custody, how does he manage to get transferred to a prison like Hazelton in the first place? There had already been a couple of recent prisoner killings at Hazelton; it was known to be a serious joint. Other organized crime figures from mafia families who had been ratted on by Bulger were doing time there—convicts who are serious men serving life sentences for murder, men who have nothing to lose and only much to gain in underworld status and personal satisfaction by killing a famous and despised rat like Bulger.

Clearly, there is something wrong here. In the first place, given how well-known Bulger's long history with the FBI as a Top Echelon Criminal Informant is to prisoners throughout the federal prison system, Whitey should have been in protective custody. He never should have been transferred to Hazelton in the first place, and he never should have been allowed in the general population or left alone in an open cell where other convicts could get their hands on him. Even if he declined PC, the Bureau should have been required to keep him separated from known organized crime figures and convict killers under what is known in the system as a separation order. Bulger should have been designated to a federal prison where there were no other organized crime figures who may have known Whitey or been ratted out by him, and so wanted him dead. He should have been locked up in one of several federal prisons where there are isolated, protected units specifically set up to house organized crime rats. None of this happened. Leading me to believe that Bulger was set up to be killed.

It must have been a raucous murder. One can only imagine that Bulger did not go quietly to meet his maker. Yet no one did anything to stop it. A killing like this can happen only with high-level compliance and even coordination by Bureau of Prisons officials from the top echelons in Washington, DC, and down to the warden at Hazelton, the captain and lieutenants on duty, and the unit guards in Receiving and Discharge where Bulger was to meet his unwelcome welcoming committee.

It makes perfect sense when you understand that prison staff, guards, and most administrators hate informers and jailhouse rats almost as much the convicts do. Snitches think they deserve special treatment; they expect to be coddled by the prison staff for having assisted law enforcement, and so they gripe and complain and make demands when they are not accorded the acceptance, comfort, and advantages they feel they deserve. This engenders resentment and even malice. Prison guards live, at least for the time they are on duty, in the same moral world as the convicts. From all I've read, Bulger was a pain in the ass to staff at every prison where he served time. Typical narcissist, he believed the institution should be run on his terms. Apparently, he was still running his games: manipulating a female contract employee into letting him use her cell phone to make unauthorized calls; signing his name to some other convict's drawings and paintings so they could be sold to suckers on the street, with Whitey getting a piece of the proceeds. And just generally acting like he was special when the only thing special about him was his relationship with the FBI.

No sooner was Bulger summarily dispatched to that great penitentiary in perdition than an equally evil, perhaps an even more heinous human, the pedophile rapist and scam artist Jeffrey Epstein, met a similar fate at the federal holding facility in Manhattan, the Metropolitan Correctional Center. Here is another case where, to me at least, no matter what they say, it was a hit sanctioned, set up, and coordinated by prison staff under direction from higher-ups in the Bureau. There are two things you don't want to be if you get locked up in the federal prison system at any of these higher-level institutions: a rat or a pedophile; Epstein was both. Maybe not an active rat, but a rat in the making—a potential rat with some major players on his snitch list. Perhaps he was already cooperating. Clearly, the guy had to go.

Again, fuck him. He got what he deserved—but not what we deserve. We deserve better: we deserve to know the truth of what goes on in our prisons and in our criminal justice system. We are told Epstein killed himself; that he somehow managed to strangle himself when he was on suicide watch. Oh, but wait; no, we're told he had been taken off suicide watch. Of course—but, why? Who made that decision, and what was the basis of their reasoning? Was he no longer considered a threat to himself? Perhaps not. The man was a narcissist, after all. People like Epstein don't usually kill themselves; they are convinced they are special and can get out of whatever unhappy situations they find themselves in. Hadn't he managed to weasel his way out of previous sex charges? His lawyer claims Epstein was convinced he would beat this case as well. And, even if he had been taken off suicide watch, why was he provided with whatever means he supposedly used to choke himself to death?

Again, none of this adds up to anything except a well-coordinated BOP-sanctioned and -executed hit. I spent over two years in that facility, the MCC in Manhattan, as recounted in my previous book, *Kingpin: Prisoner of the War on Drugs*. I was housed on the same maximum-security floor as Epstein. It's not easy to kill yourself in that place, especially when you're as important a prisoner as was Epstein. There is nearly constant monitoring of prisoners such as Epstein or El Chapo or World Trade Center bomber Ramzi Yousef. You don't really have the opportunity or the uninterrupted time and privacy it takes to manage to hang yourself or choke yourself to death without a little assistance from either staff or a prisoner given the means and opportunity to help you die.

The truth is, we will never know the truth; we will never know what really happened to either Bulger or Epstein. The Bureau of Prisons may be the most impenetrable of government bureaucracies; they answer to no one outside the system. And for good reason: the bureau has responsibility for housing and containing some of the most sophisticated, richest, violent, and dangerous men and women criminals in the world. The bureau masters may claim with a reasonable degree of credibility that they need to keep their procedures and systems secret for security purposes.

They may issue some sanitized version of the events; they may even claim to be charging individuals involved in the incidents—transferring the warden at MCC for instance, which actually means giving him a promotion and a better position at a prison outside the city; or suspending a couple of guards, giving them a paid vacation. But neither investigation will expose any of what actually happened. There will never be any real consequences for the people who allowed and facilitated these killings. BOP officials may squawk that they are understaffed, and so they can't monitor and control everything that goes on in their prisons, but that's nonsense. The federal prison system is an extremely efficiently run gulag archipelago of more than one hundred prisons of varying degrees of security, ranging from low-level work camps to maximum security penitentiaries and even supermaxes and super-max Security Housing Units (SHUs) in several multilevel prison compounds. Rarely if ever do any of the one hundred thousand or so prisoners under their control escape from the medium or maximum security prisons, and there are few disturbances, riots, work stoppages, or hunger strikes—at least that we know of, because, as I say, we don't really know what goes on in there. If, as Dostoyevsky wrote, "The degree of civilization in a society can be judged by entering its prisons," our prison system is proof we have entered into an Orwellian era of total government control, secrecy, and mendacity.

What I do know is that I made it out, I am free, and I am now more convinced than ever that no matter how tough it gets out here in the world at times, it beats the hell out of being locked up in the federal or state prison system. I am assured that to be a good citizen, a good American, means to be aware of what those in power are doing, whether it be waging foreign or domestic wars, building border walls, or separating families by locking up innocent people in government containment and concentration camps. It means to be ever vigilant that our leaders are never allowed to let the degree of civilization in the United States come to resemble anything like what goes on in our prisons. Or are we already there?